MONACO

The Colors of Time's Passage

MONACO

The Colors of Time's Passage

Photographs by Jean-Baptiste Leroux
Texts by Mic Chamblas-Ploton

Foreword by H.S.H. Prince Albert II of Monaco

ABRAMS, NEW YORK

CONTENTS

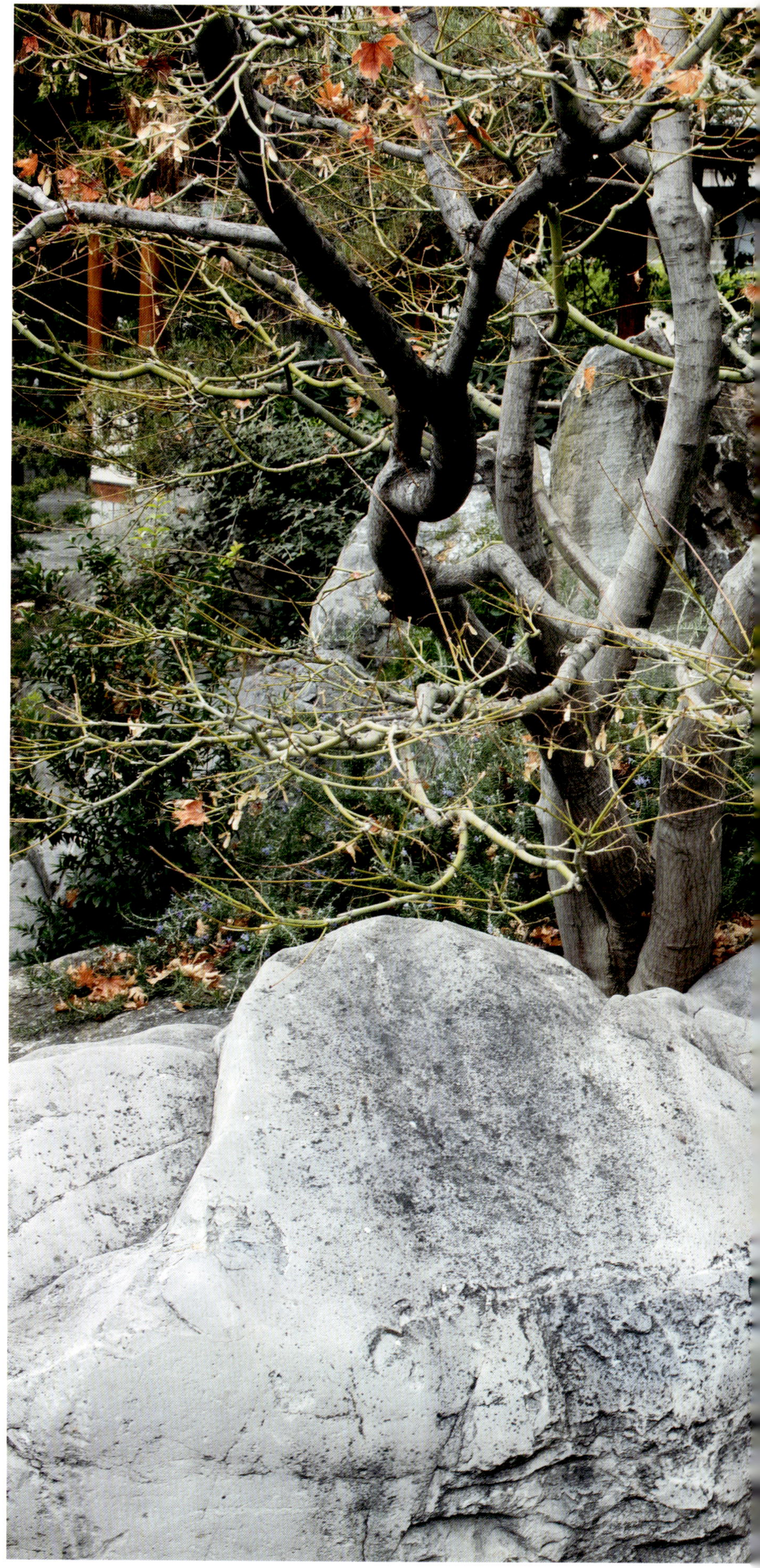

Japanese garden waterfall on a winter morning. January 1, 2016, 11:36 a.m.

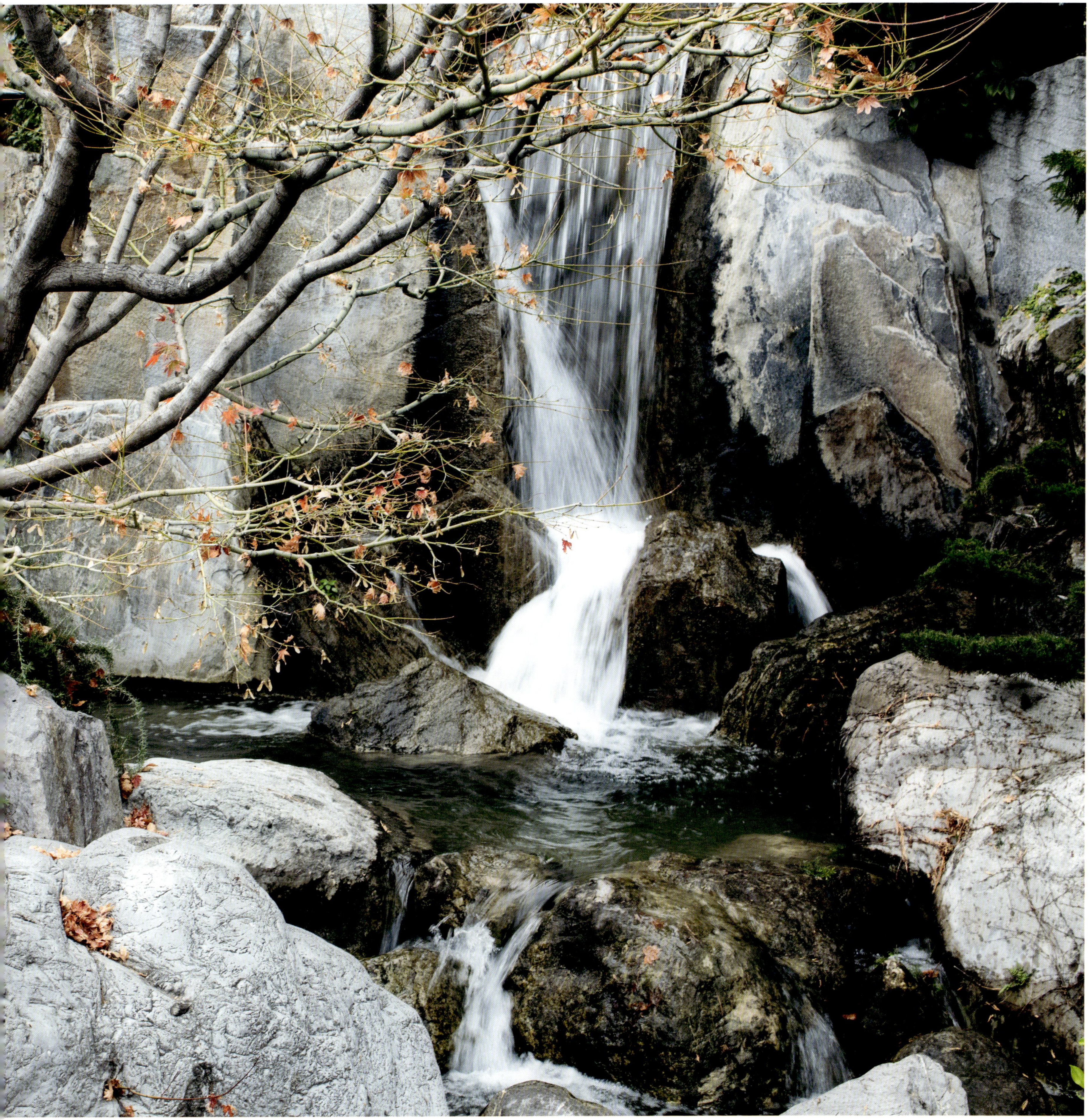

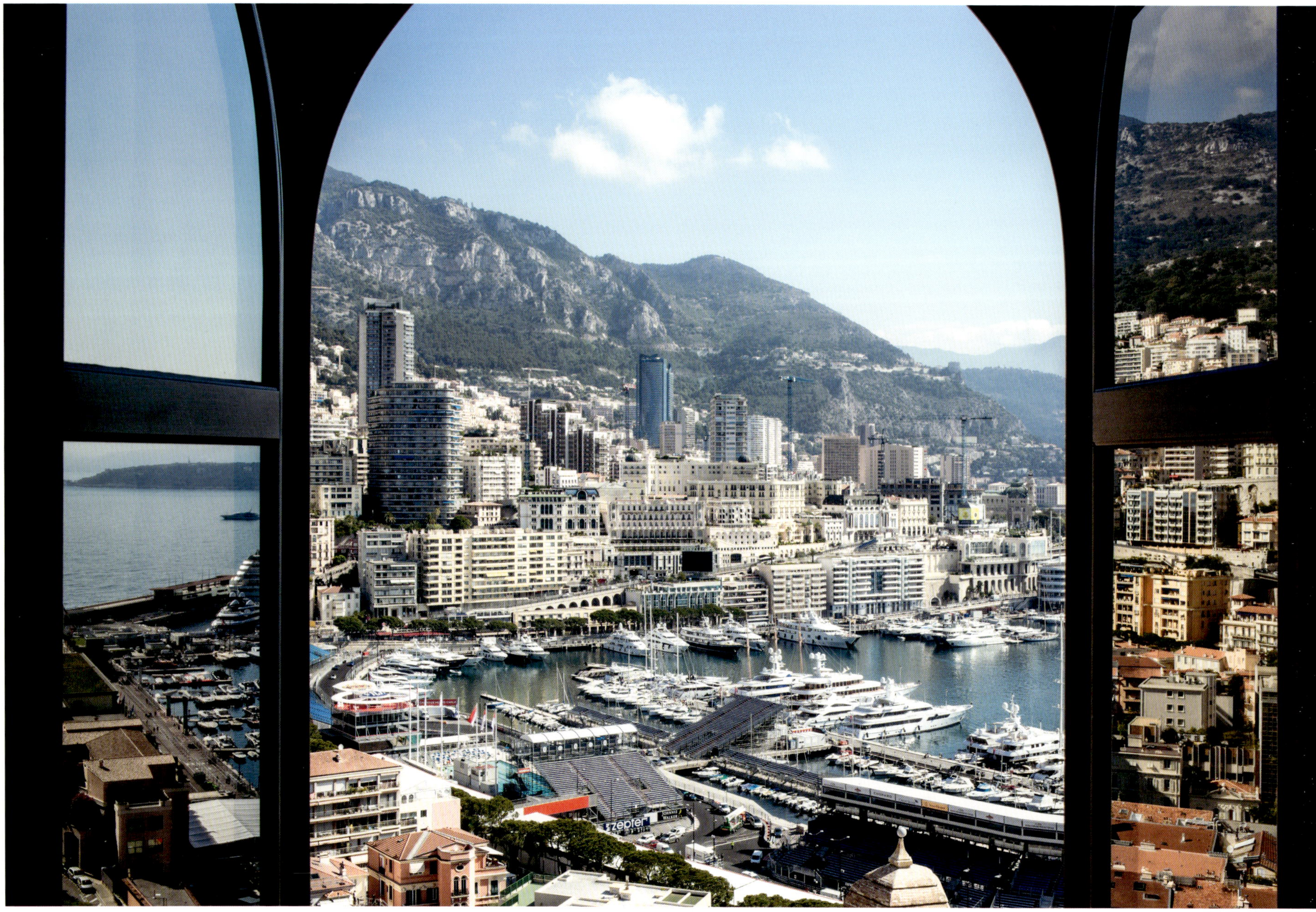

View of Port Hercules from a window of Prince Albert II's office in Prince's Palace.
May 17, 2016, 9:03 a.m.

FOREWORD

Perceiving Monaco differently through the lens of a photographer who follows the evolution of the seasons and the light.

This beautiful book is a wonderful way to escape from our busy lives and pace ourselves with the artist's rhythm. Readers will gain intimate access to a dynamic country they may have only glimpsed until now; the Rock of Monaco proudly delineated against the intense blue of the sea, to gradually fade in an evening haze before blending into the night; the historic Sainte-Dévote Chapel looking out toward vibrant Port Hercules underneath an ever-changing sky.

Inspired by emotions felt while discovering the Principality, the text accompanying the photographs enhances their impact and invites readers to discover the riches of a country whose blossoming culture, poetry, music, dance, and art are a timeless and inextricable part of its heritage.

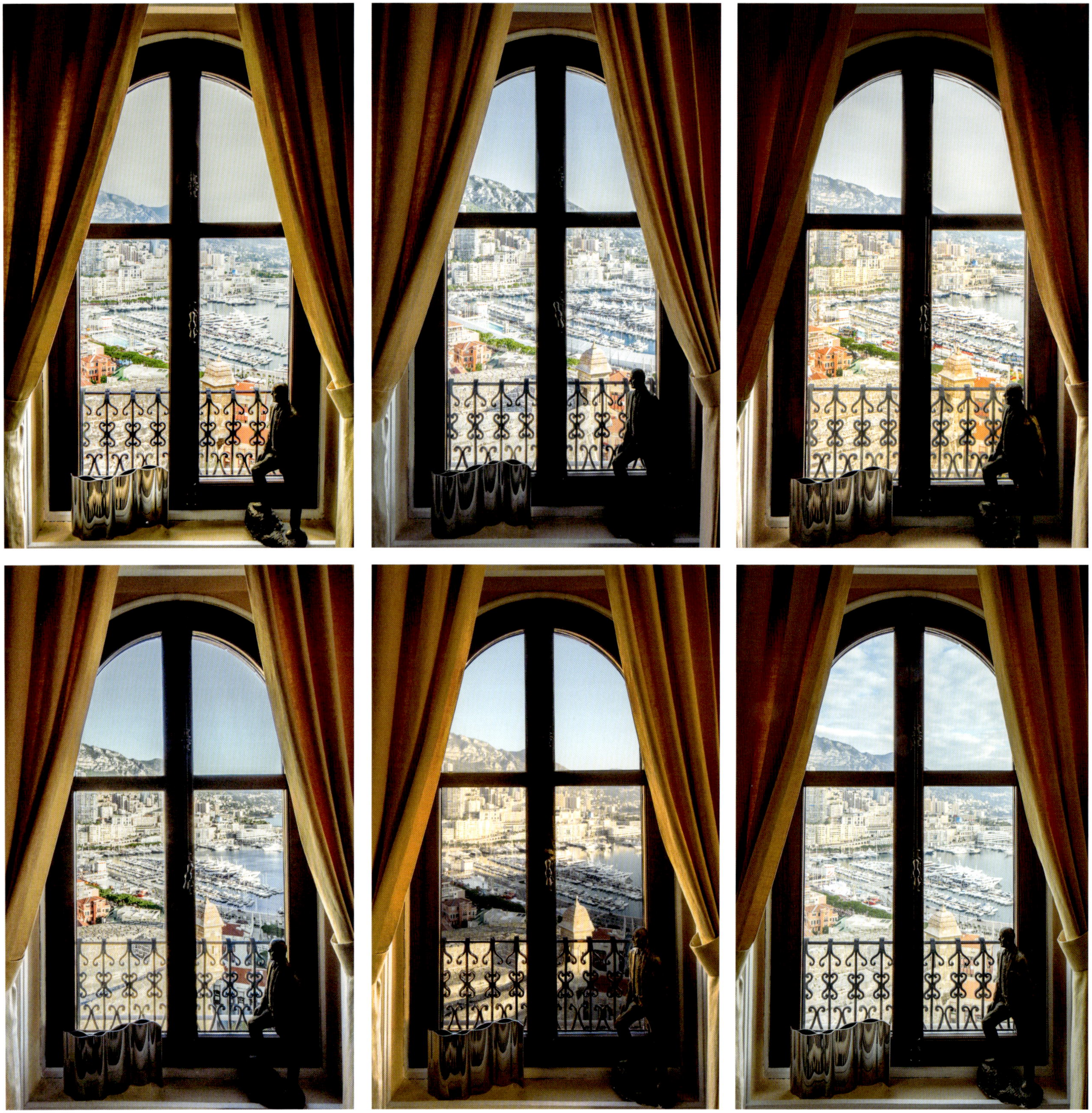

Taken from the prince's office at 9:00 a.m. on the 24th day of every month over one year,
the photographer captures the changing scene as seen by Prince Albert II from his window.

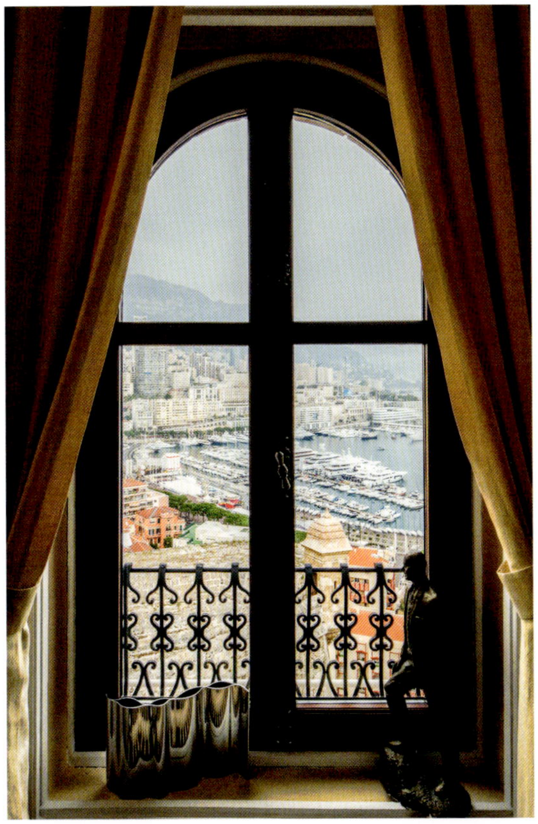
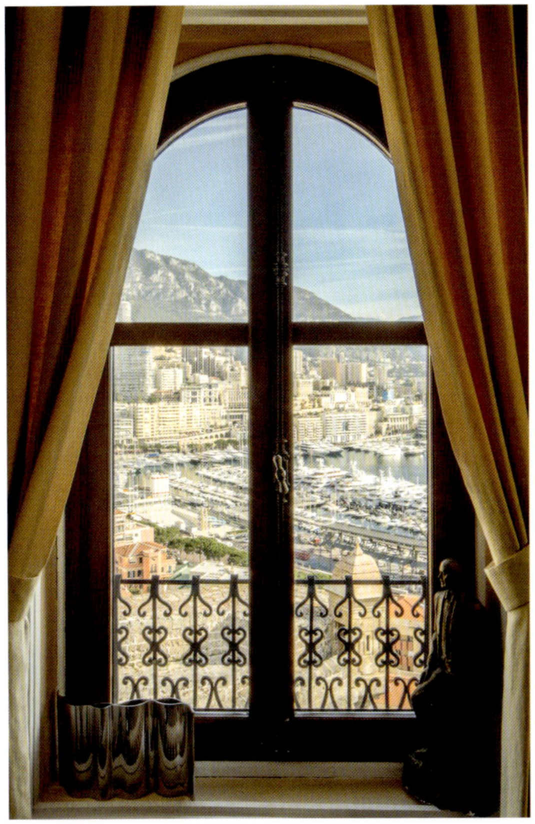
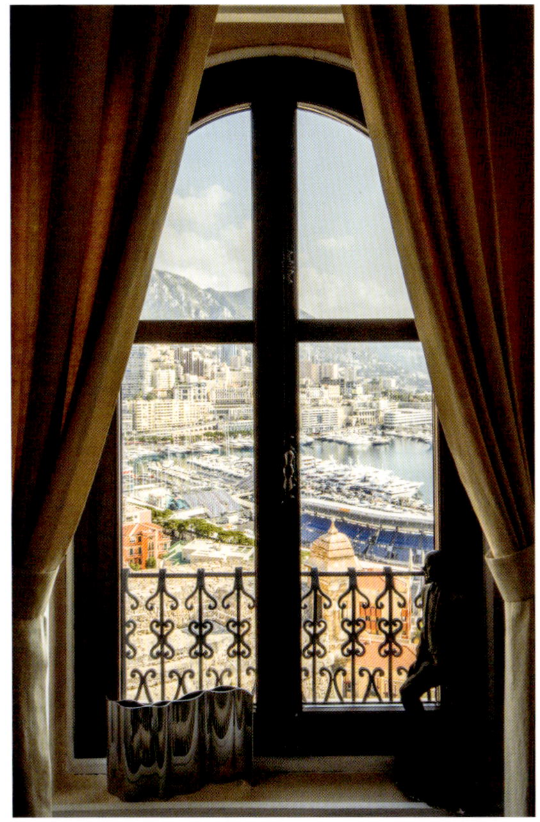
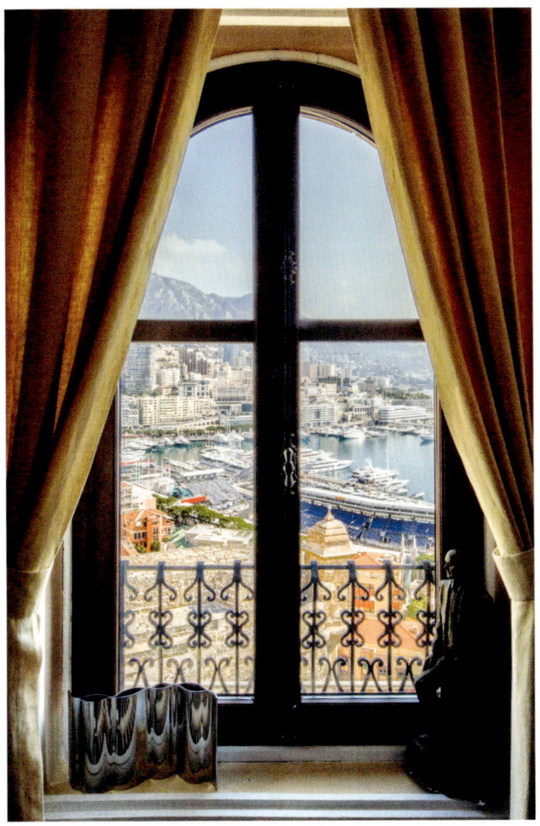
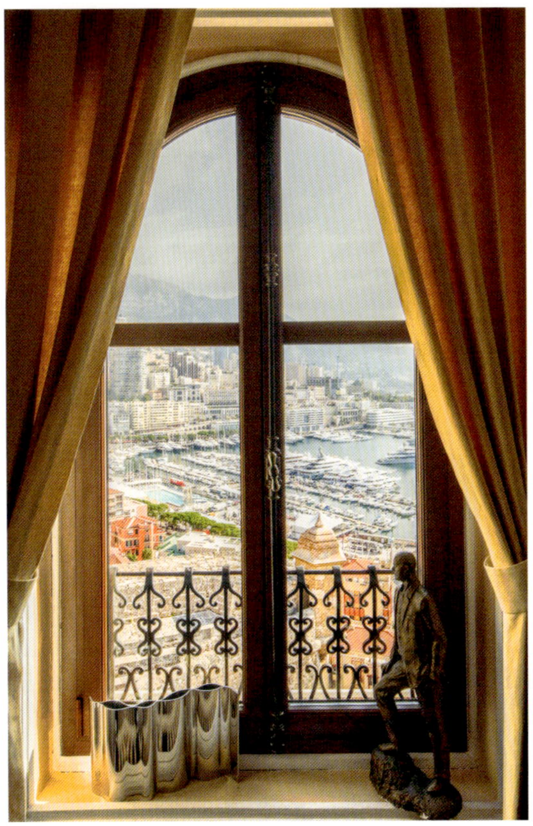
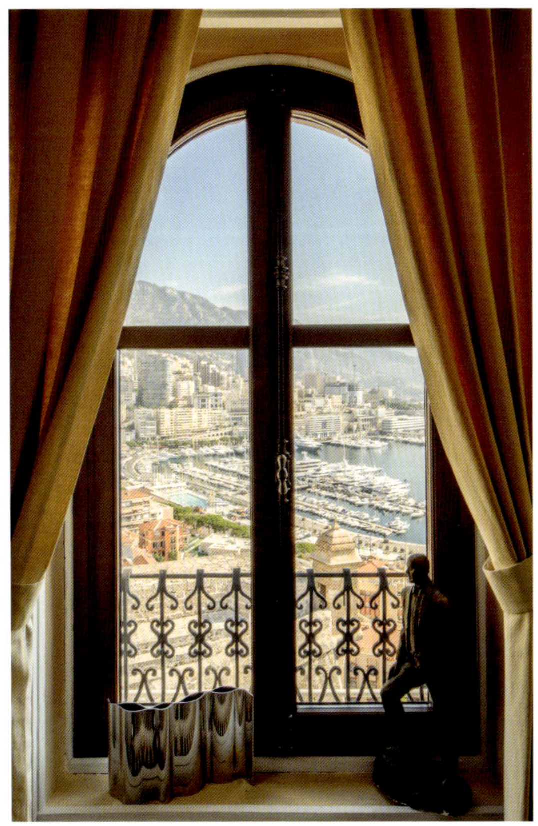

Following spread. Port Hercules in the afternoon
from the top of Rampe Major. December 28, 2015, 4:01 p.m.

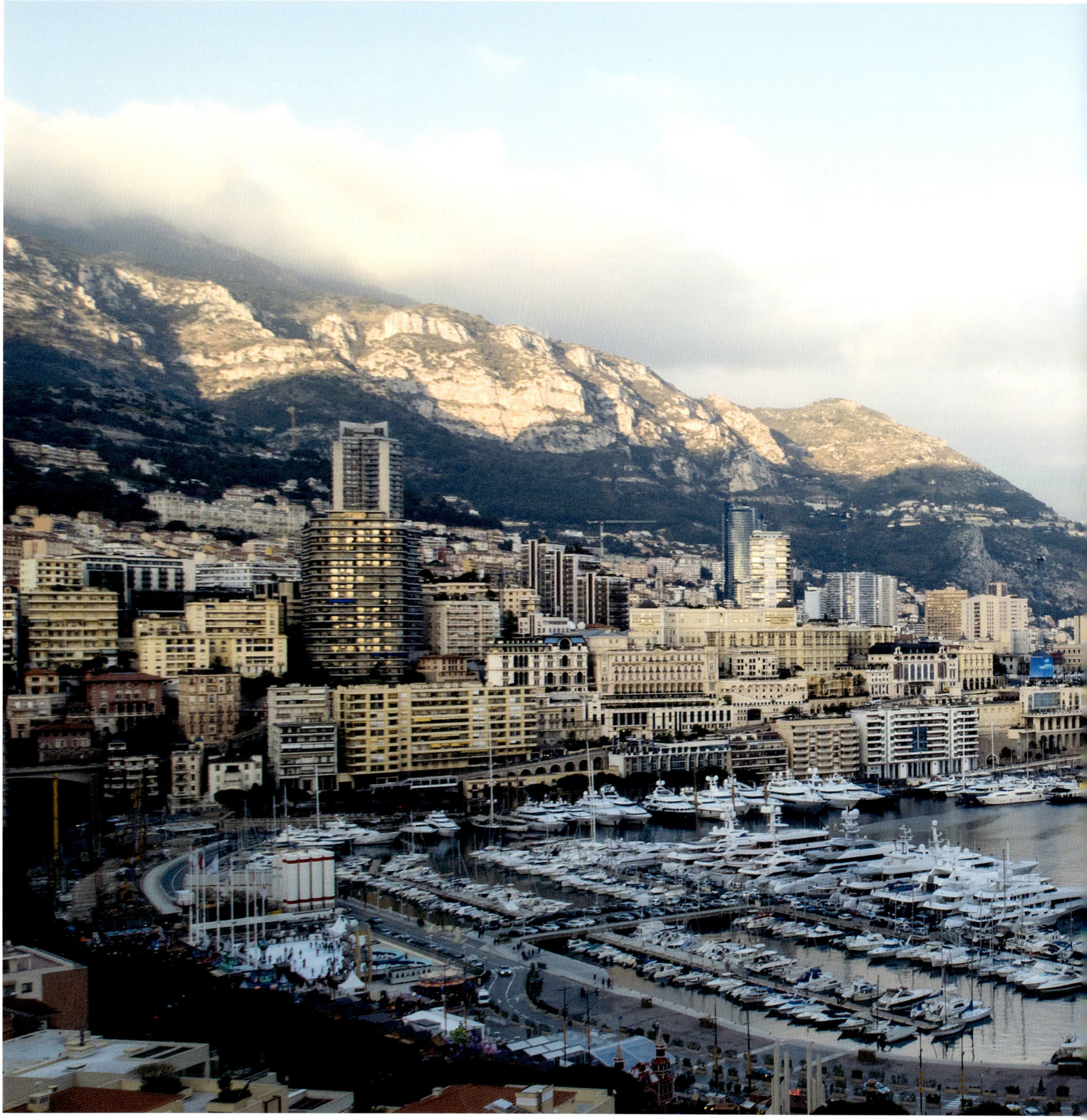

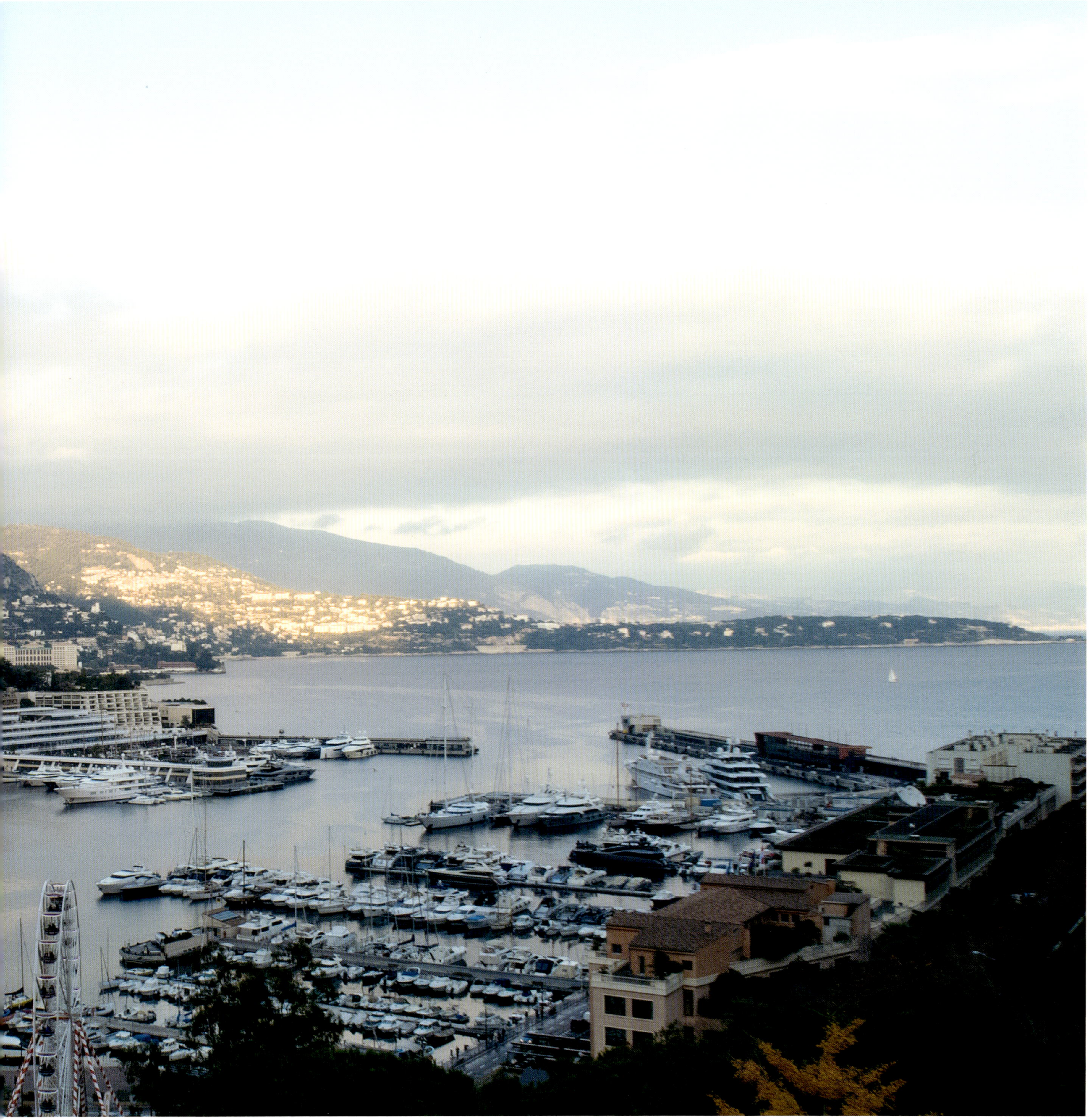

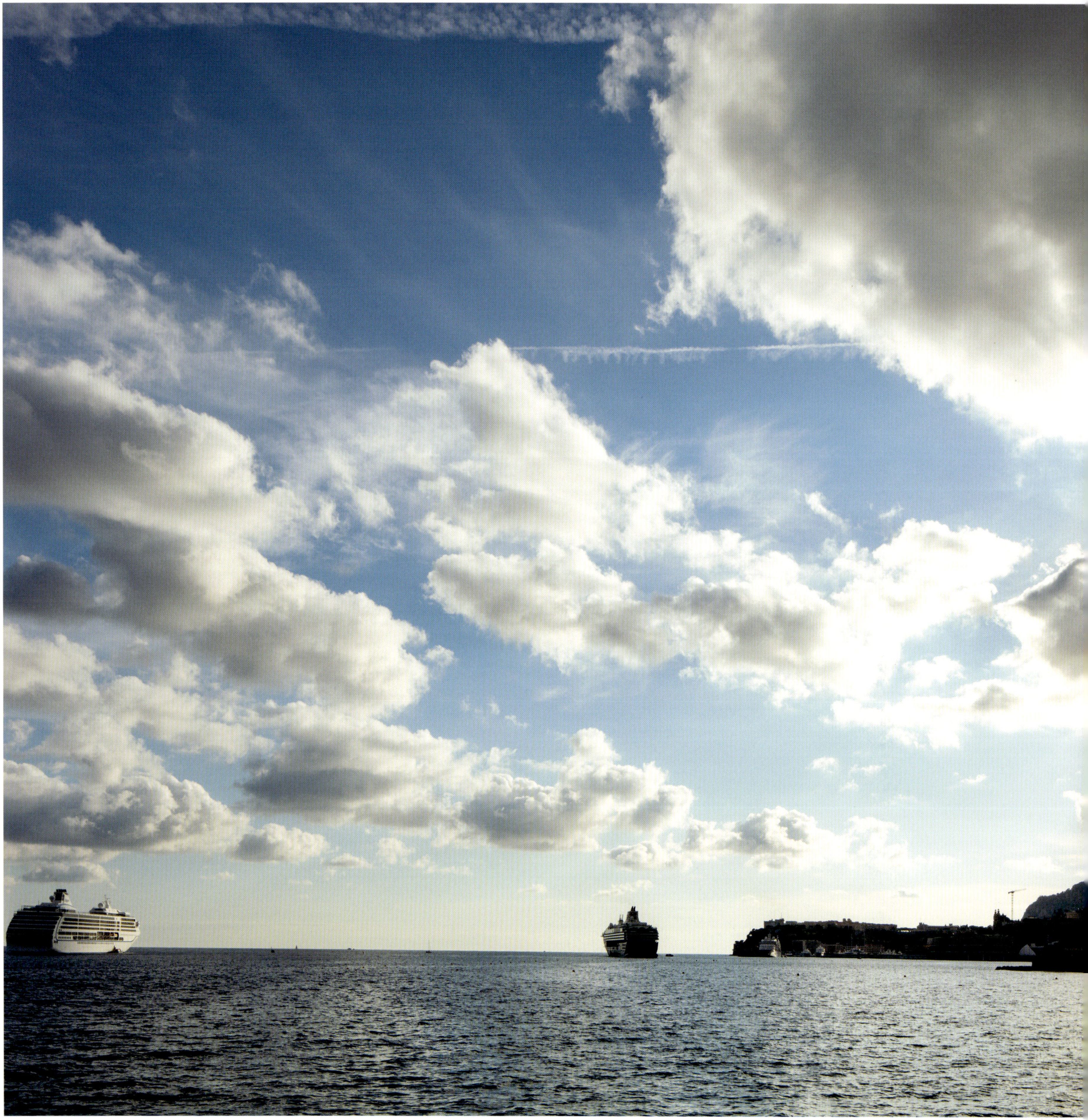

I

SHIFTING SKIES

Arriving by boat at the entrance of Port Hercules, Monaco's marina that lies protected under the Rock, spectacular cloud formations suggest a land full of promise. The words of Colette, describing the Principality as "the only country whose borders are flowers . . . " seem as apt and seductive now as they did in 1950 when they were first penned and addressed to Prince Rainier III. Gliding among the seven hundred moorings of the marina with this intoxicating view ahead, the imagination soars as it starts to explore through the eyes of the photographer's lens:

"I'm watching the light shift, and I stand still to better observe the subtle passage of clouds and sun. I notice the extremely wide color palette and the beautiful natural setting. It is right on the waterfront, between the winds of sea and land, that we often witness scenes normally hidden to us inland. It might be the way cloud lines harmonize with old baroque architecture. Or it might be a Saharan sky with sandy winds agitating the palm trees. There are always great pictures. Sometimes you have to be quick and other times patient. But you always have to be on the lookout, behind you and in front. The 'shot / reverse shot' between the sea and the city is a great example."

U-shaped Port Hercules is protected from sea swells by innovative breakwaters commissioned by Prince Rainier III and his son, Albert II. It is the only deep-water harbor on the French Riviera and can now welcome cruise ships. It lies in a natural bay, an ancient harbor for Greek and Roman ships—that is how it got its name. It still retains its renowned elegance and continues to attract hundreds of pleasure boats to its jetties each day. Like in Venice, small ferries provide a shuttle service between the opposite sides of the marina, between Quai des États-Unis and Quai Rainier I. A ride on these solar-powered water taxis provides the perfect opportunity to fully appreciate the port's geographical setting, nestled between the Mediterranean Sea, the district of La Condamine, the sovereign Rock of Monaco, and Monte Carlo, the resort created by Prince Charles III in 1861.

"I wanted to capture that fleeting moment when sunset turns to dusk and the lights of the city come alive. I spent two hours on Rampe Major which leads to the palace, waiting and watching as the sun leaves Port Hercules and eventually slips behind Tête de Chien rock. Standing on this historic path, I was struck by how the past and present collide over a scene where the heritage and life of the port come together with nature as their link."

Walking up Rampe Major from Place d'Armes at the foot of the Rock of Monaco, passing by the wonderfully vibrant La Condamine market with its explosion of colors, is like stepping back in history. The higher up the Rock's orange-paved flank one climbs, the stronger the sense of traveling back in time. Visitors of all nationalities brush shoulders with one another as they pass the two sixteenth-century doors before finally arriving at the statue of François Grimaldi, aka "Malizia," disguised as a Franciscan friar to immortalize his cunning capture of the fortress in 1297. The experience is even more captivating if timed to arrive at 11:55 a.m., when the changing-of-the-guard ceremony begins and the period of history changes once more. Built in the thirteenth century and expanded over time, the Prince's Palace reveals further details about the Rock's history. And in the Gallery of Hercules, with its mythological frescoes adorning the colorful lounges and throne room, visitors gain intimate access to seven hundred years of reign. The journey through time is continued by strolling the streets lined with painted houses within the medieval fortifications. This is where to find the grand Monaco Cathedral, the Chapelle de la Miséricorde, the Oceanographic Museum, and the Saint Martin Gardens with their sublime views over the sea. Here, a series of paths wind through the beautifully landscaped ramparts, offering glimpses of the waves below and the promise of new discoveries at each new turn.

Once inside the Principality, between the sea and mountains, it is hard to believe the astonishing statistics of Monaco's true size. Less than 1 square mile in area and with just 2.5 miles of Mediterranean coastline, this patch of land 11 miles from Nice, 7 miles from the Italian border, and nestled between Beausoleil, Cap d'Ail, Roquebrune-Cap-Martin, and La Turbie, is strikingly diverse for its size. And even though its highest point is just 538 feet, it is given a strong impression of height by Mont Agel in the French commune of Peille, which overlooks Monaco from 3,766 feet.

When the prevailing winds from Genoa to the east and the tail end of the mistral to the west fill the sky with impressive clouds of subtle colors and fiery hues, they seem to suspend a theater curtain between the land and sea that scatters the sun's bright light. "Never have I seen elsewhere such fairy-like sunsets, such conflagrations of the whole horizon, such an effulgence of clouds, such a clever and superb arrangement, such a daily renewal of extravagant and magnificent effects which call forth admiration, but would raise a smile were they painted by men," writes Maupassant in *Afloat (Sur l'eau)*. It is easy to imagine the great Raoul Gunsbourg, the famous director of the Opéra de Monte-Carlo between 1893 and 1951, conducting the clouds' performance over the city. The grand master of ceremonies put on some of the biggest operas and was behind the introduction of Diaghilev's Ballets Russes to Monaco. With its baroque architecture, Les Spélugues plateau—once planted with olive, lemon, and orange trees—became Monte Carlo, the most coveted place in high society under Prince Charles III of Monaco, thanks to its casino, opera house, gardens, and luxury hotels, which we can still visit today

Previous spread. Looking to the west of the Principality and the ballet of boats leaving Port Hercules in the late afternoon. October 2015, 17, 4:59 p.m.

Raising the curtain over spectacular Monte Carlo Bay. October 2015, 17, 10:56 a.m.

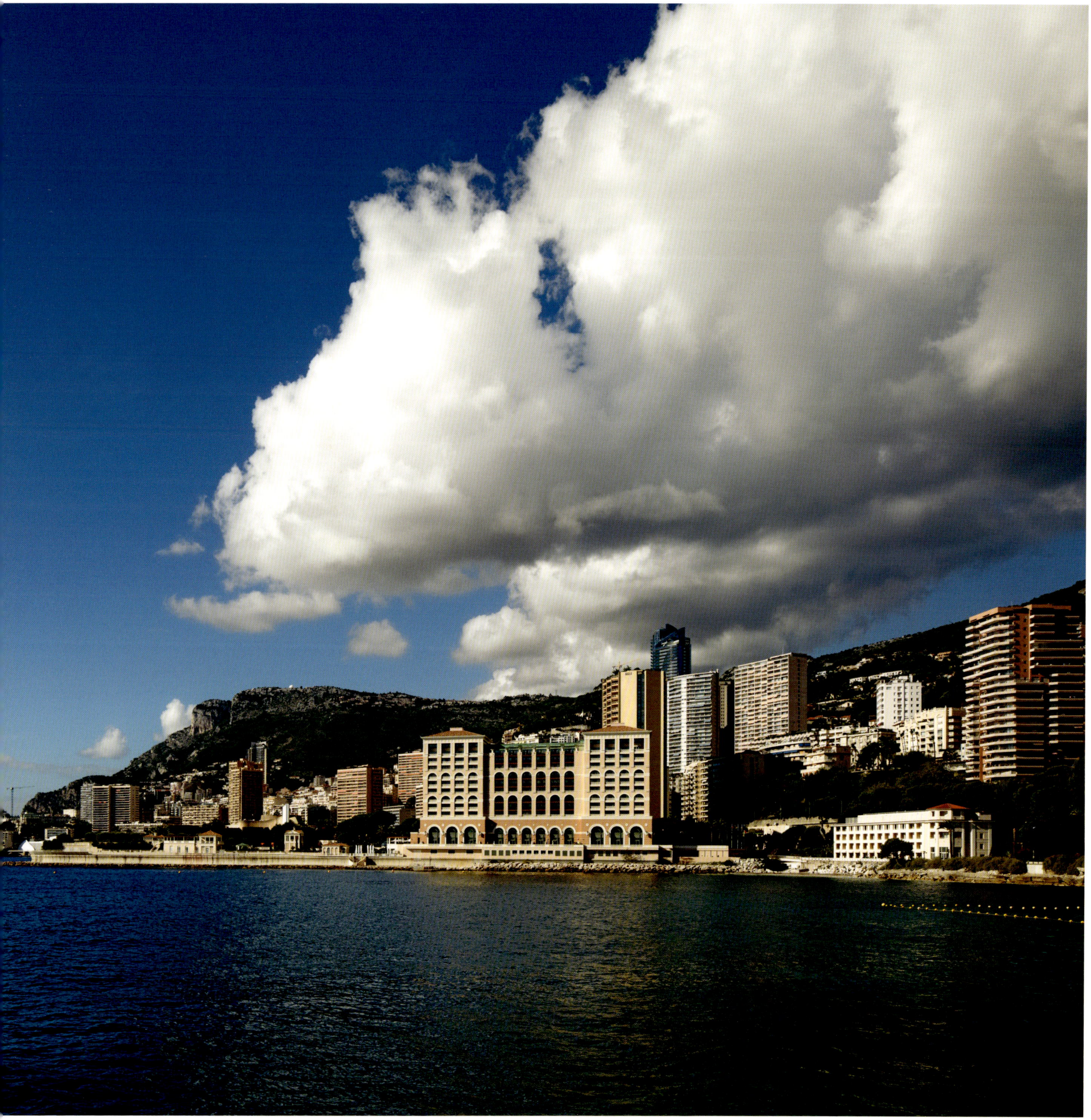

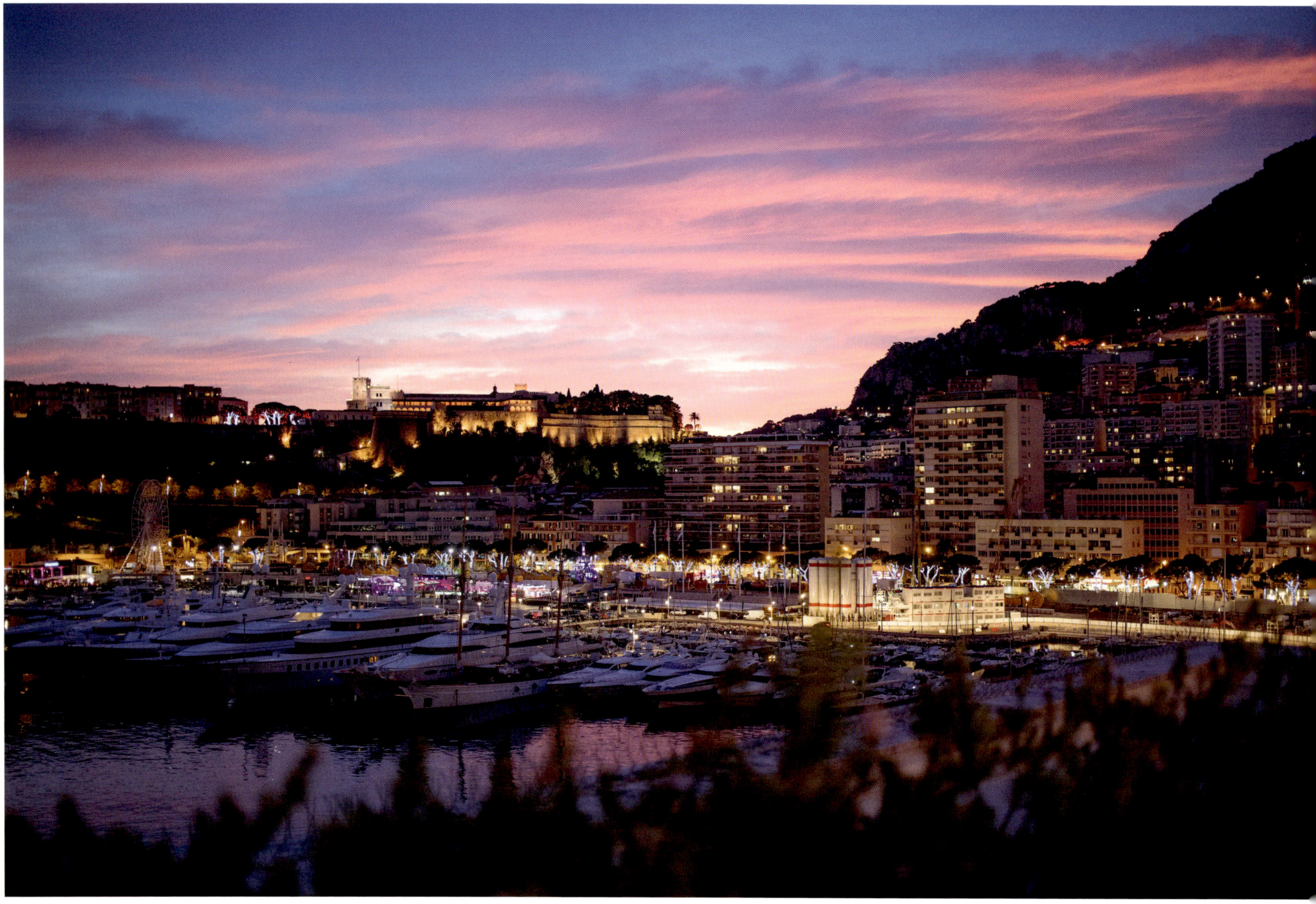

Port Hercules and the Rock of Monaco at sunset and dusk.
November 29, 2015. Left page, 6:23 p.m.; right page, 6:39 p.m.

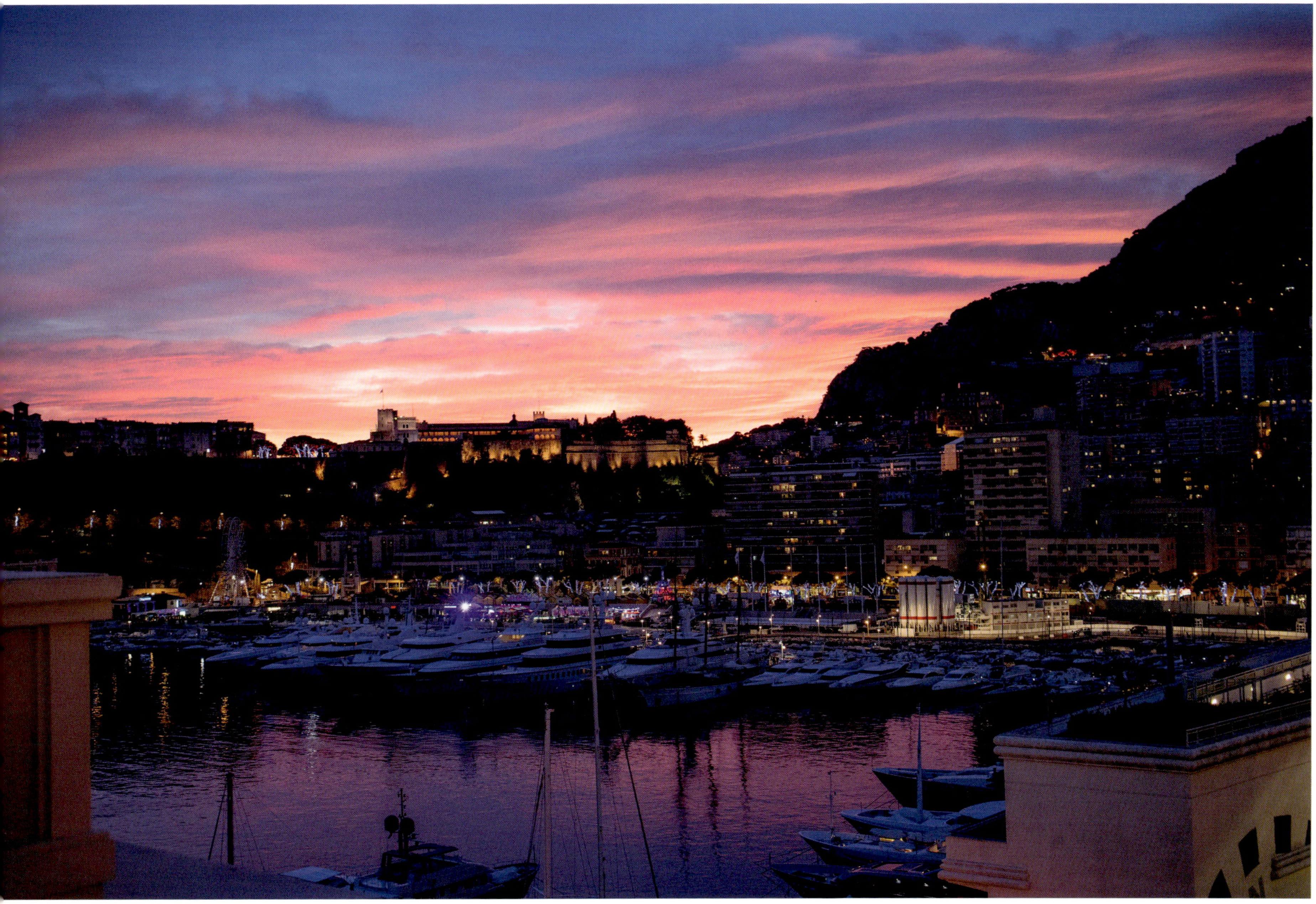

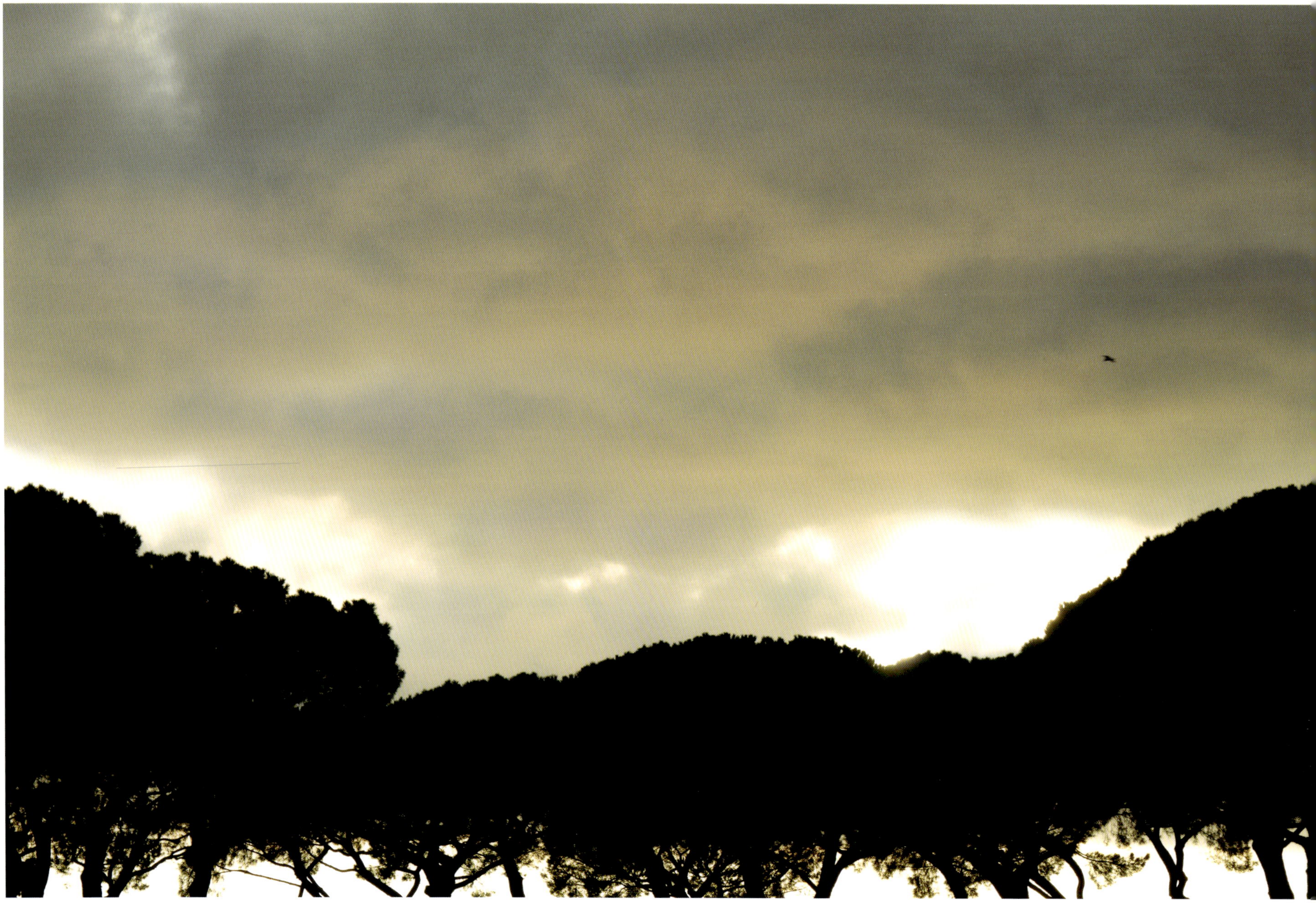

Frozen in time, colors fade at the end of a winter's day at Place du Palais.
December 28, 2015. Left page, 4:03 p.m.; right page, 4:11 p.m.

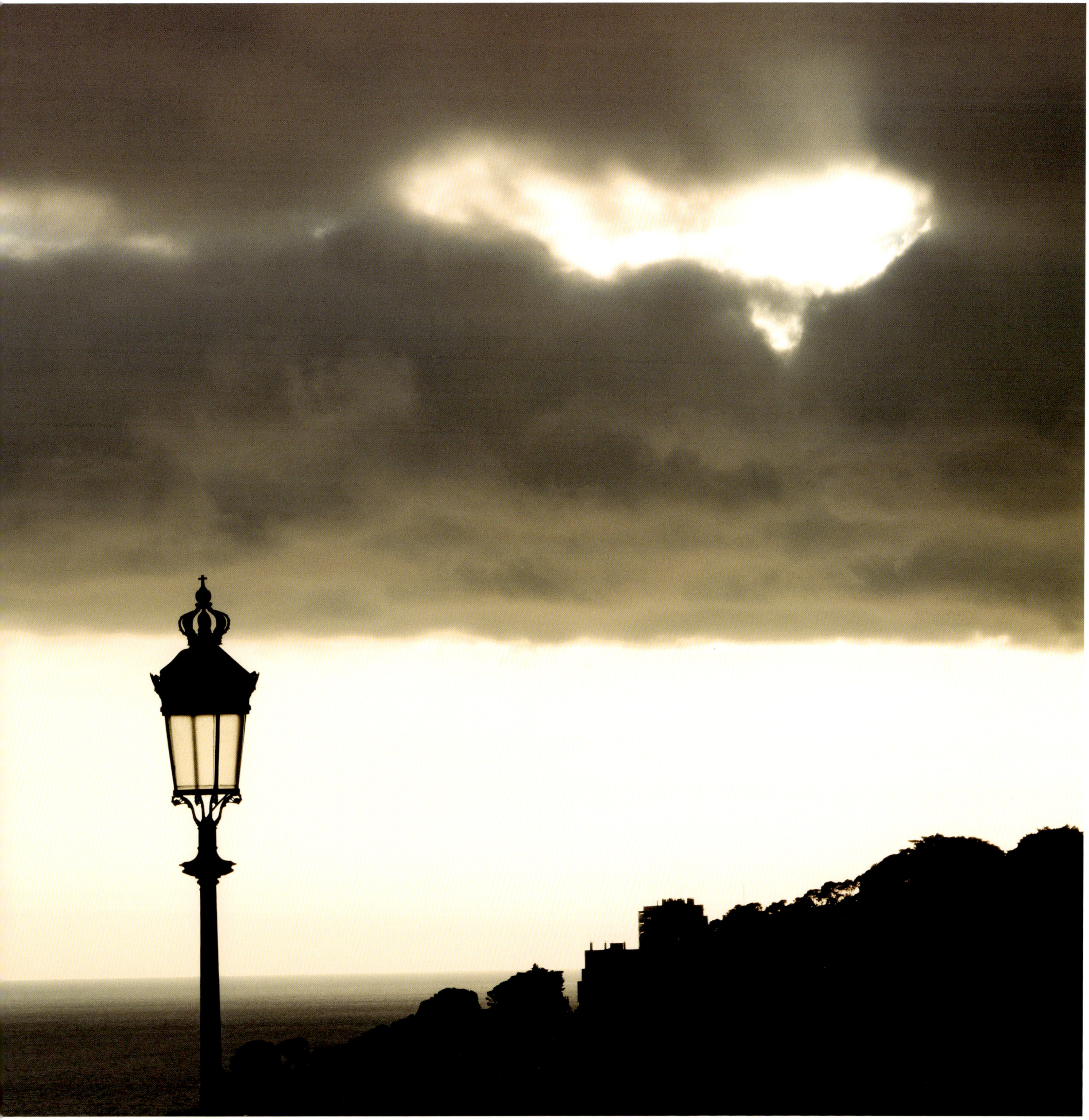

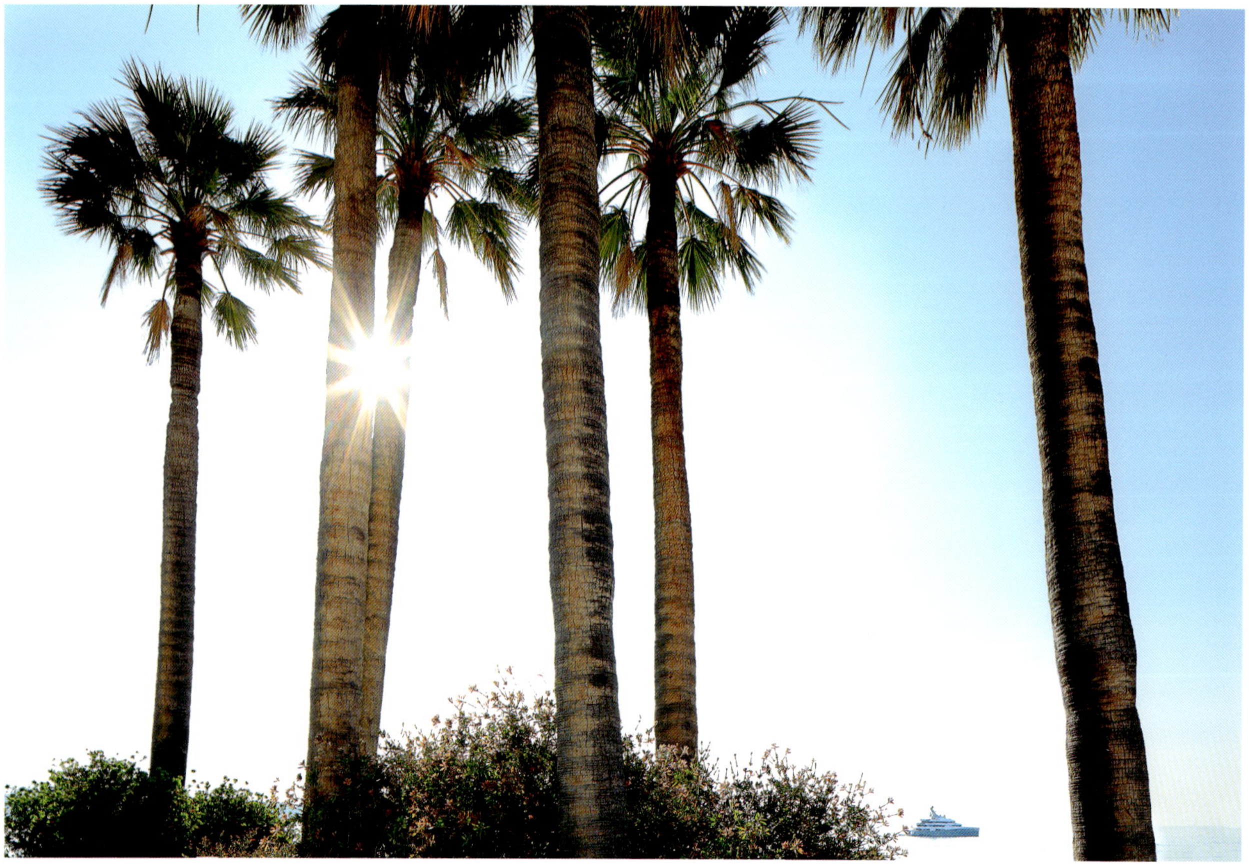

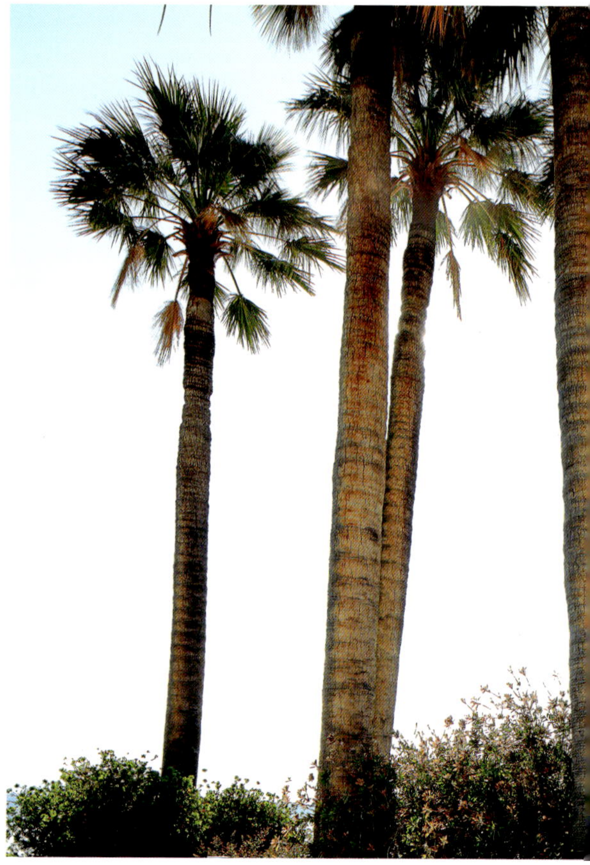

Like the tip of a watch hand, the sun counts down the minutes, represented here by palm trees.
June 21, 2015. Left, 7:31 a.m.; center, 7:41 a.m.; right, 7:47 a.m.

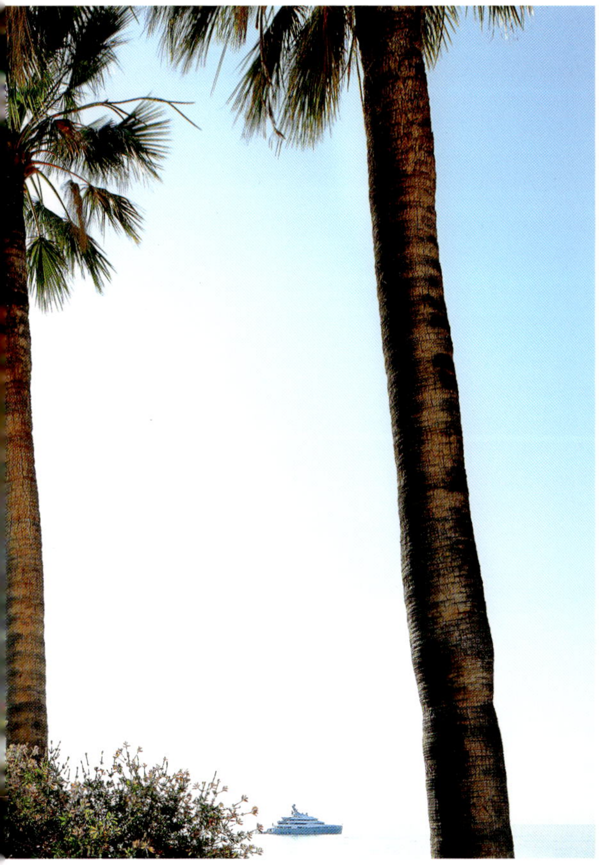

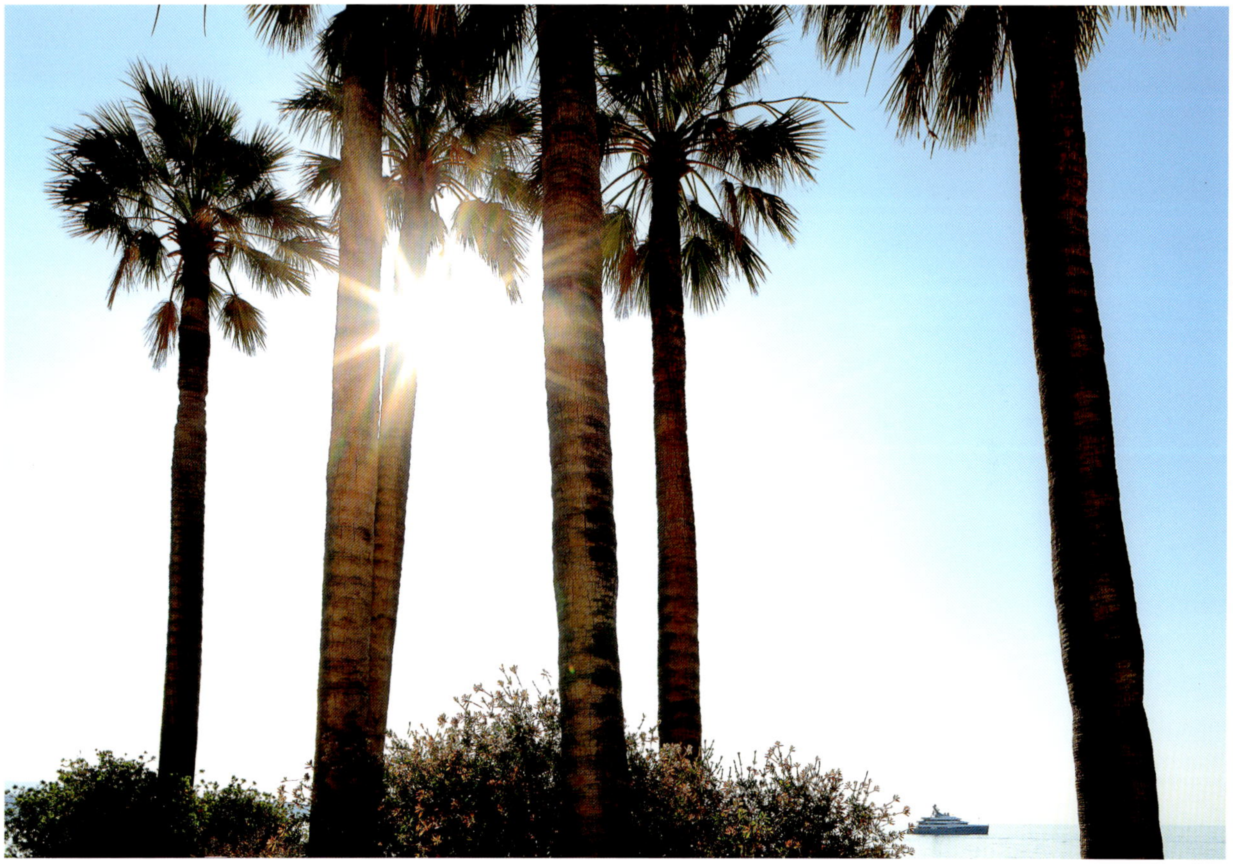

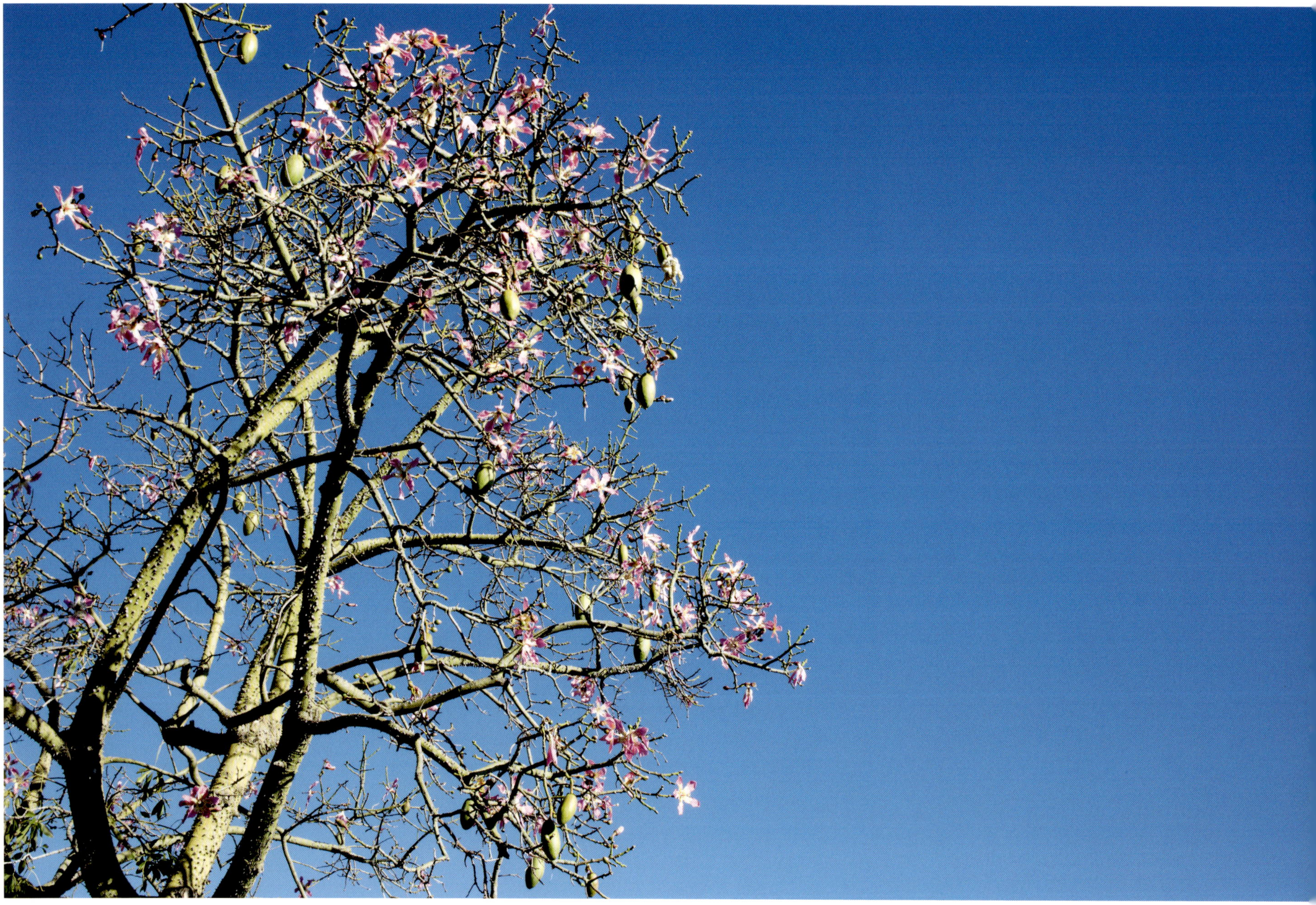

The sun points its spotlight at a magnolia's magnificent flowers,
then moves on before returning the next day with renewed splendor.
October 31, 2015. Left page, 11:15 a.m.; right page, 5:31 p.m.

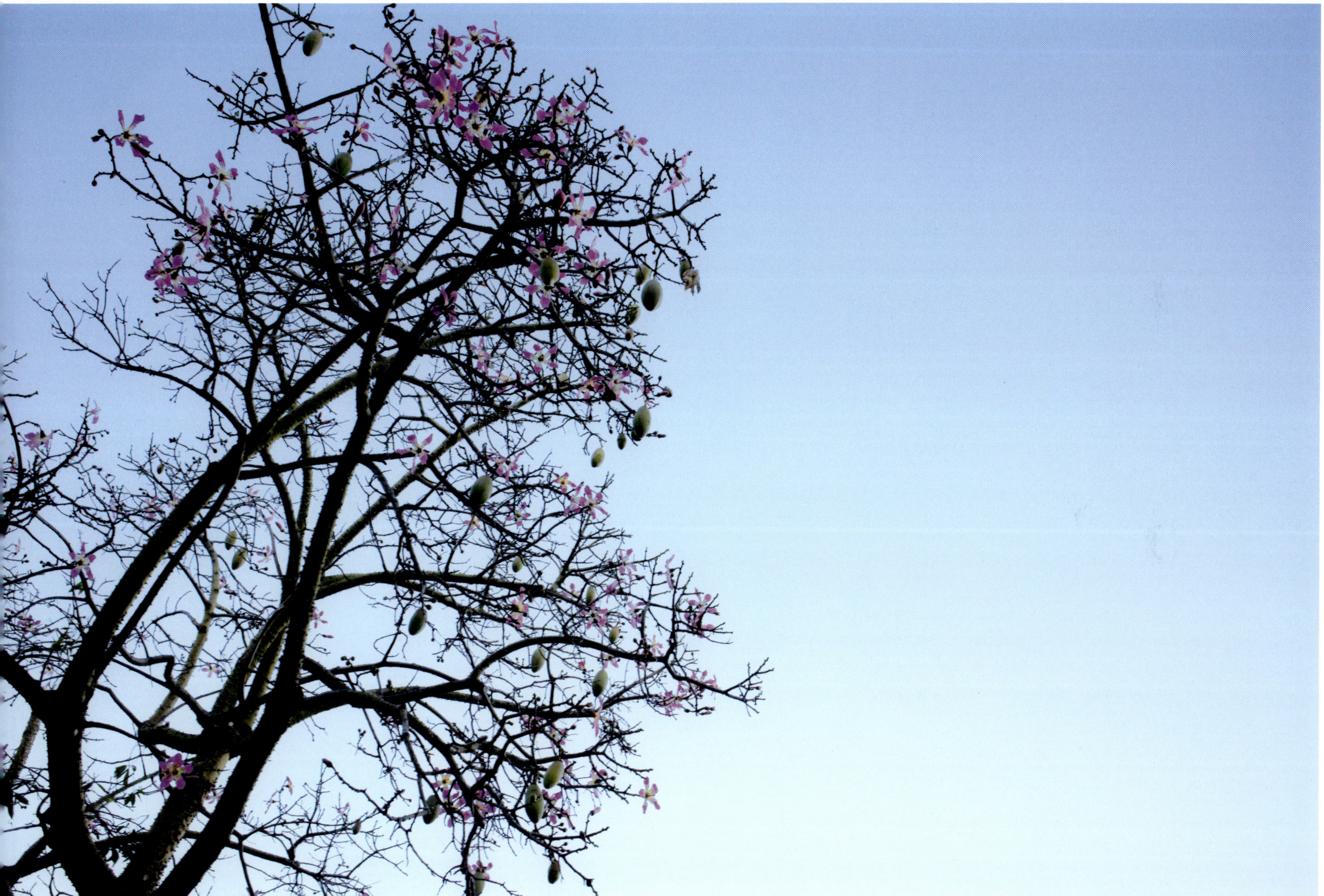

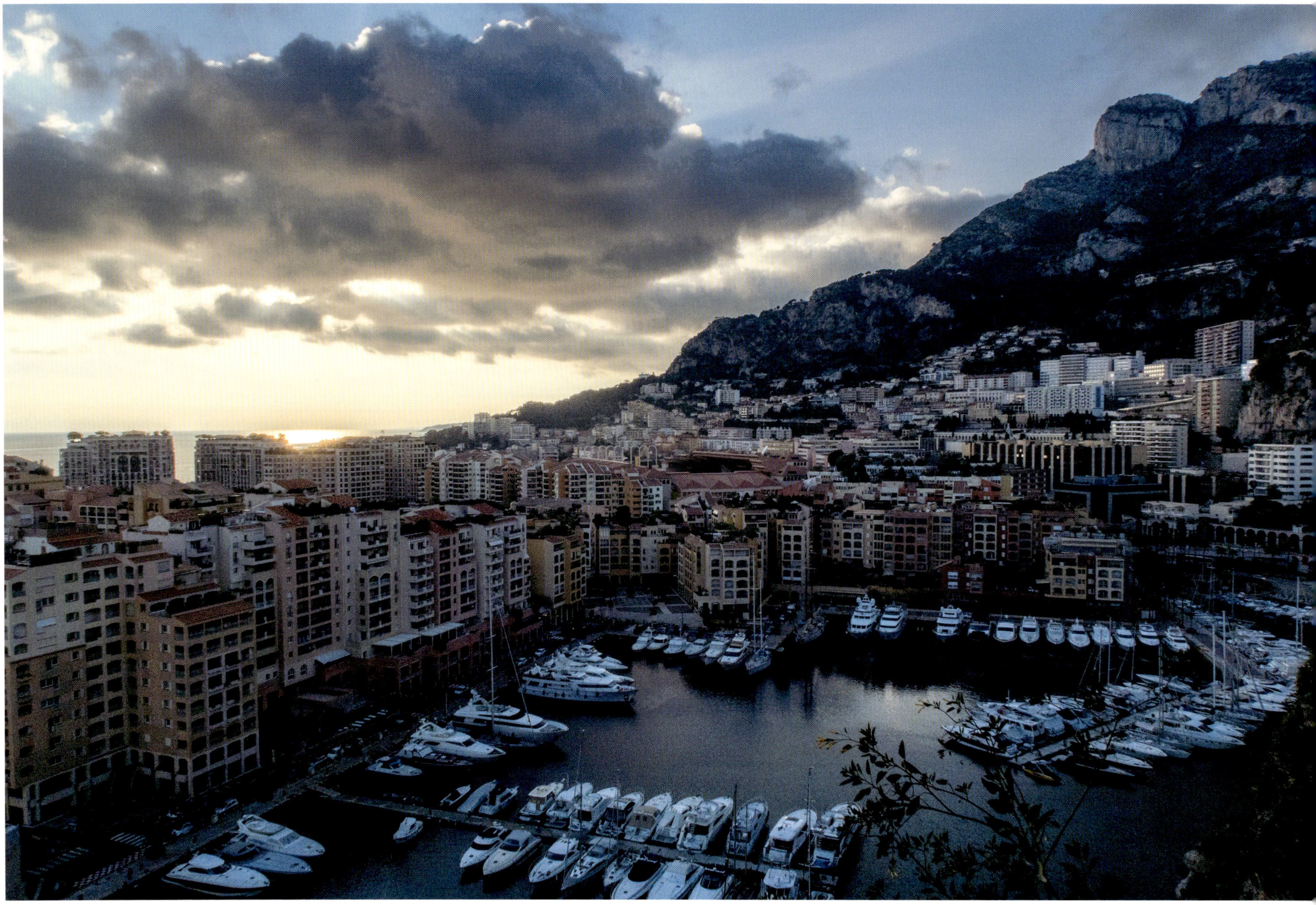

Dramatic cloud formations over Fontvieille's harbor on a winter's afternoon.
December 28, 2015. Left page, 11 seconds after 3:42 p.m.; right page, 35 seconds after 3:42 p.m.

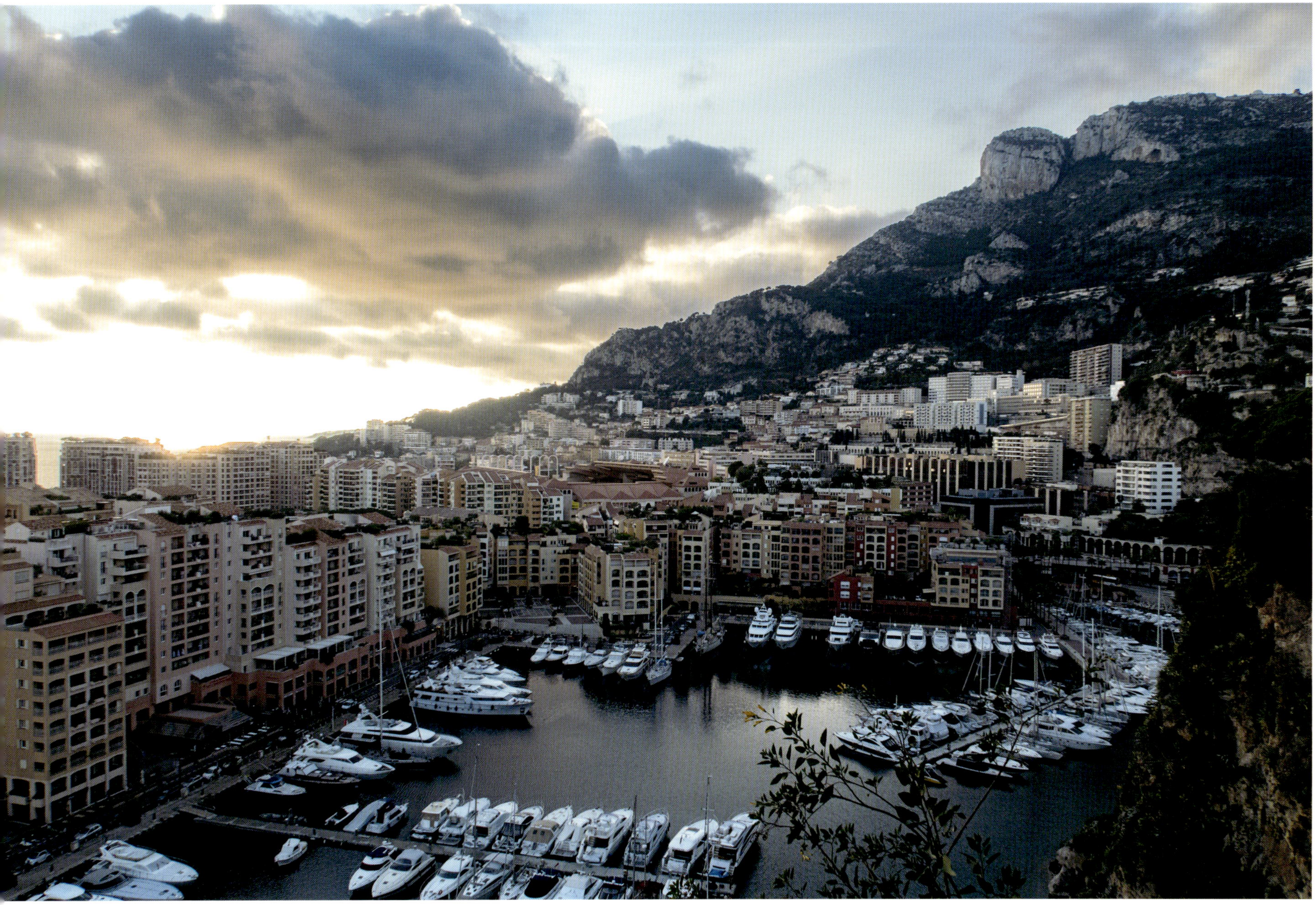

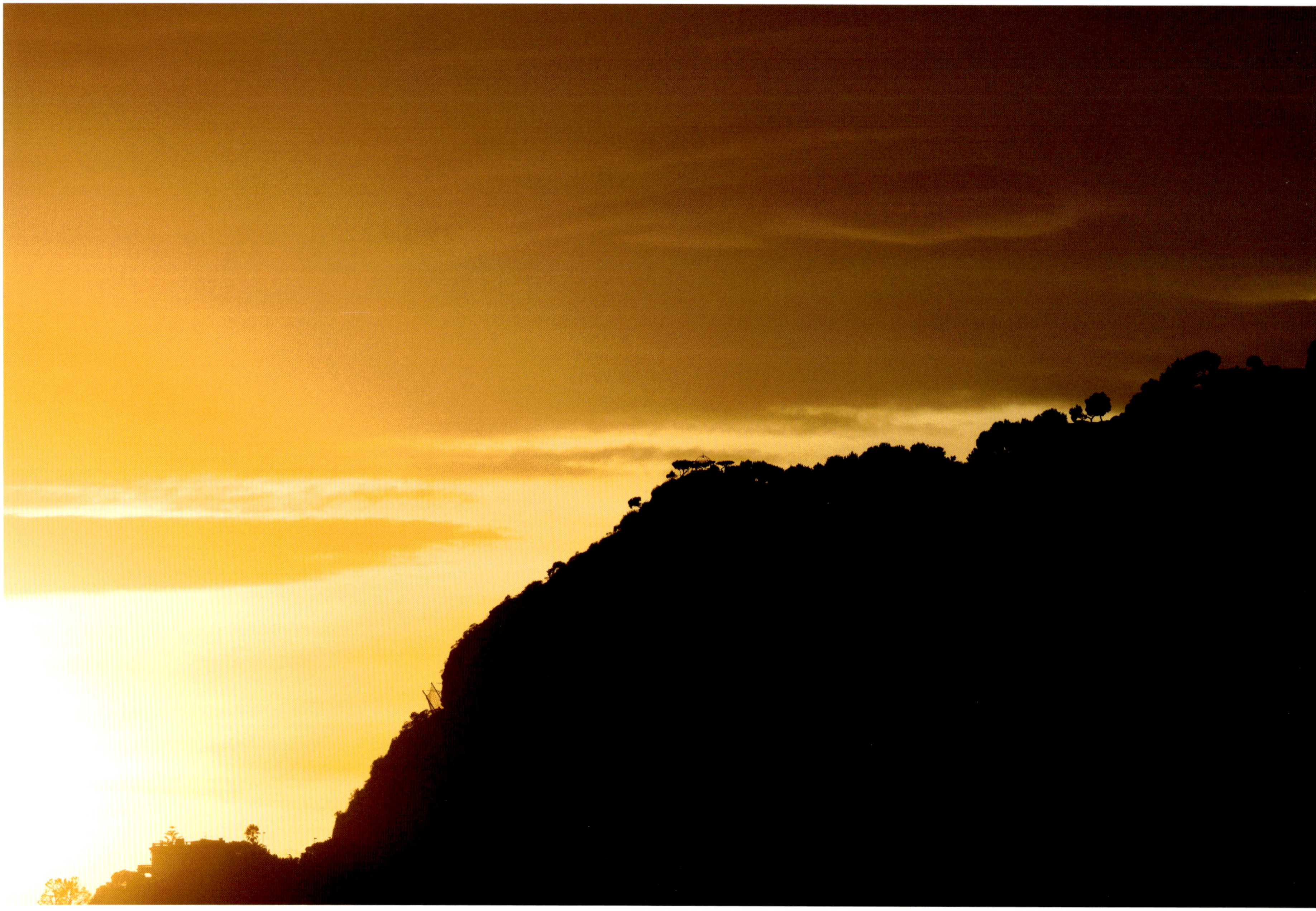

Previous triptych. Taken a few days apart, from the terrace of the Oceanographic Museum, the view over Fontvieille reveals dynamic color changes over time.
From left to right, January 31, 2016, 5:23 p.m., and 5:48 p.m. February 4, 2016, 11:30 a.m.

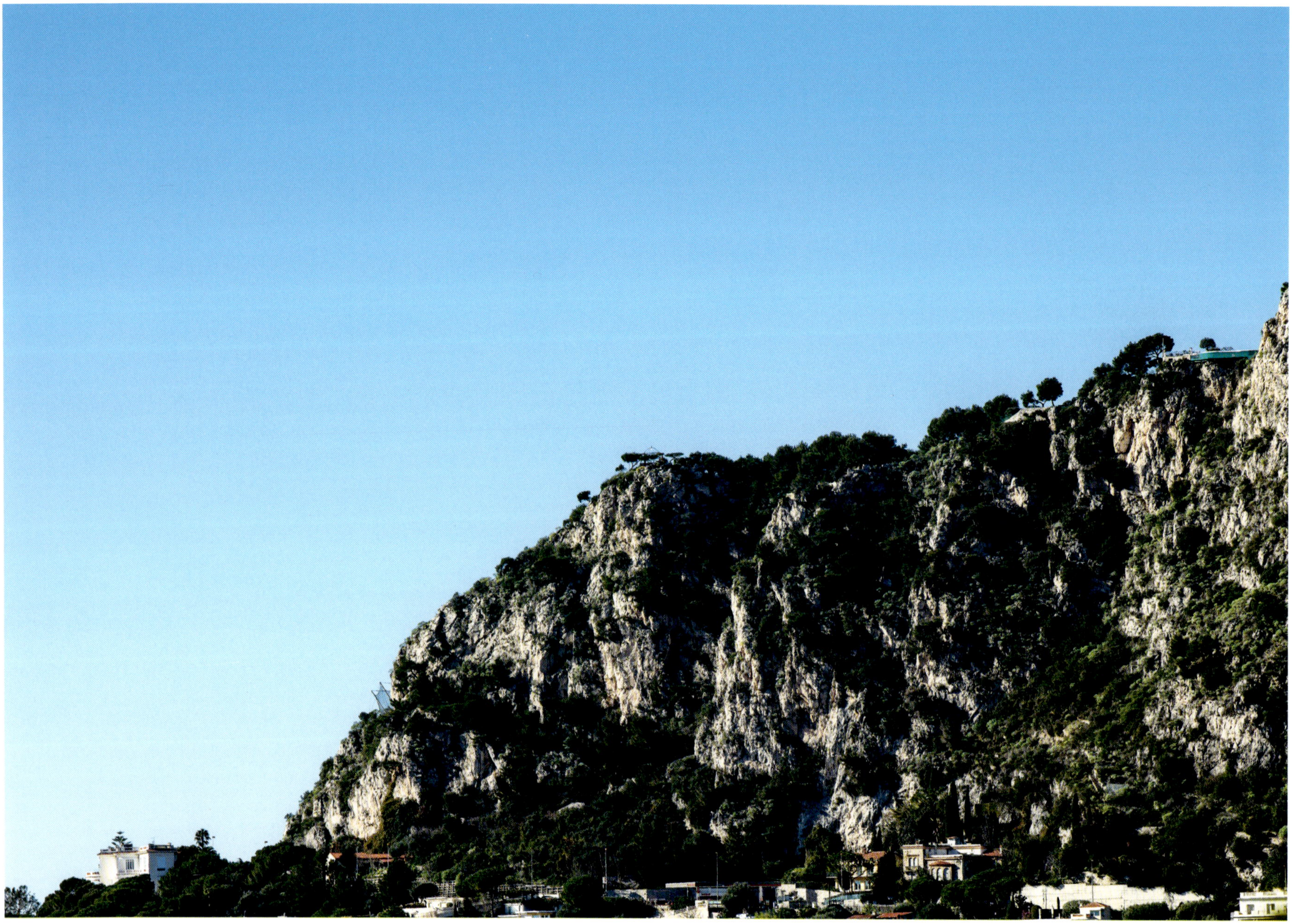

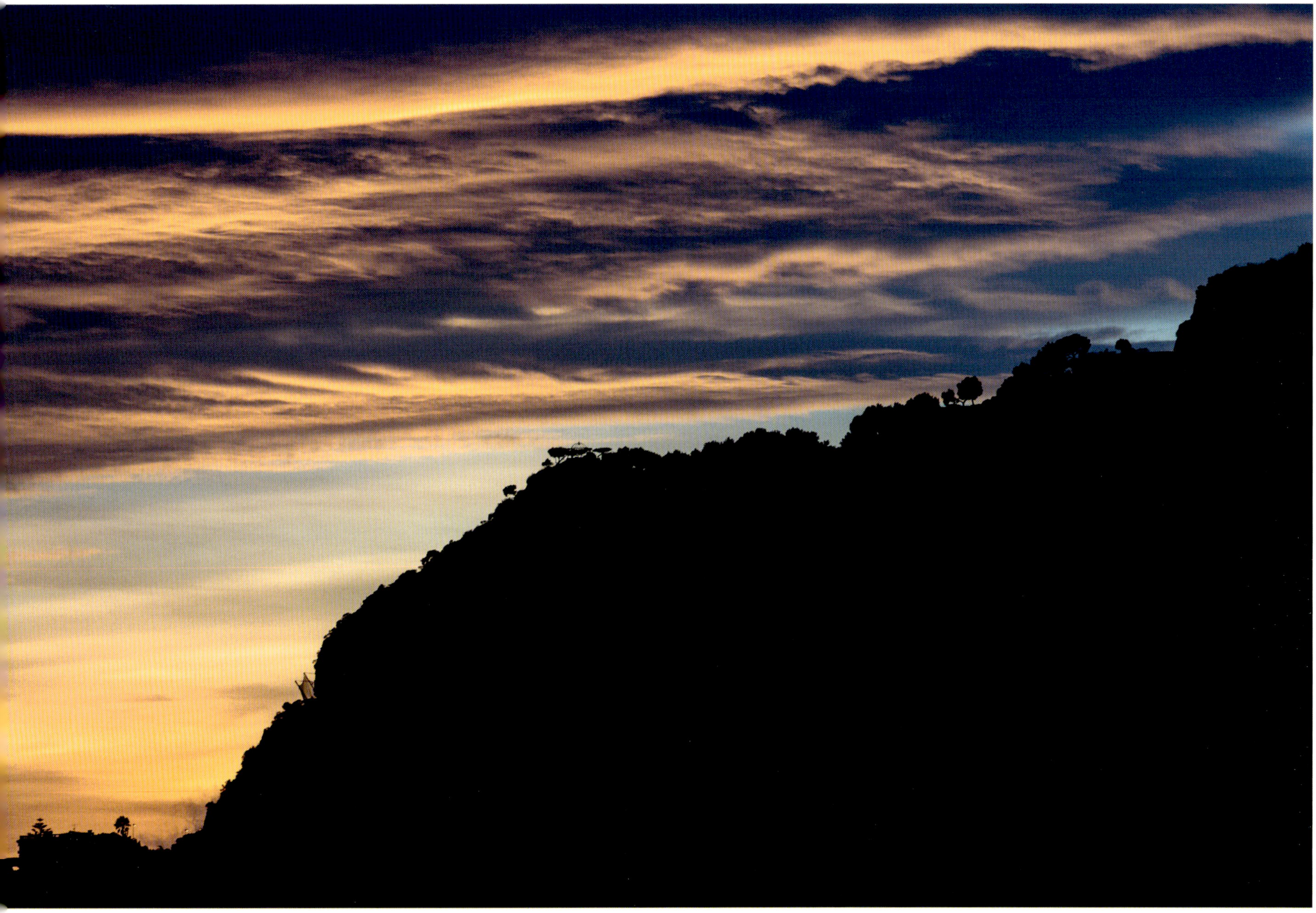

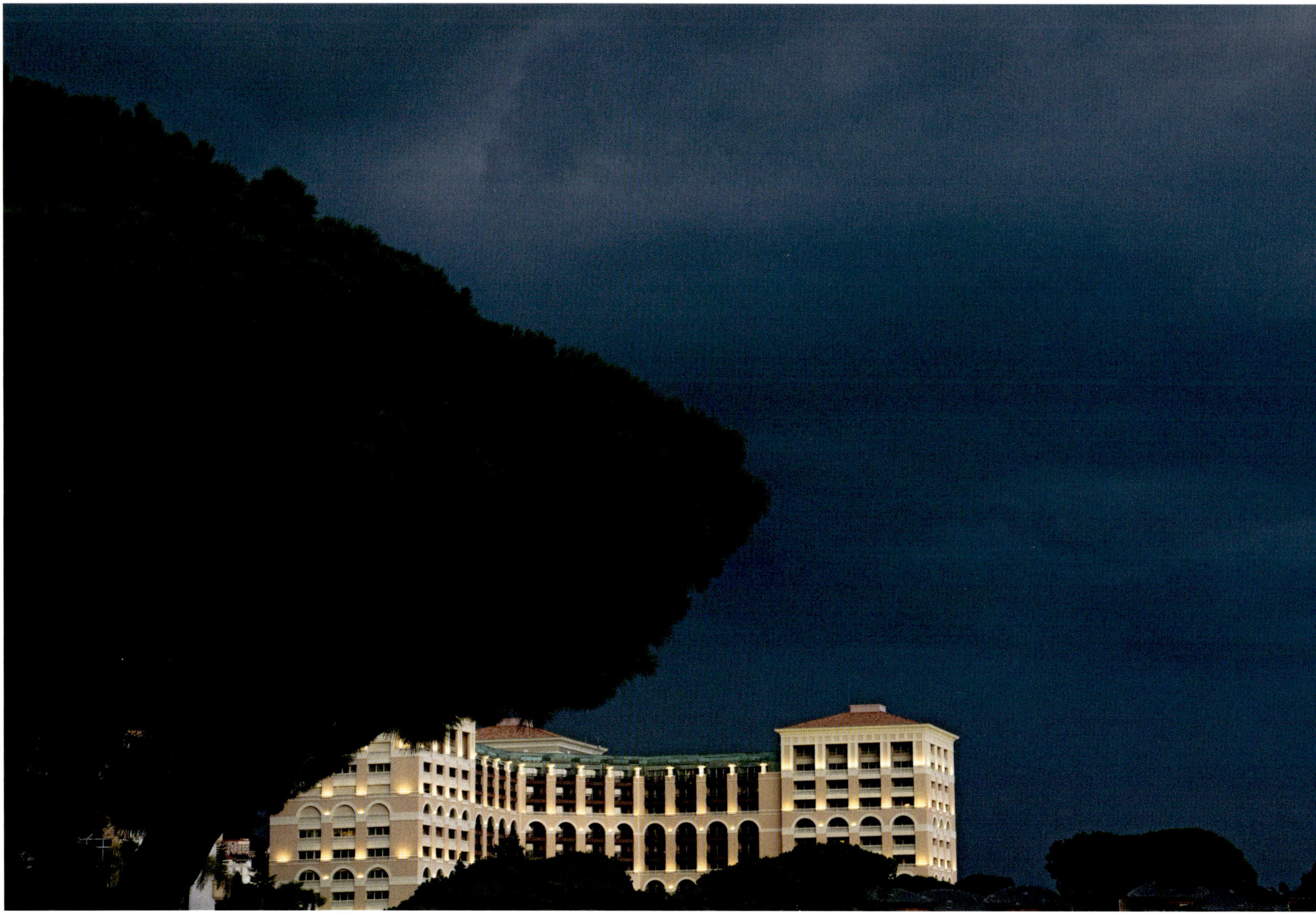

Behind the scenes in Monte Carlo Bay.
Left page, November 22, 2015, 5:12 p.m. Right page, March 5, 2016, 4:31 p.m.

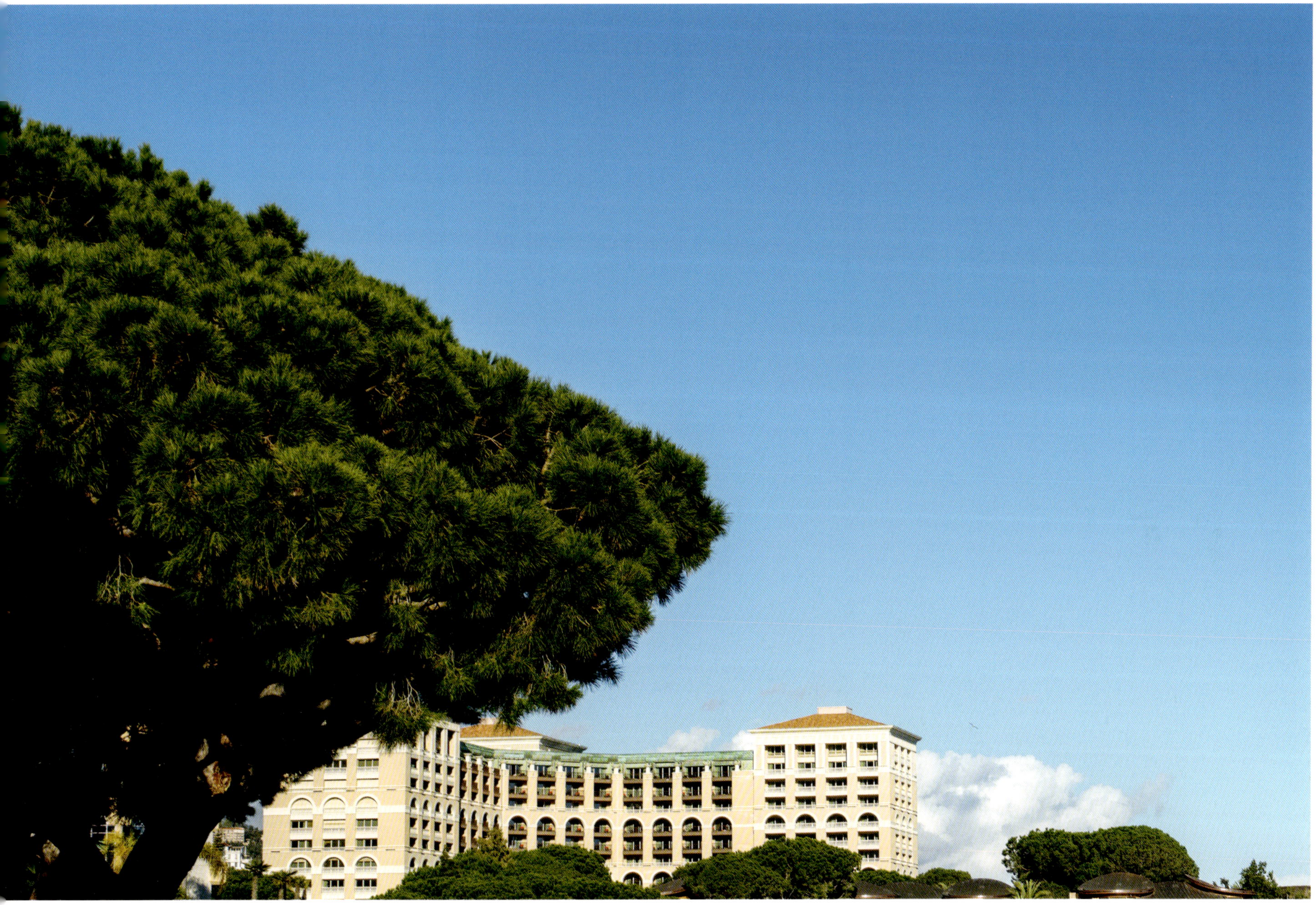

Following spread. A nod to the Impressionists is made by capturing the delicate color palette variations that come and go at the mercy of time and air temperature. November 30, 2015. Left page, 5:33 p.m.; right page, 5:58 p.m.

II

A SEA OF COLORS

Arriving in Monaco by car is an exciting experience. From the top of the boulevard du Jardin Exotique, a spectacular view opens up. Below, the Rock dominates between Port Hercules and Fontvieille, its old fortified walls protecting the medieval town like a precious jewel. The green belt of the palace and Saint Martin Gardens contrast with the town's red roofs, while the imposing white cathedral and Oceanographic Museum catch the eye against a backdrop of a vast and shimmering sea. "At sunset, a pink sky paints the sea purple and prepares the Rock for sleep, while twenty hours later the sun directs its spotlight onto the Rock to accentuate its natural setting," explains the photographer.

Weaving down the hills between the houses or following a road like boulevard des Moulins along the top of the Principality, the sea constantly demands attention as it appears in gaps between buildings, prompting a stop at the top of a staircase or a walk to the shore to observe it more closely. And when the sun is out, which is three hundred days a year in Monaco, the expanse of sand at Larvotto Beach right next to the town center always beckons.

"I spent ten hours at Larvotto," admits the photographer, "but even though it was a long day, it never dragged because capturing the ever-changing scene was so enjoyable. In the morning, the building façades are illuminated, while the pure blue of the sky intensifies the deep blue of the sea and of the waves that constantly break in the foreground. At times the clouds change the color of the sea. When the sun goes down, they are stained pink and reflect this dominant color onto the sea. And then they disappear, revealing a rising full moon, which itself casts its own special light across the water."

Below the buildings bordering Larvotto Beach, an array of restaurants and terraces draws in those seeking refreshment. There are tables to suit every style or craving, the perfect place to sit, order a drink, and pull out a copy of Maupassant's *Afloat (Sur l'eau)* and share the emotions he felt when he wrote these words: "The gentle ripple of water on the sandy shore or on the rocky granite affects and moves me, and the joy that fills me as I feel myself driven forward by the wind and carried along by the waves, proceeds from the abandonment of myself to the brutal and natural forces of creation, from my return to a primitive state."

The earth's natural forces he mentions were the subject of scientific research throughout the life of Prince Albert I, great-great-grandfather of the Sovereign Prince, HSH Prince Albert II. A protector of the seas, Albert I governed his country with a humanistic vision, created the Monegasque Constitution, and founded the International Institute for Peace, a precursor of the League of Nations and the United Nations. His greatest passion was for oceanography, and his mission was to understand, cherish, and protect the oceans. This led him to explore the Mediterranean, the Azores, and Spitsbergen, among other areas, for much of his life. To house and study the many marine samples he brought back from his expeditions, he built the Oceanographic Museum. This monument dedicated to the seas and oceans was built on the Rock between 1899 and 1910, and features the imposing architectural design of Paul Delefortrie. This masterful neoclassical building rises 279 feet straight up from the coastal cliff face, inspiring a sense of awe which continues once you go inside. Browsing the 70,000-square-foot museum, which is open to the public, is an exhilarating adventure into the marine world, which takes in the grandeur of the place, its cliffside position, its decor, and its 6,000 fascinating specimens. Between the historical collections (the Prince Albert I Room, the Whale Room, measuring instruments, treasures of the deep, the Cabinet of Curiosities, and artists' creations) and the aquariums (tropical seas, the Mediterranean, a 20-foot-deep shark lagoon, and a touch tank where you can pet a baby shark), the importance of understanding and protecting this living heritage is clear to see. Prince Albert II, honorary president of the Oceanographic Museum, is continuing the inspiring work of his great-great-grandfather by raising awareness and protecting the environment both within and outside the Principality by working with the United Nations and his own foundation.

The sea around Monaco has been a place of wellbeing and relaxation to spa guests since 1863 when Prince Charles III, father of Albert I, built Monte Carlo in an effort to revive his country's economy after it lost the two territories of Menton and Roquebrune. Like the great German spa resorts of Baden-Baden and Wiesbaden, an international and wealthy clientele would come in winter for the rejuvenating benefits of the Monegasque seawater and climate. And they also wanted to have fun by going to the famous casino (which was impossible in France at the time), the ball, the opera for lyrical works and ballets, the theater, the gardens, and by enjoying the luxurious comfort and fine dining of the grand hotels. After various unsuccessful attempts in La Condamine, initially with the Villa Bellevu casino, the prince approached François Blanc, one of the top casino operators of the time and the brains behind the Homburg casino. Blanc was awarded a fifty-year concession with the Société des Bains de Mer (SBM) to manage the Monte Carlo casino. It was a resounding success, and with the construction of new hotels, villas, and avenues—all accessible by train starting in 1867—the district of Monte Carlo was born. Today, the luxury resort services of SBM continue to create the magic of Monaco through its glamorous hotels, Belle Époque casino rooms, Michelin-starred gastronomy, and world-class shows. Its Thermes Marins is one of the most beautiful spas in Europe, where expert hands can massage away guests' troubles as they gaze out to sea.

Previous spread. A vanishing horizon creates an illusion at sea. April 16, 2016, 3:16 p.m.

A harmony of blues as the harbor lights sparkle into life over Port Hercules and the Rock at dusk. October 17, 2015, 6:56 p.m.

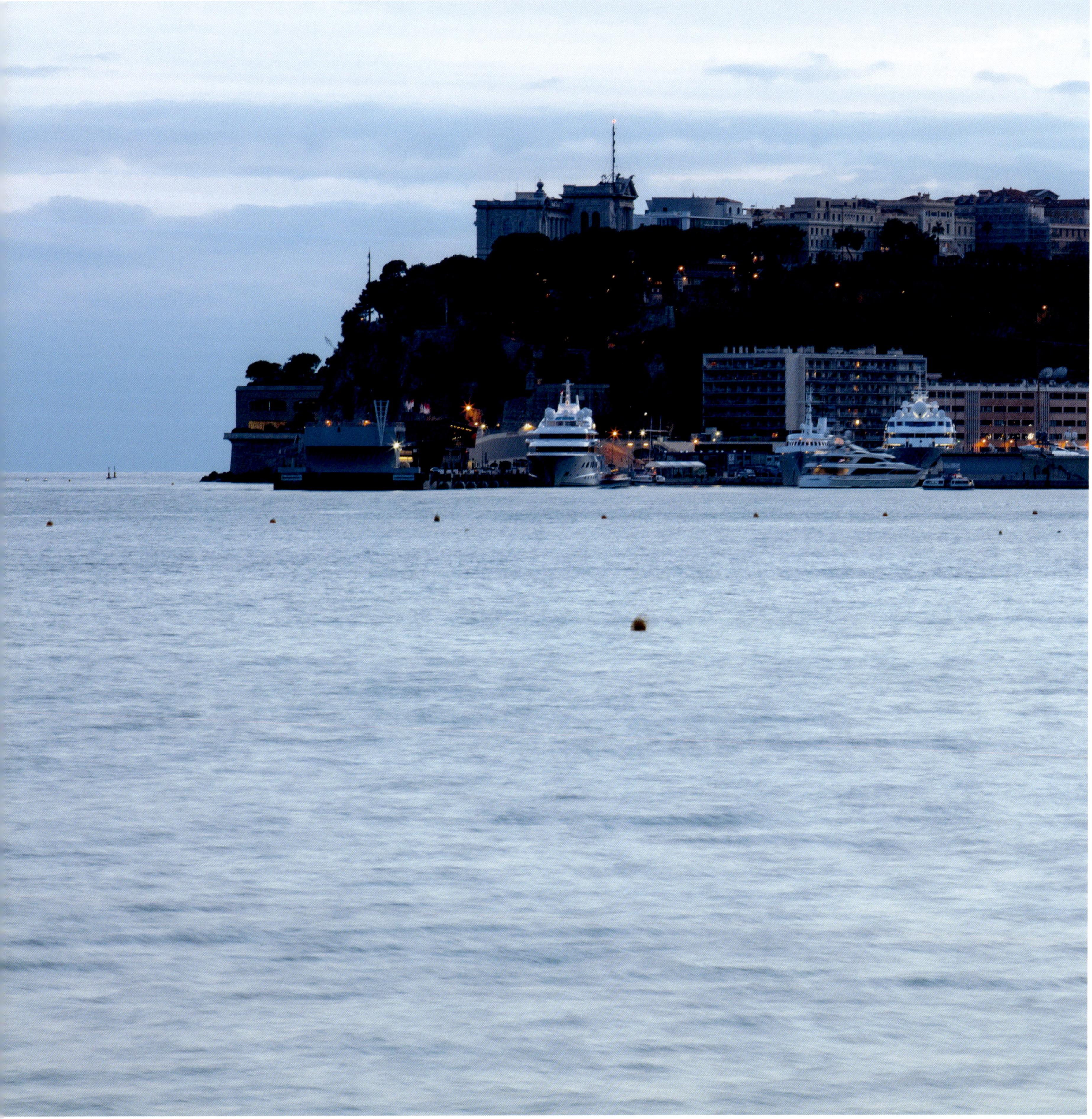

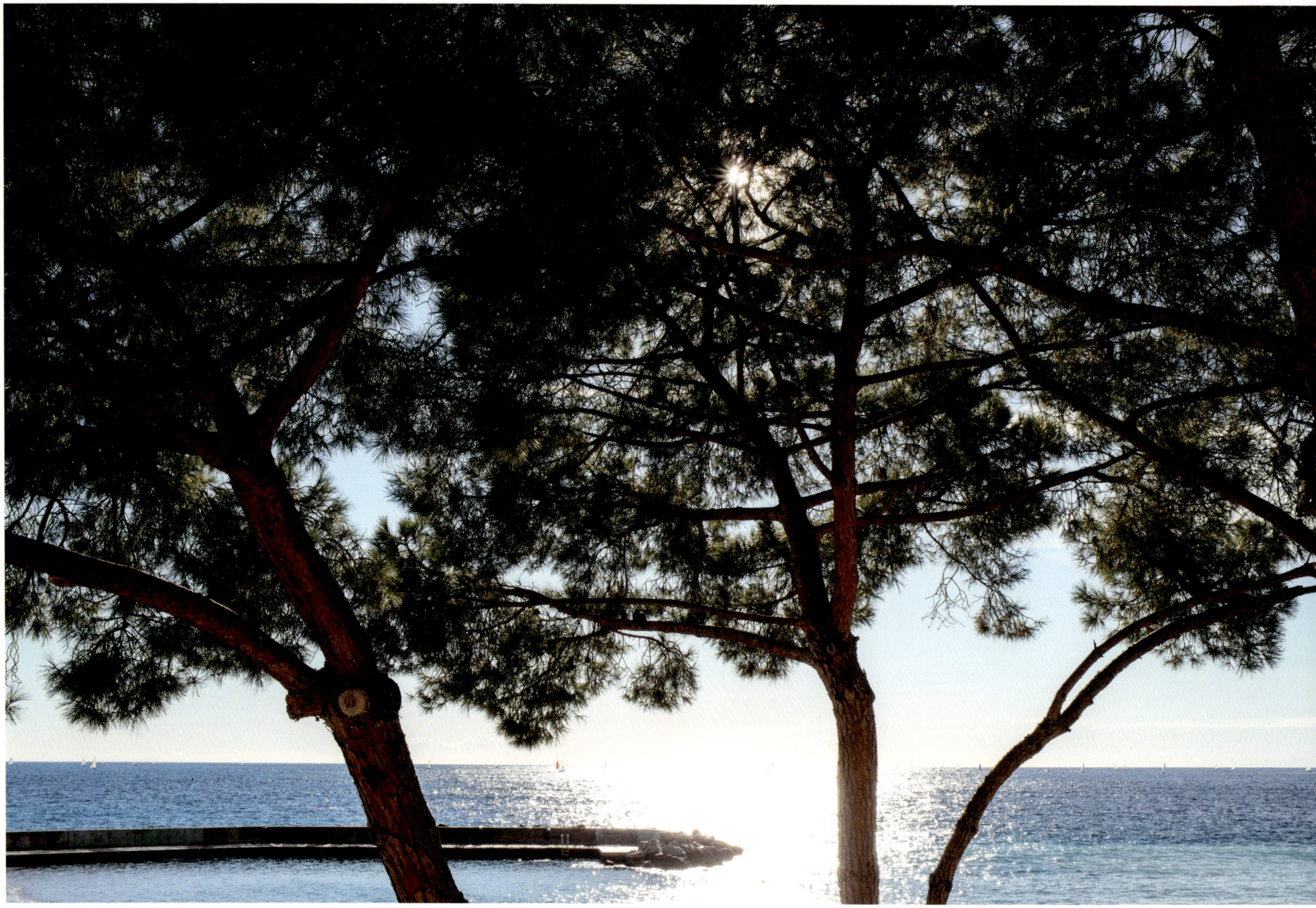

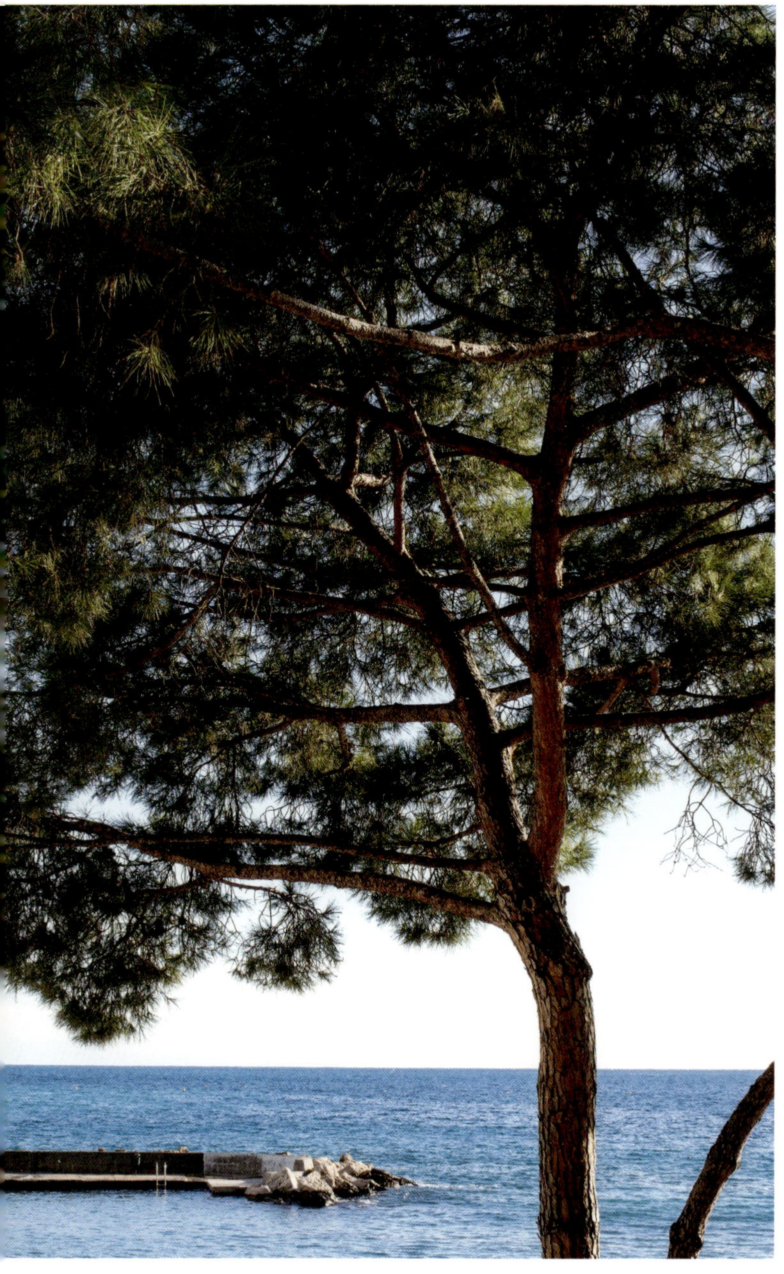

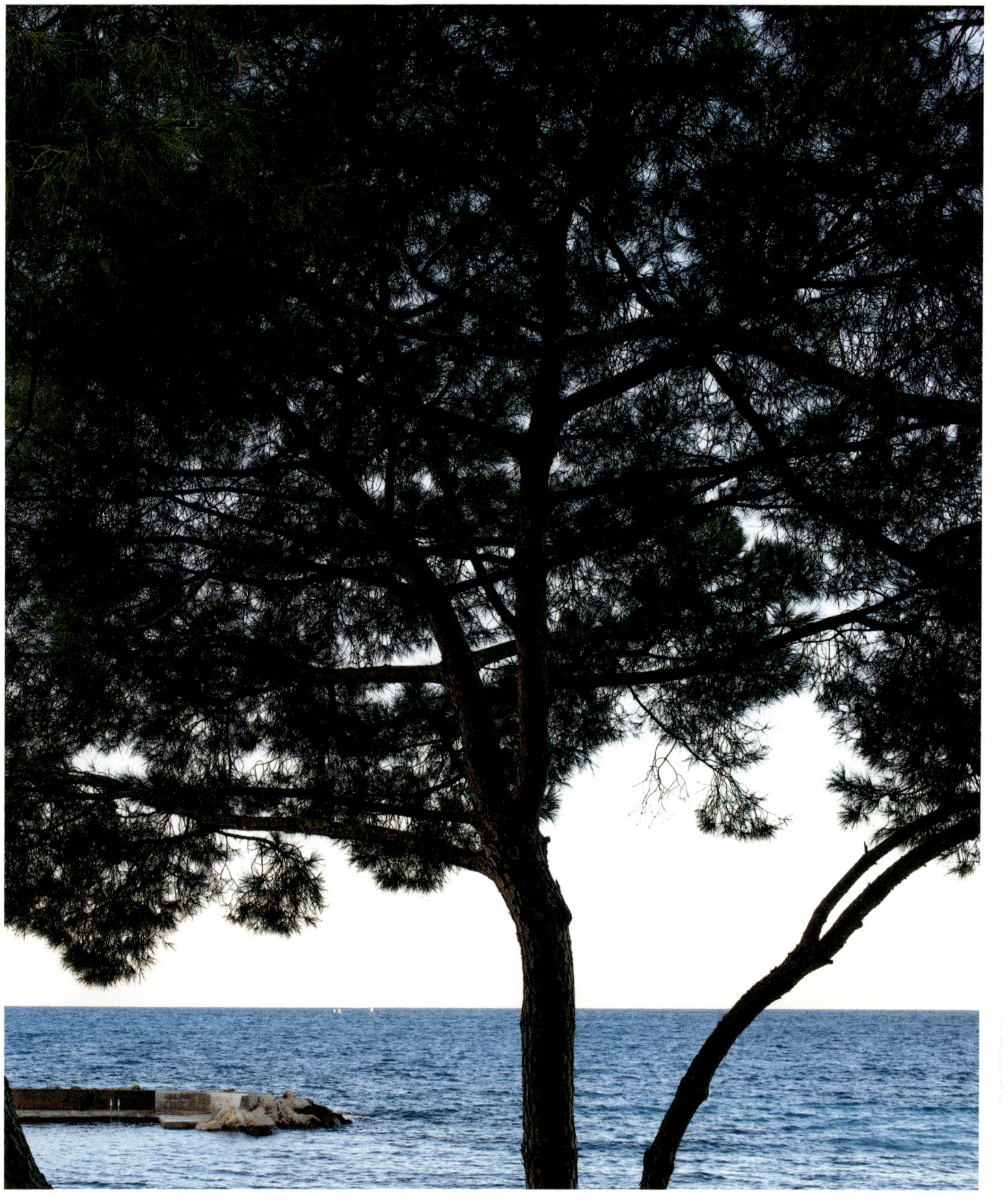

After several hours of hide-and-seek with the sun, it paints the sea a wonderful sky blue.
Strong sunlight reflecting off the water creates an intensely backlit scene, replaced a few hours later by silhouetted trees.
November 22, 2015. Left, 11:41 a.m.; center, 3:36 p.m.; right, 5:42 p.m.

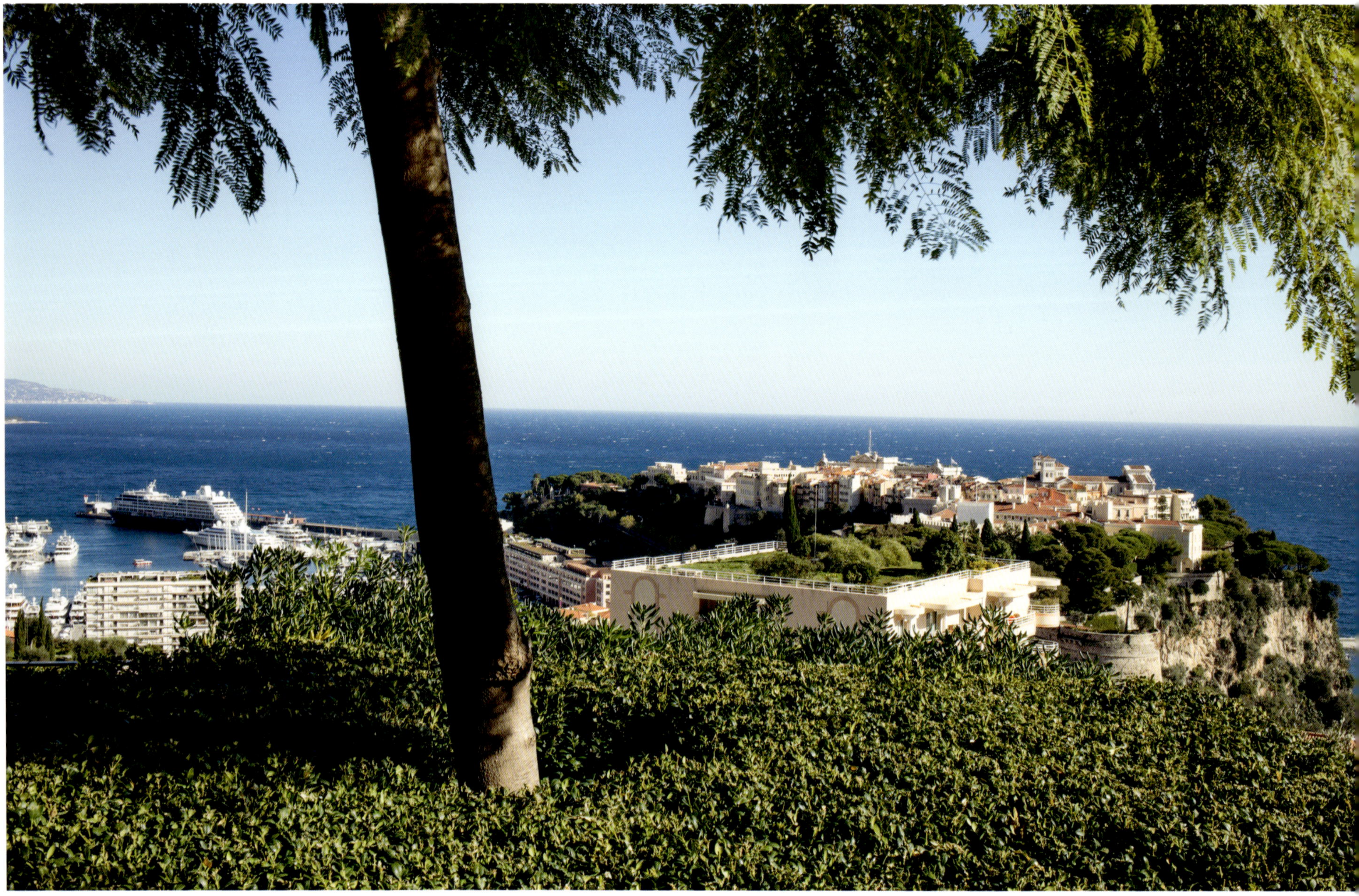

The majestic Rock of Monaco. As the scene opens, the Rock's outline stands out against the pure blue of the sea, but the sunlit vegetation in the foreground steals the show. A few hours later, the Rock takes center stage under the spotlight after the tree pulls the curtain down on the first act. October 31, 2015. Left page, 2:26 p.m.; right page, 4:10 p.m.

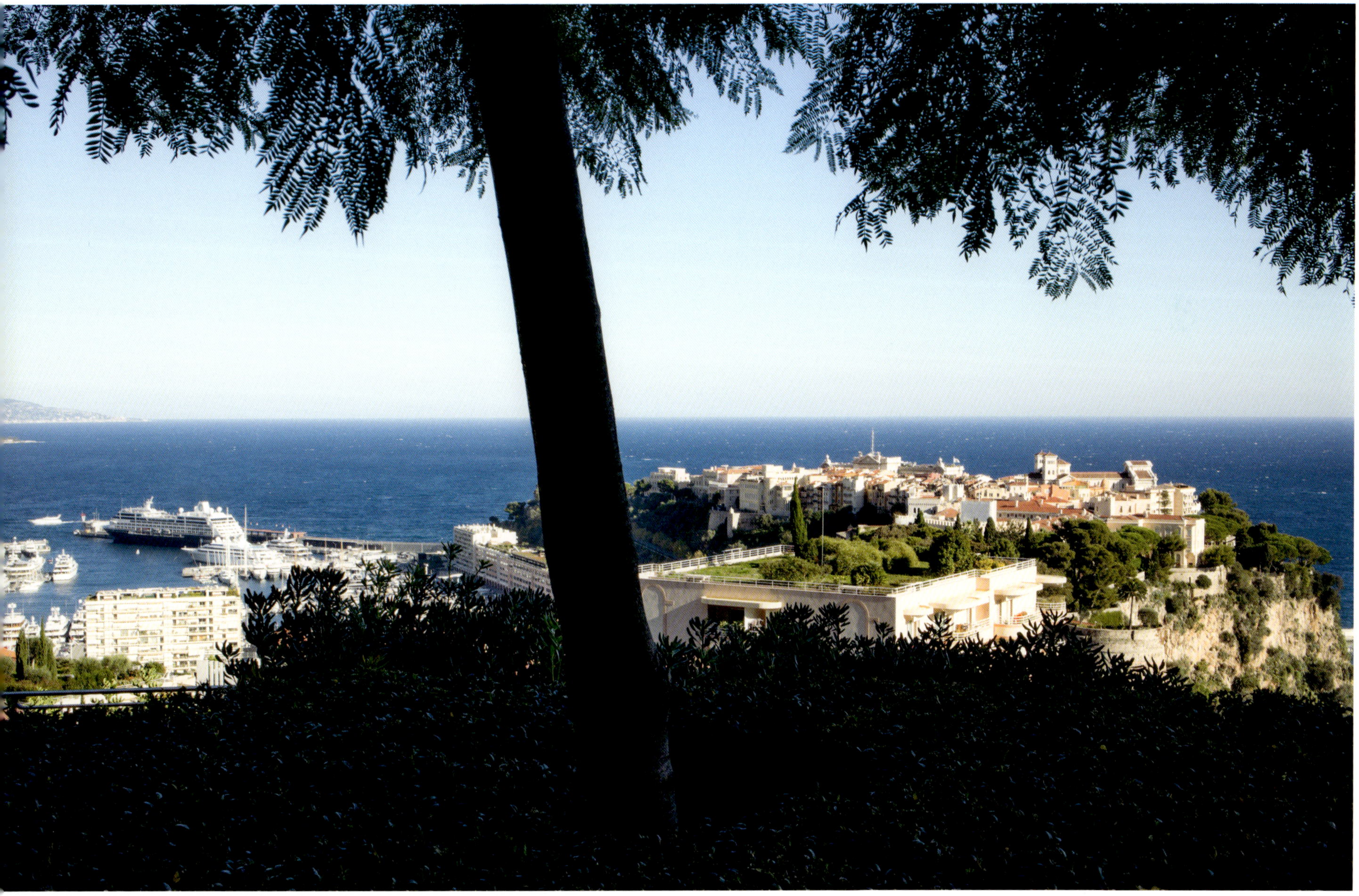

Following spread. At twilight the sky bathes the sea and city with its dusky blue. The following day, the sun sits high in a pure blue sky over a translucent sea. Left page, January 31, 2016, 5:40 p.m. Right page, February 22, 2016, 3:33 p.m.

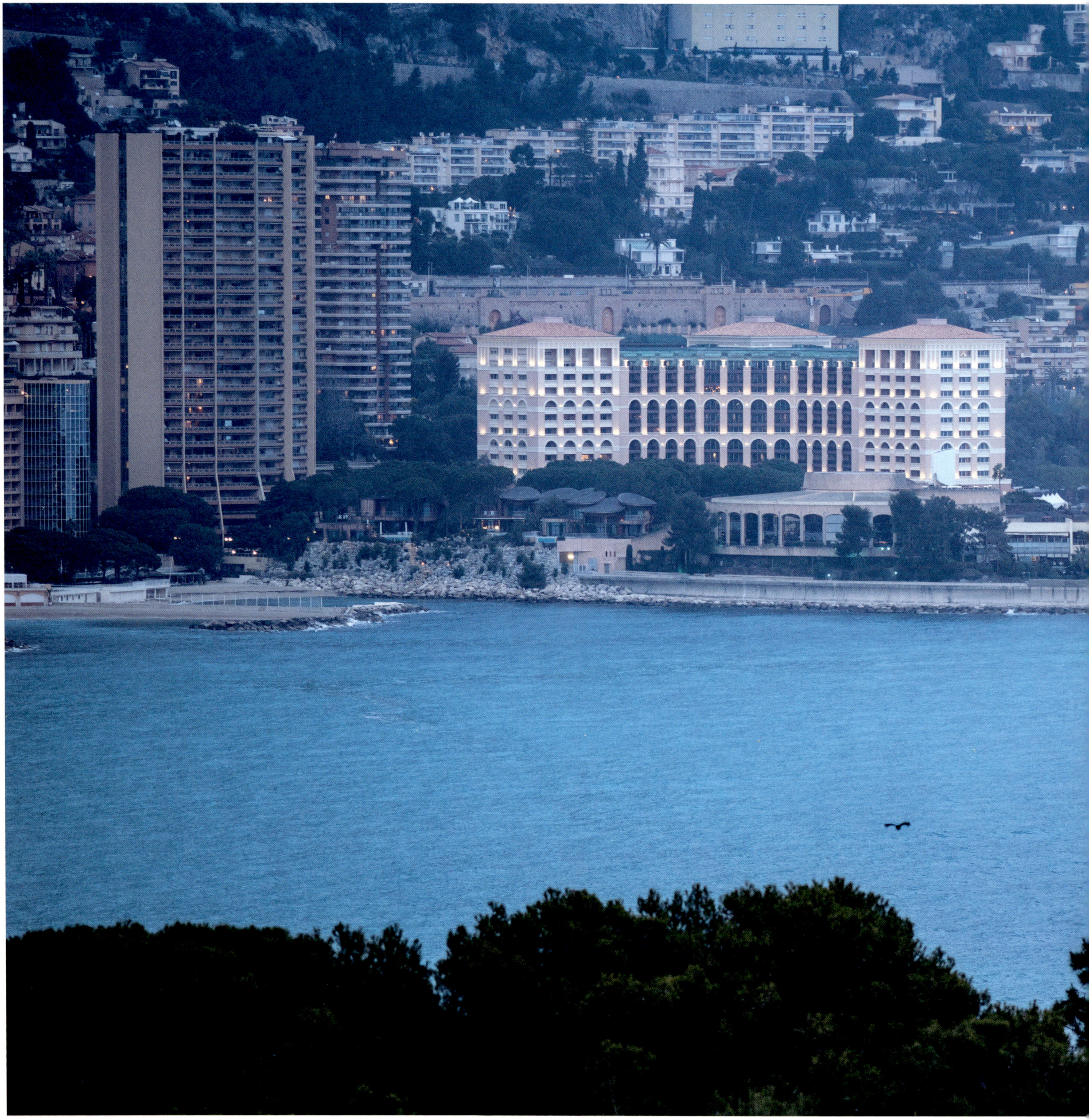

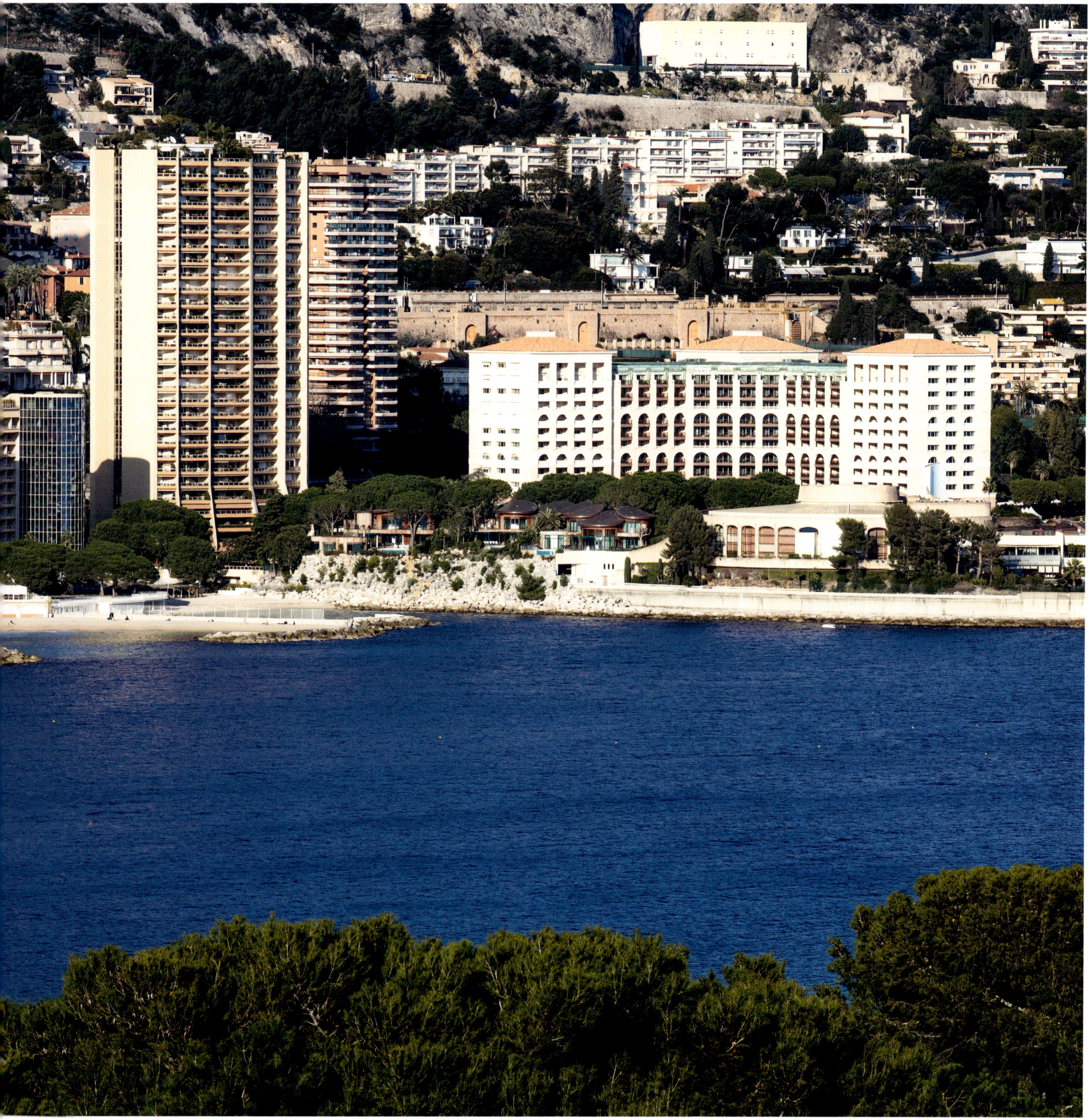

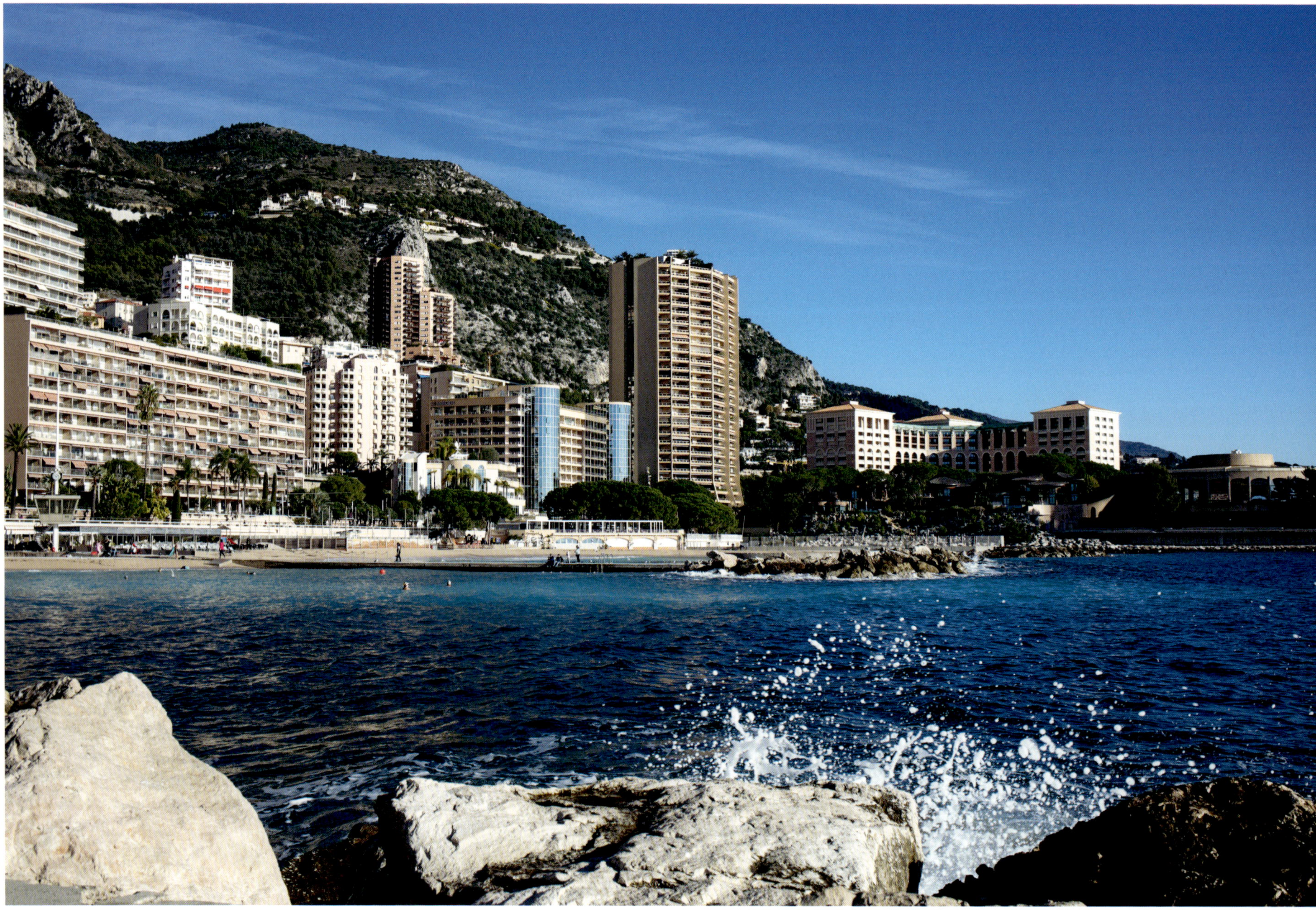

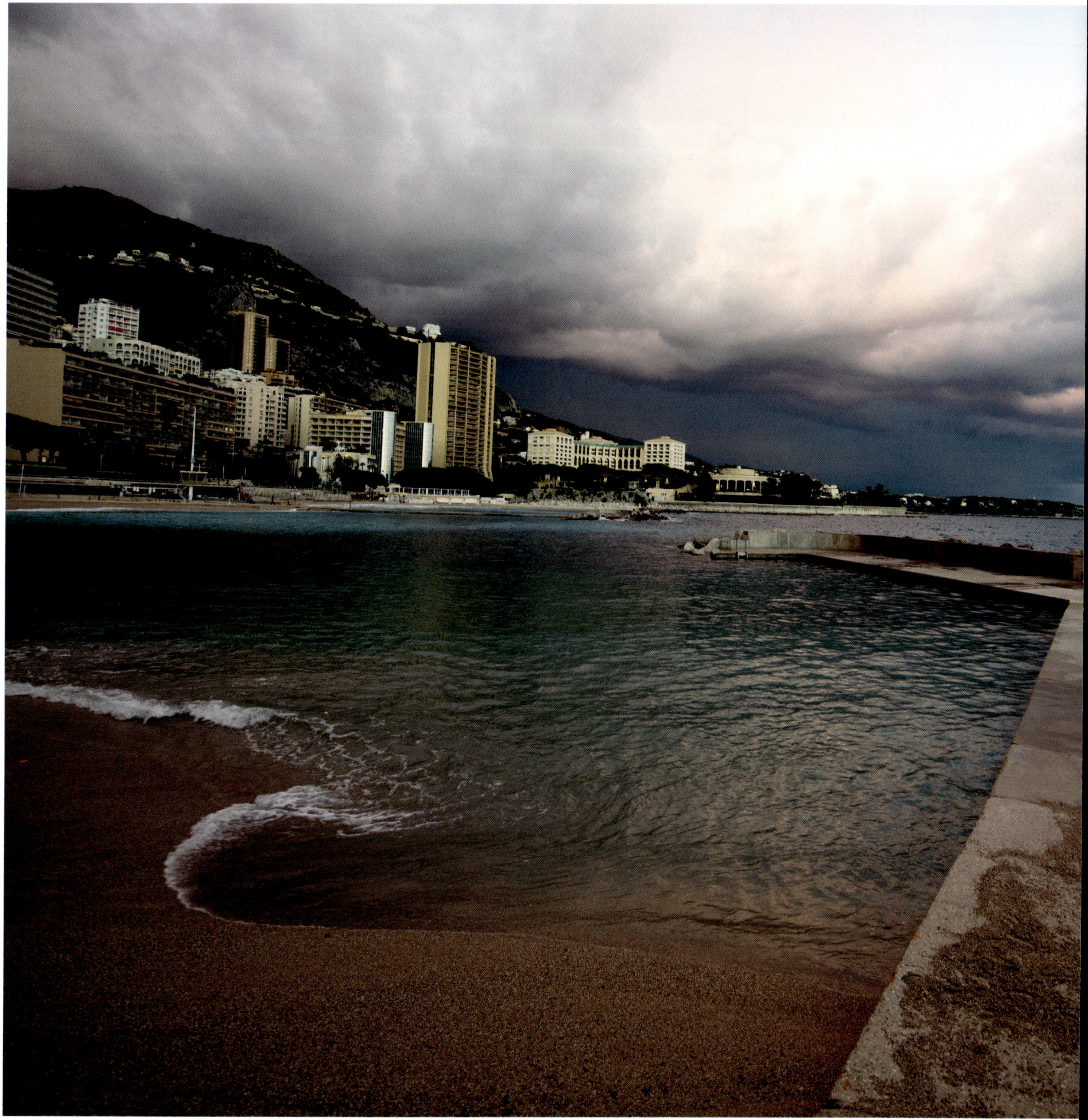

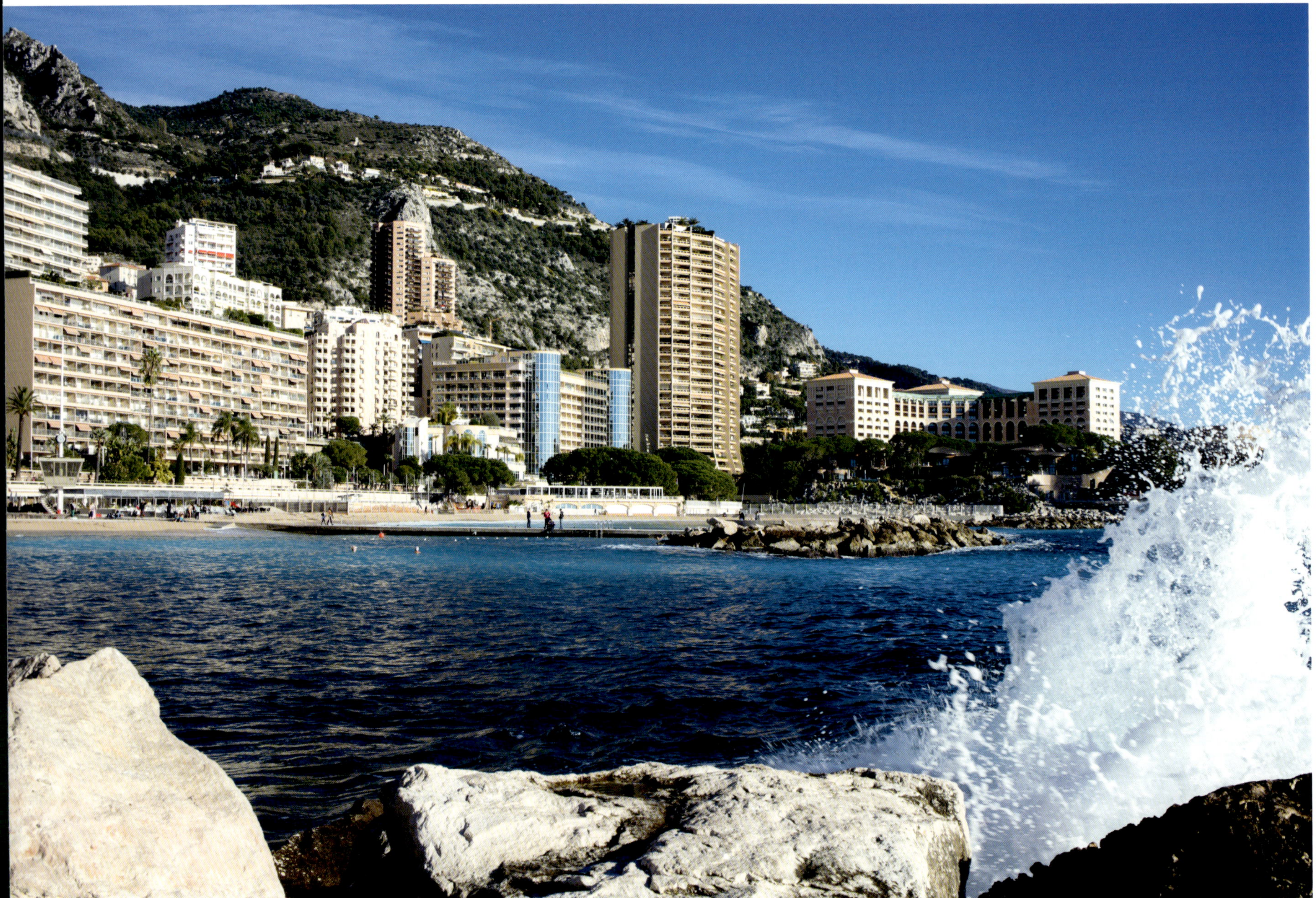

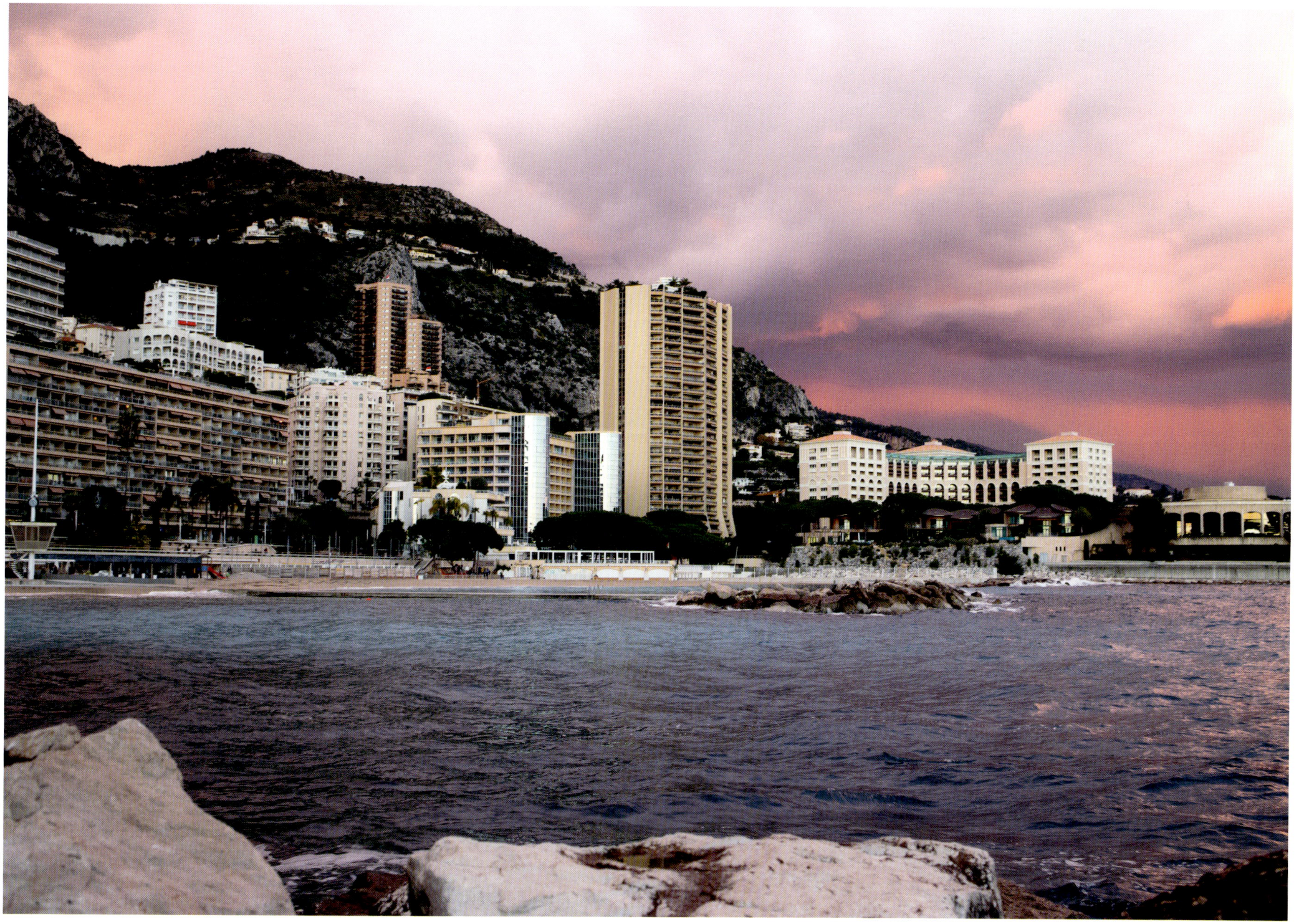

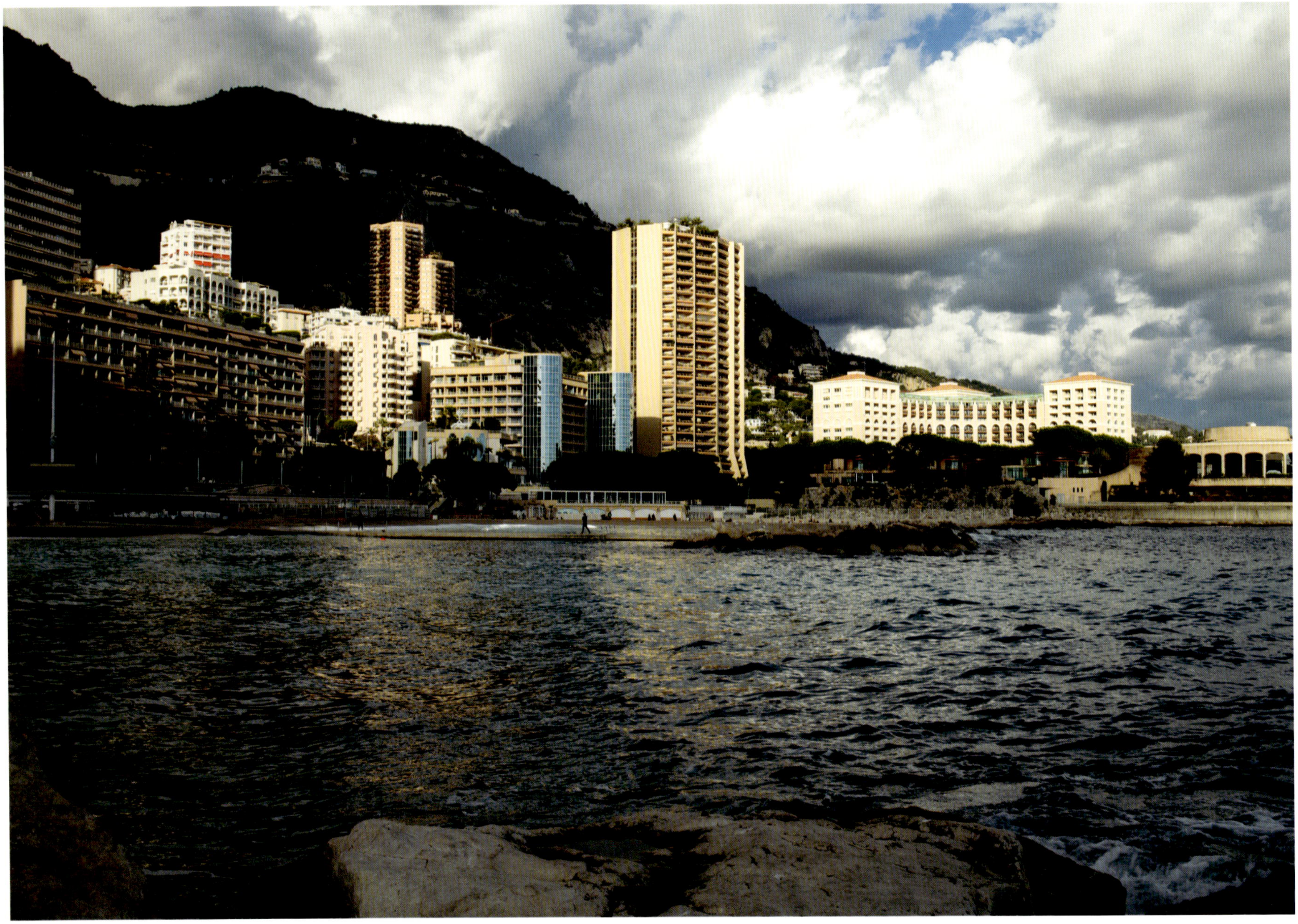

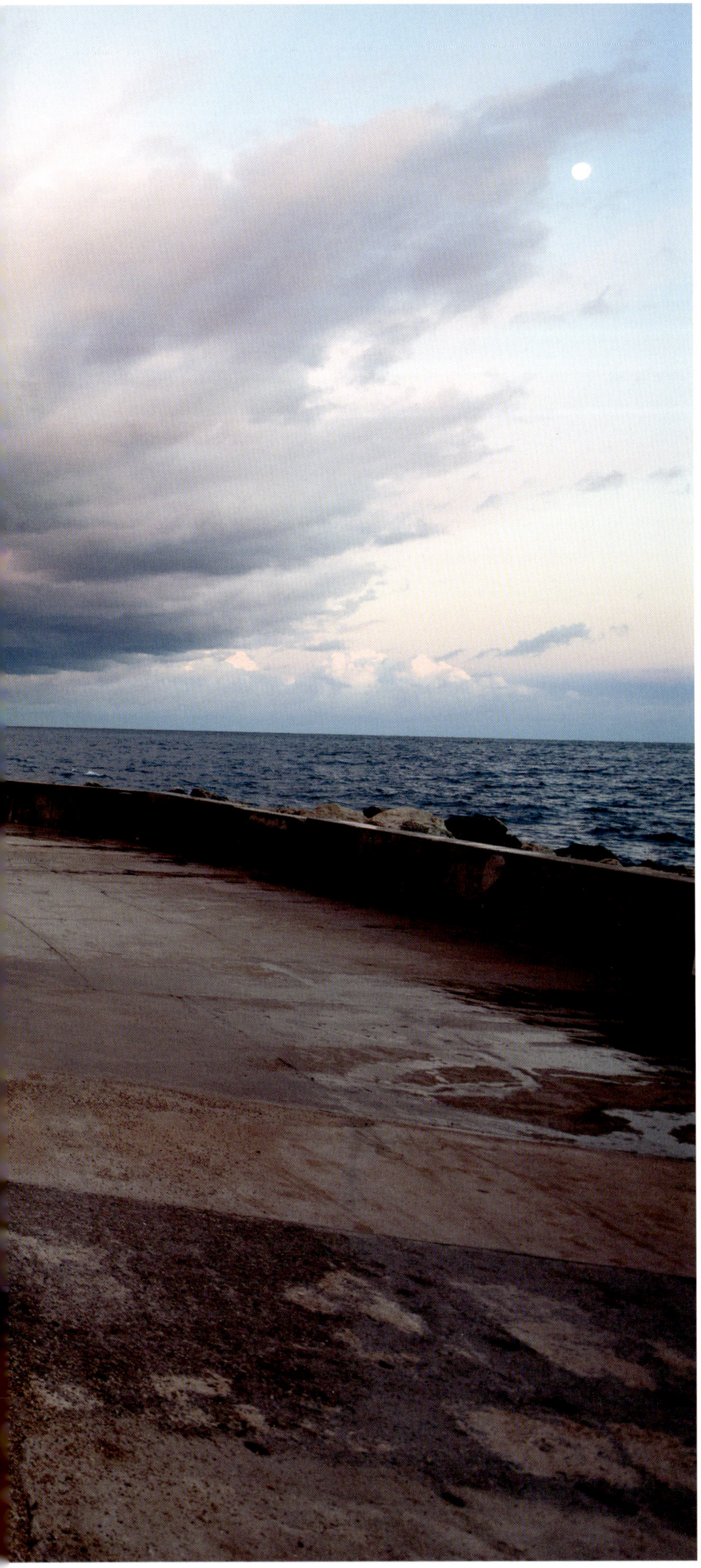

"And in the calm of the evening, I'd ride wildly toward the horizon tinged pink in the setting sun, for at twilight, everything turns pink..."

Guy de Maupassant, *Afloat*

Previous spreads. At morning on Larvotto Beach, the sun illuminates the building façades, while the blue sky intensifies the deep blue of the sea. At sunset the clouds turn pink, reflecting this dominant color onto the sea before making way for the full moon, which bathes the sea in its pearly light. November 22, 2015.
Previous pages. From left to right, 11:11 a.m.; 11:14 a.m. 4:24 pm; 6:03 p.m. Opposite, 6:05 p.m.

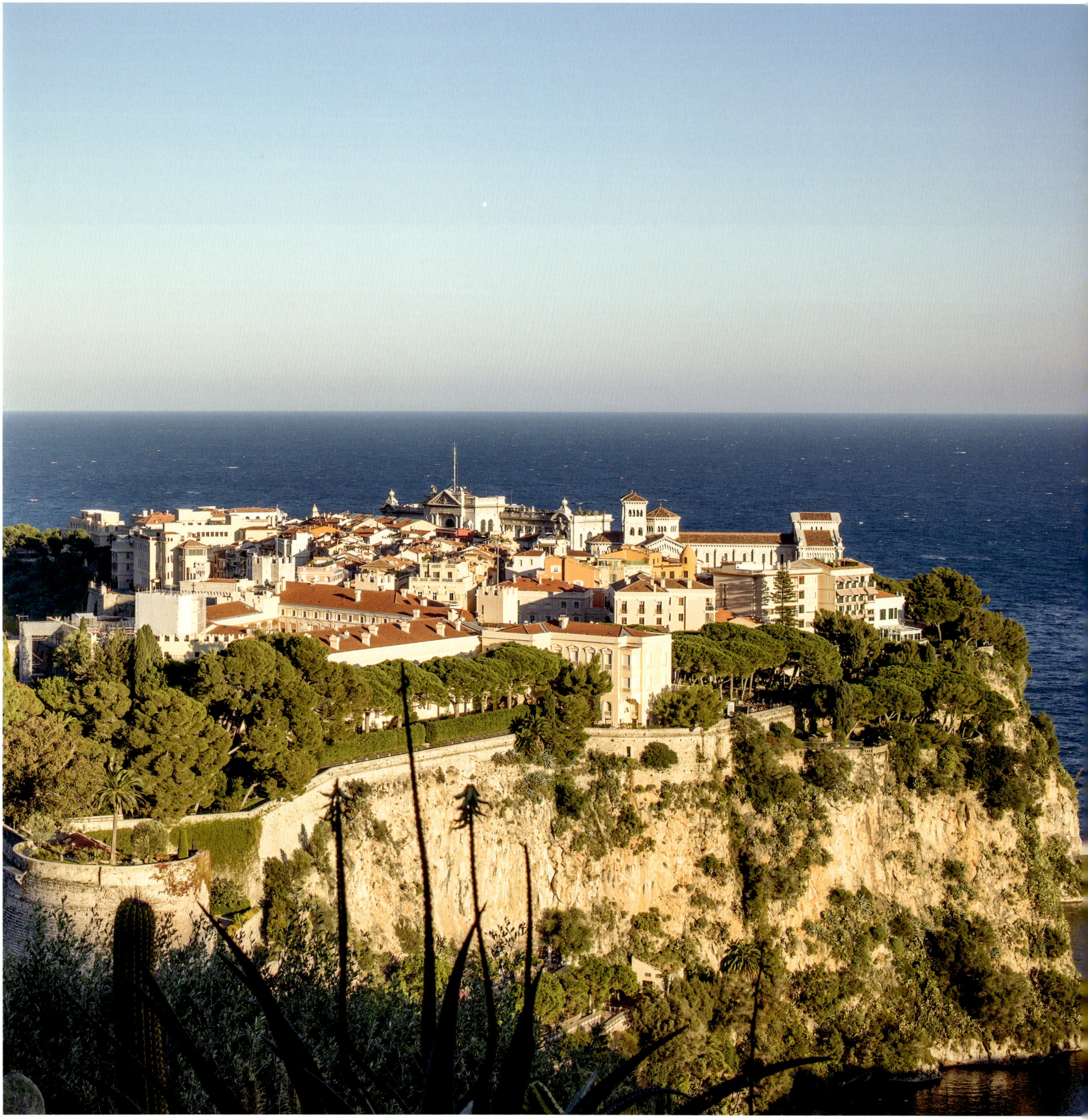

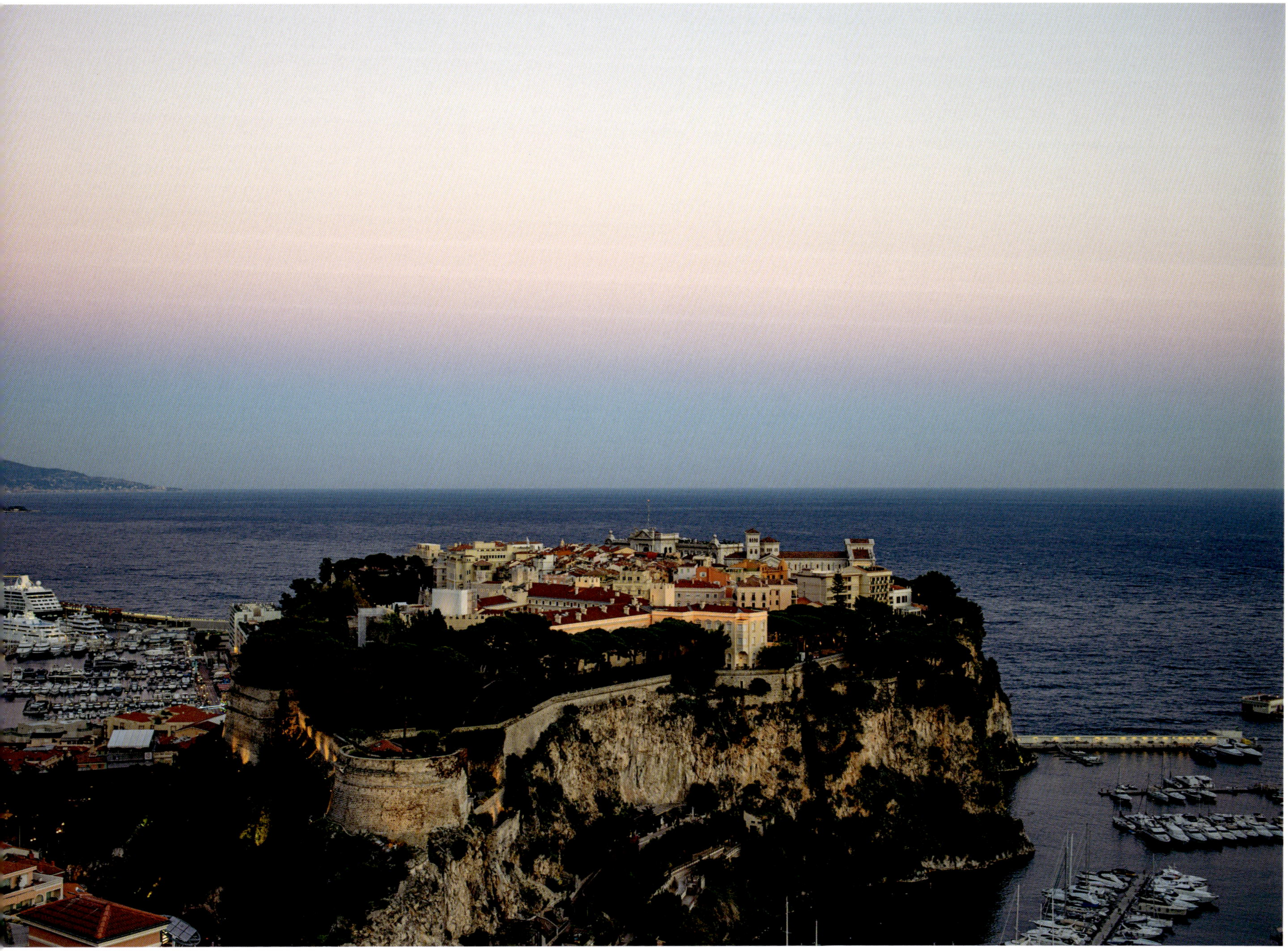

The sun's last rays highlight the Rock in its natural setting.
As the sun sets, a pink sky hangs over a plum-colored sea as the Rock prepares for sleep.
October 31, 2015. Left page, 5:25 p.m.; right page, 6:35 p.m.

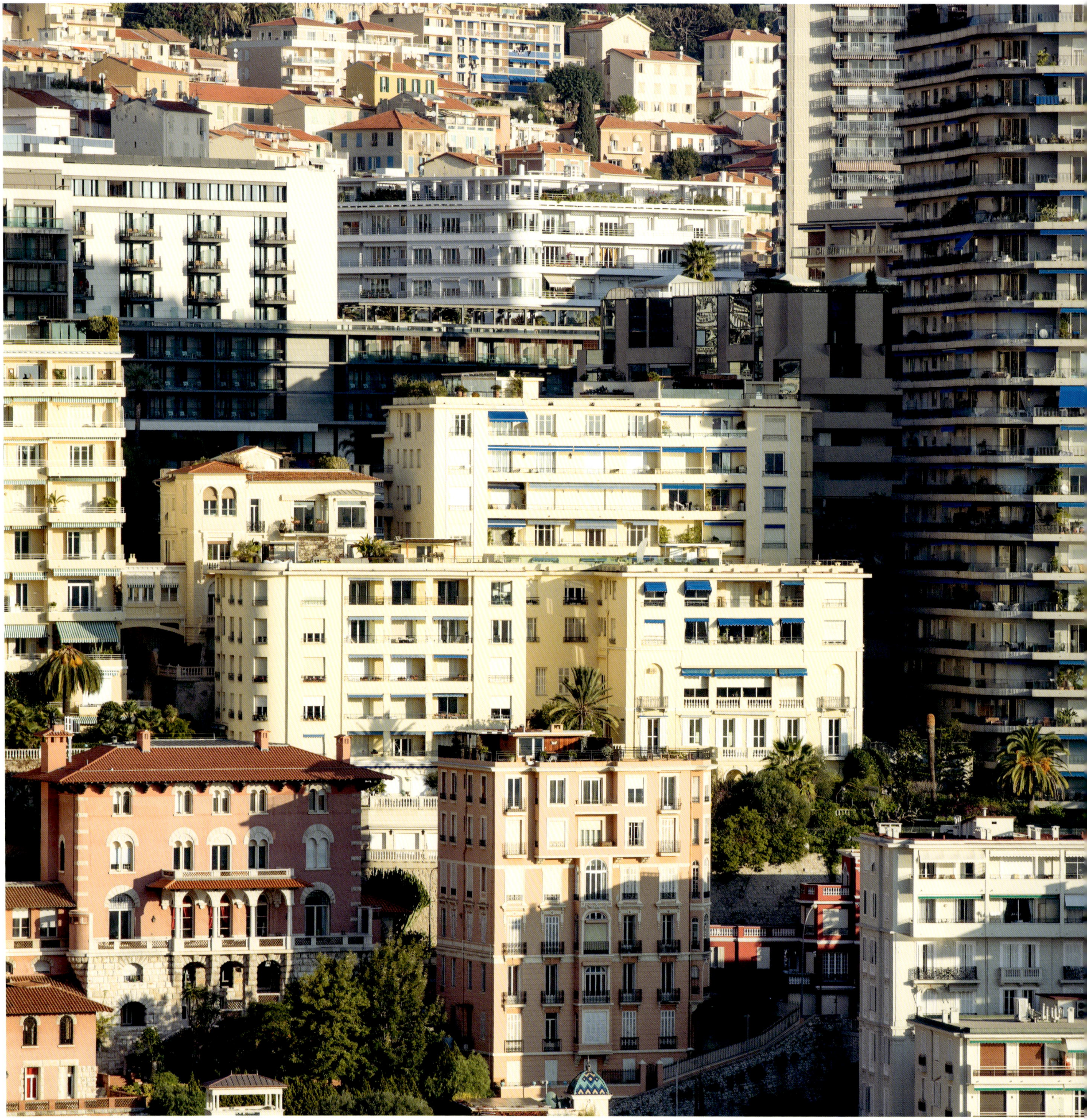

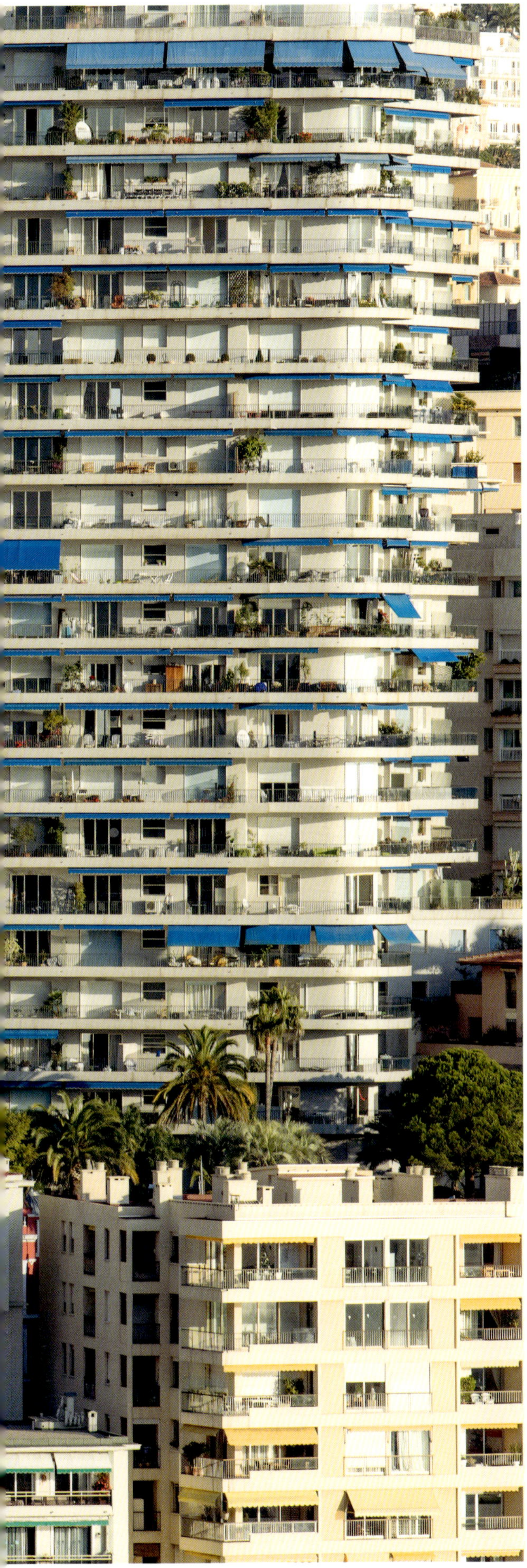

AN ARCHITECTURAL MOSAIC

"Hong Kong in miniature" or "Singapore of the Riviera." Such statements made to describe the architectural appearance of Monaco are only made by those prone to lazy clichés. Wandering around the Principality is like looking through a wonderful compound eye, as demonstrated by the photographer during one of his shoots. "My approach to Monaco's architecture makes use of interplay, like a time machine that allows me to see the positive aspect of everything; in other words, appreciating the past through the present, and the present through the past."

The color palette of the façades is superb, ranging from soft pink to red ochre, with peach, tea, salmon, crimson, grenadine, and raspberry all in between and providing colorful contrast to the bright whites and muted ivories of the towering new buildings. This radiant palette is regulated through an official façade color chart, which has been constantly evolving ever since the first apartments and properties of wealthy winter residents were built. The chart includes color tones that fall within the main palette for all the architectural components: façades, foundations, door and window frames, and decorative elements. As for windows, wrought-iron work, doors, and shutters, they are included in additional palettes. The principles of façade coloring are based on historical periods: heritage, Belle Époque, modern, and contemporary. A whole range of color combinations—including strong contrasts, natural harmonies, hot-cold contrasts, and warm shades—are all available. And you can really let your creativity flow with the possibilities, as long as everything is approved by the Department of Forward Studies, Urban Planning, and Mobility!

The warm neutral shades and graduated colors of the buildings, verandas, balconies, and undersides of balconies create a link between the buildings of different styles. Like precious jewels between the modern buildings, the Belle Époque, neoclassical, Florentine, art deco, and eclectic-style villas add interest to any walk and constantly remind the visitor of the country's rich history. To increase housing opportunities in the state while maintaining its attractive heritage, Prince Albert II made an inventory of its historical buildings.

The curious can seek out and marvel at some of them: the neoclassical Villa Miraflores on avenue Saint-Michel near the casino in Monte Carlo, or Villa Troty on rue de Ténao, painted peach pink and boasting a hanging garden. Villa Blanchy with its panoramic views and Villa Colombe with its large bay windows can be found near the Sainte-Dévote Chapel, while Villa le Nid nestles against the arch of the stairs. As for the spectacular Villa Danichgah—built in 1910 for Prince Mirza Riza Khan Arfa, a politician, a former soldier, and an Iranian writer who wrote an ode to peace for all heads of state—its Moorish blue domes can still be admired upon arriving in Monaco on boulevard du Jardin Exotique.[(1)]

Each encounter with one of these decorative villas reveals a new creative flourish: Massier de Vallauris urns, turquoise balusters, ceramics with colorful four-season floral designs, sculpted marble lintels on the Rock's antique doors, Italian frescoes, stuccoed motifs, medallions decorated with Renaissance faces, and more. The refined lifestyle centered on enjoying the climate is also reflected in architectural displays: winter gardens, wrought-iron balconies, huge terraces, pergolas, Italian roofing, verandas—finding these architectural treasures is a way for art lovers to walk in the footsteps of the greats by visiting the homes or temporary residences of famous artists such as Apollinaire, Colette, Cocteau, Diaghilev, Pagnol, and van Donghen.

Born in Rome, Apollinaire was just seven years old when he arrived in Monaco with his mother and his younger brother in 1887. As Jean-Jacques Pauvert documents in his book *Apollinaire in Monaco* [(2)], the family first stayed in the apartment of the Dagnino brothers on boulevard de l'Ouest, now Rainier III, before moving to an apartment in La Condamine, Maison Canis on rue Louis Notari, at the corner of rue Princesse Antoinette. At the age of seventeen, the future poet lived in Villa Angelica in the old Passage Barriéra, Descente des Moulins, in Monte Carlo. This may be no surprise as it is well known that Apollinaire's mother regularly frequented the casino to play, and in more ways than one! As for the painter van Donghen, a popular portraitist among artists and high society, he lived at Bateau Lavoir, 7 avenue Hector Otto in La Condamine from 1949 until his death. From 1952, Marcel Pagnol lived in Villa la Lestra, 12 boulevard des Moulins in Monte Carlo. These days visitors can walk right through a square that bears his name with panoramic views of the sea. And even though these houses no longer exist, to stand where they once stood, taking in the atmosphere and surroundings and imagining the views that inspired these famous occupants is still a rare treat.

Although she never lived in Monaco, the writer Colette, who became honorary president of the literary council for the Principality in 1950, often stayed there. She was an actress there in her younger days, then a guest of Prince Rainier III, to whom she wrote many emotional letters in her later life, such as these words that come to her mind while contemplating the view from the terrace of the Hotel de Paris: "It is only 9 o'clock in the morning, but everything is so remarkable and beautiful that I cannot wait to thank you for it. This open window, this forgotten sea, the freshness of the morning air, this new experience of the month of May, it is because of you that I get to witness all these joys, which are inseparable from the dear friendship you have shown me." As for Cocteau, who worked as a poet and Illustrator for Diaghilev's company, Ballets Russes, he stayed in Hotel des Princes, next to the Balmoral Palace on La Rampe leading up to the casino, now avenue d'Ostende, and remarked in his notes: "I must admit I like Monte Carlo. The sun reflects off gold and the Café de Paris resembles St. Mark's Square. The sky-blue chairs are exquisite, the white-washed pâtisseries in the building frontages excite our lust for life; the pigeons that escape the cruel guns alight on the head of Massenet." And at the wedding of Prince Rainier and Grace Kelly: "I rest my gaze on this Rock, on this small Stendhalian city, on this esplanade guarded by ancient cannons . . . " Indeed, there are few places more serene on the Rock than the palace with its pale yellow walls and which has witnessed seven centuries of history since the Grimaldi family first arrived.

(1) Laplace, Pierre. ***Les Anciennes Villas et leurs Hôtes à Monaco***. Monaco: Victory Gadoury Editions, 2015.

(2) Pauvert, Jean-Jacques. ***Apollinaire et Monaco***. Monaco: Éditions du Rocher, 1999.

Previous spread. Looking for glimpses of the past within the Monegasque amphitheater. December 28, 2015, 9:29 a.m.

From the terrace of the Oceanographic Museum, a path of light stretches out toward the Chapelle de la Visitation. January 31, 2016, 5:54 p.m.

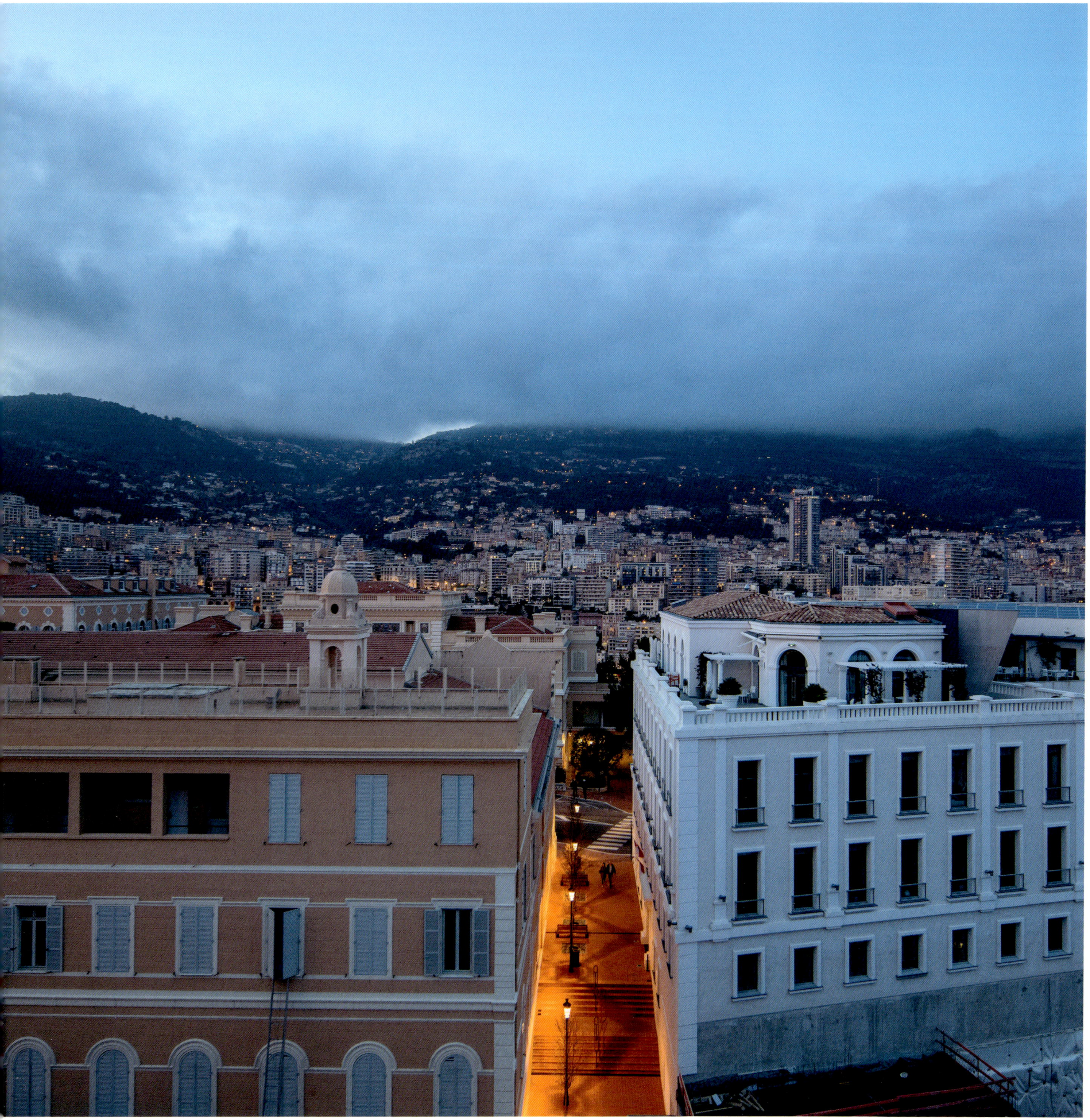

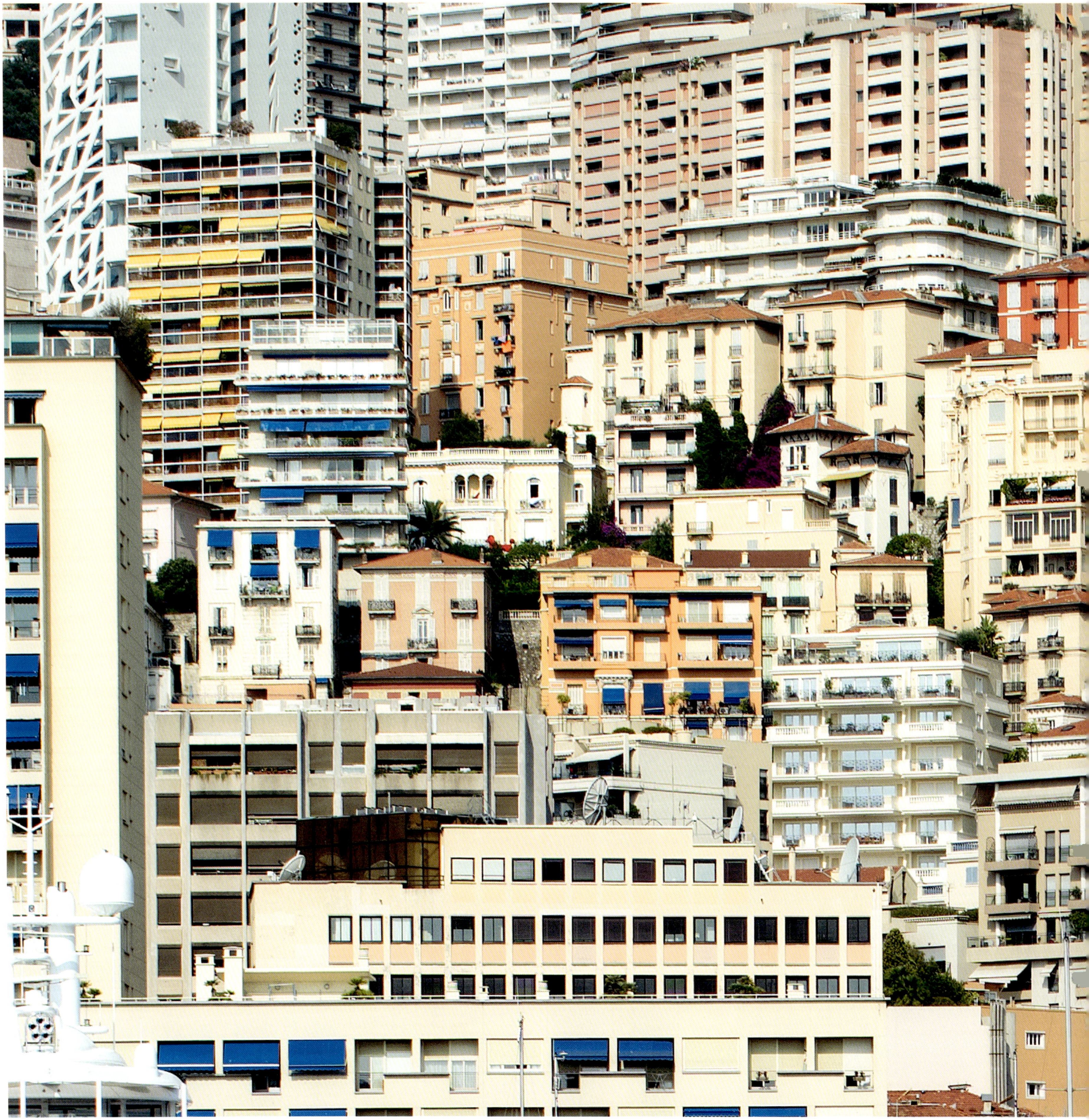

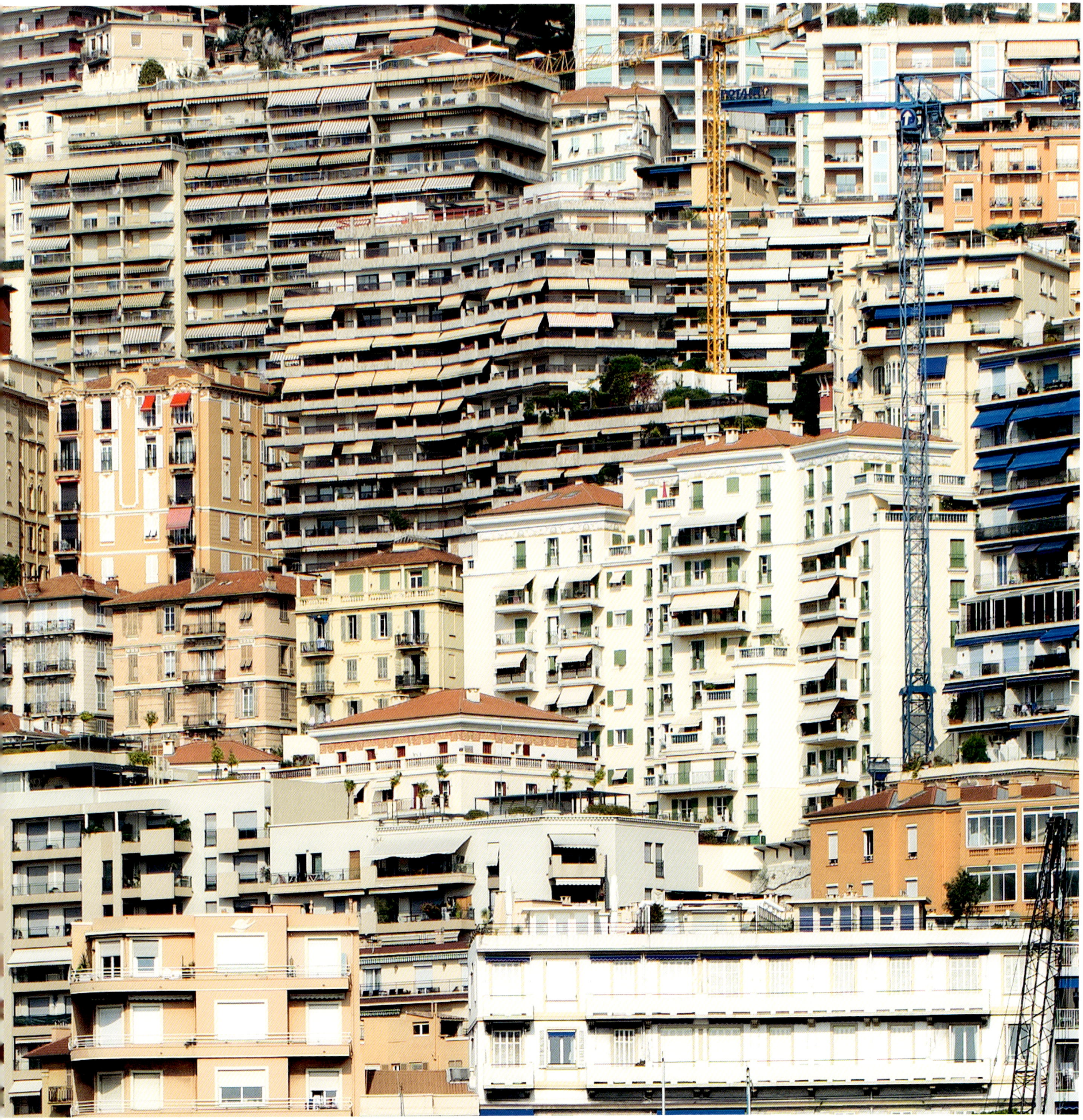

Previous spread. The sun's diffused light behind the clouds transforms the façades into a painter's palette. July 9, 2015, 9:30 a.m.

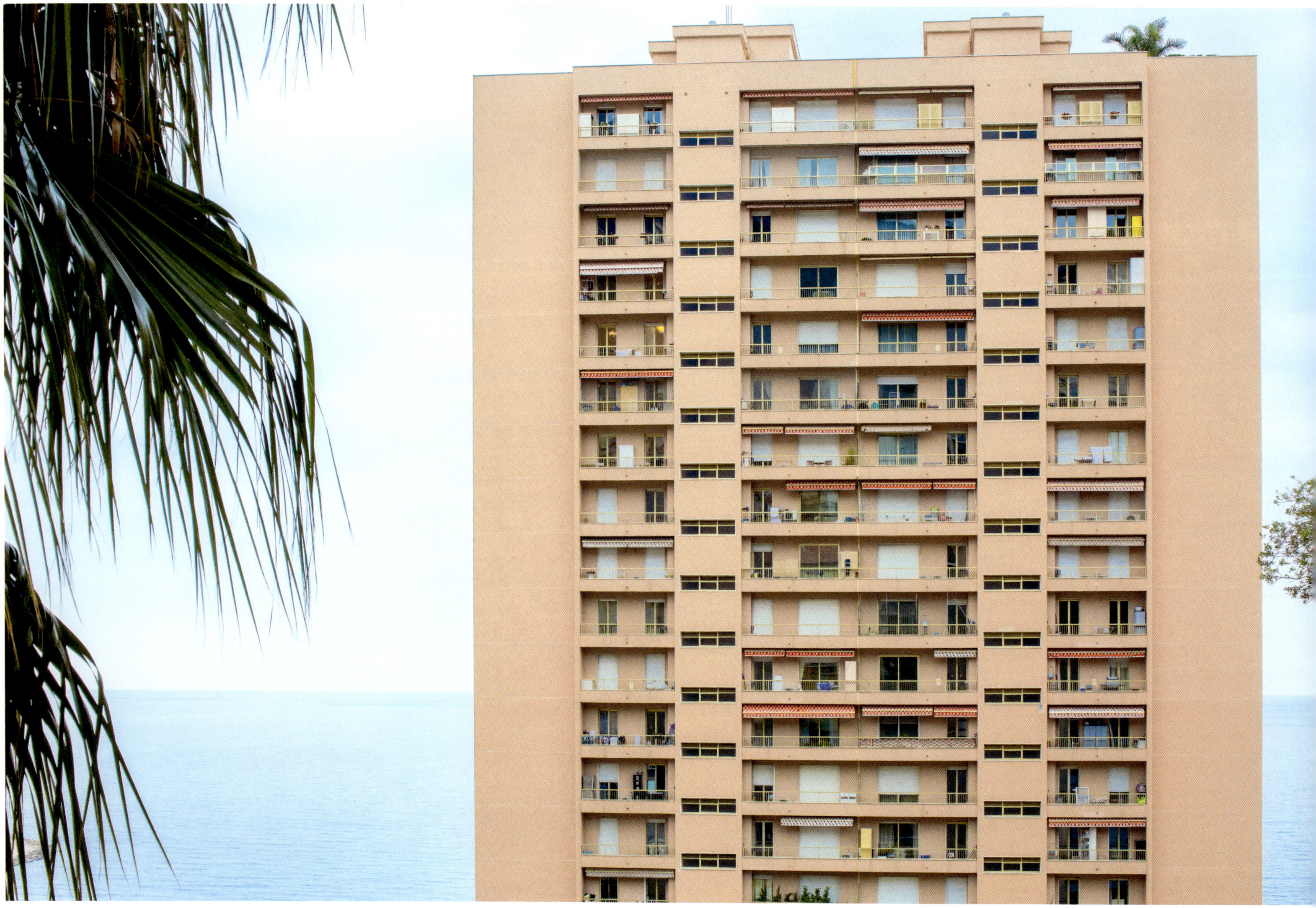

On an overcast day, the sea's pastel shades harmonize with the color of a building. A perfect tonal balance that accentuates the vegetation. January 1, 2016, 10:17 a.m.

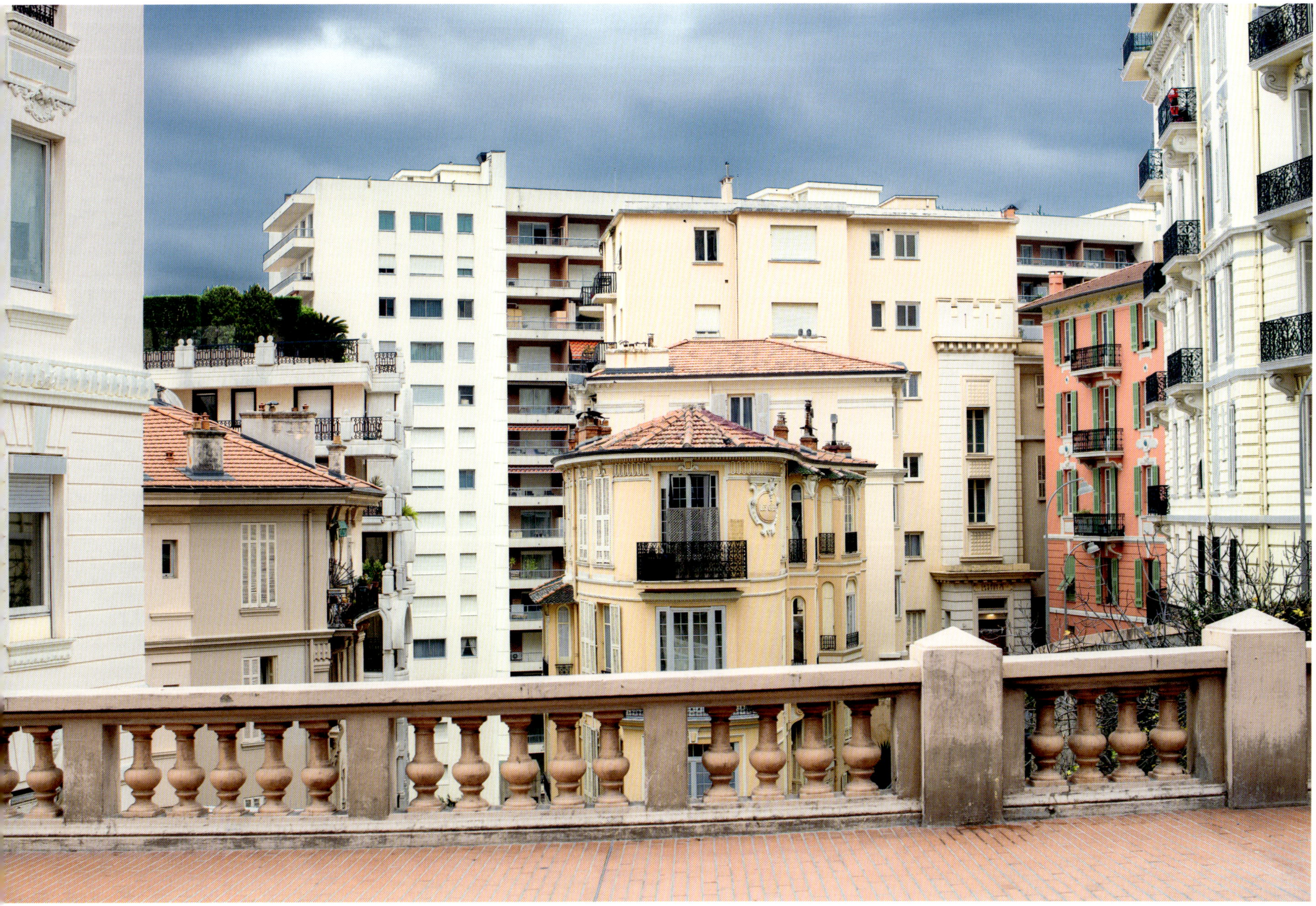

A cloudy day is the ideal time to rest against a balustrade and appreciate the subtle color scheme of Monaco's many façades. January 1, 2016, 10:30 a.m.

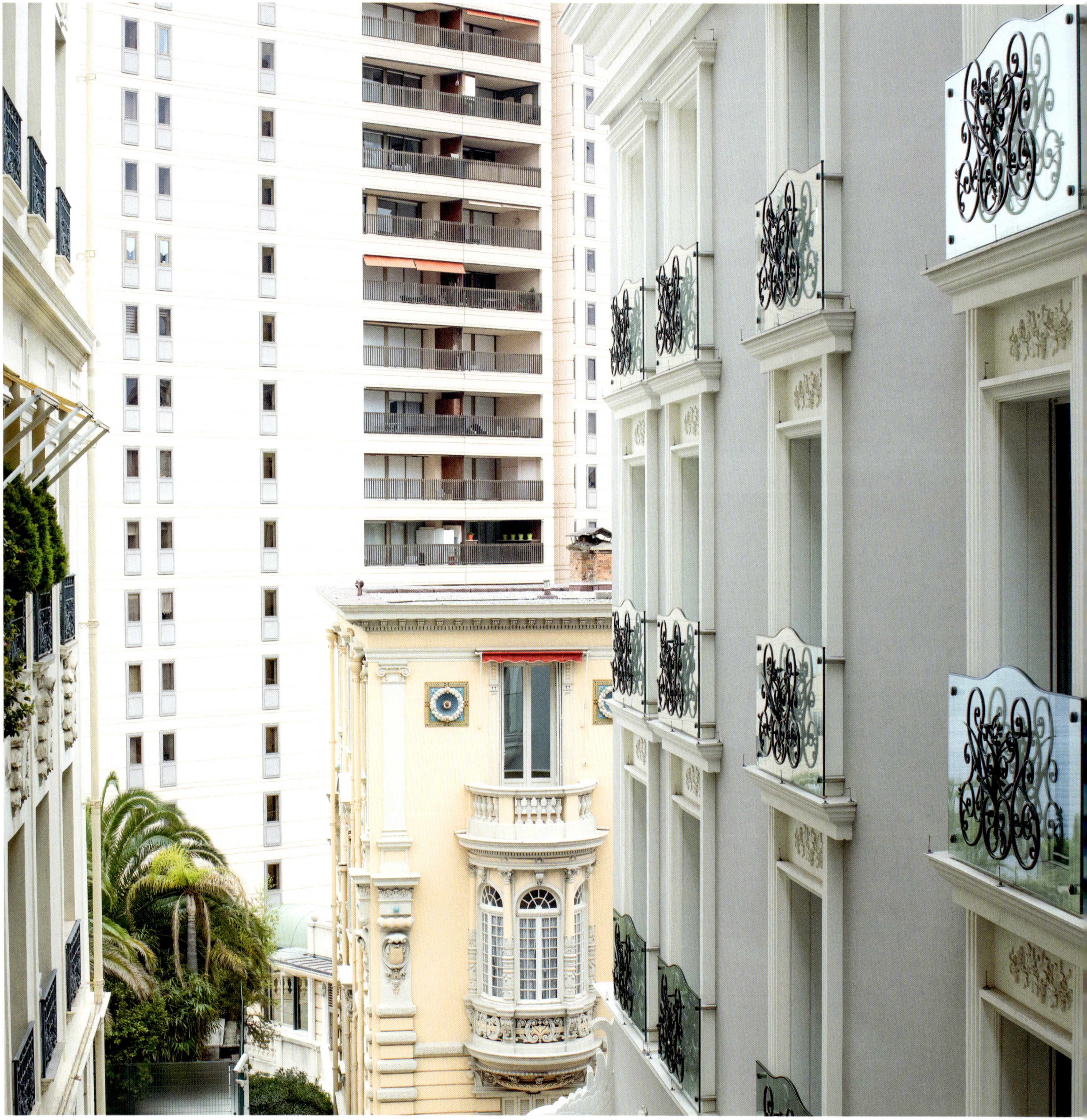

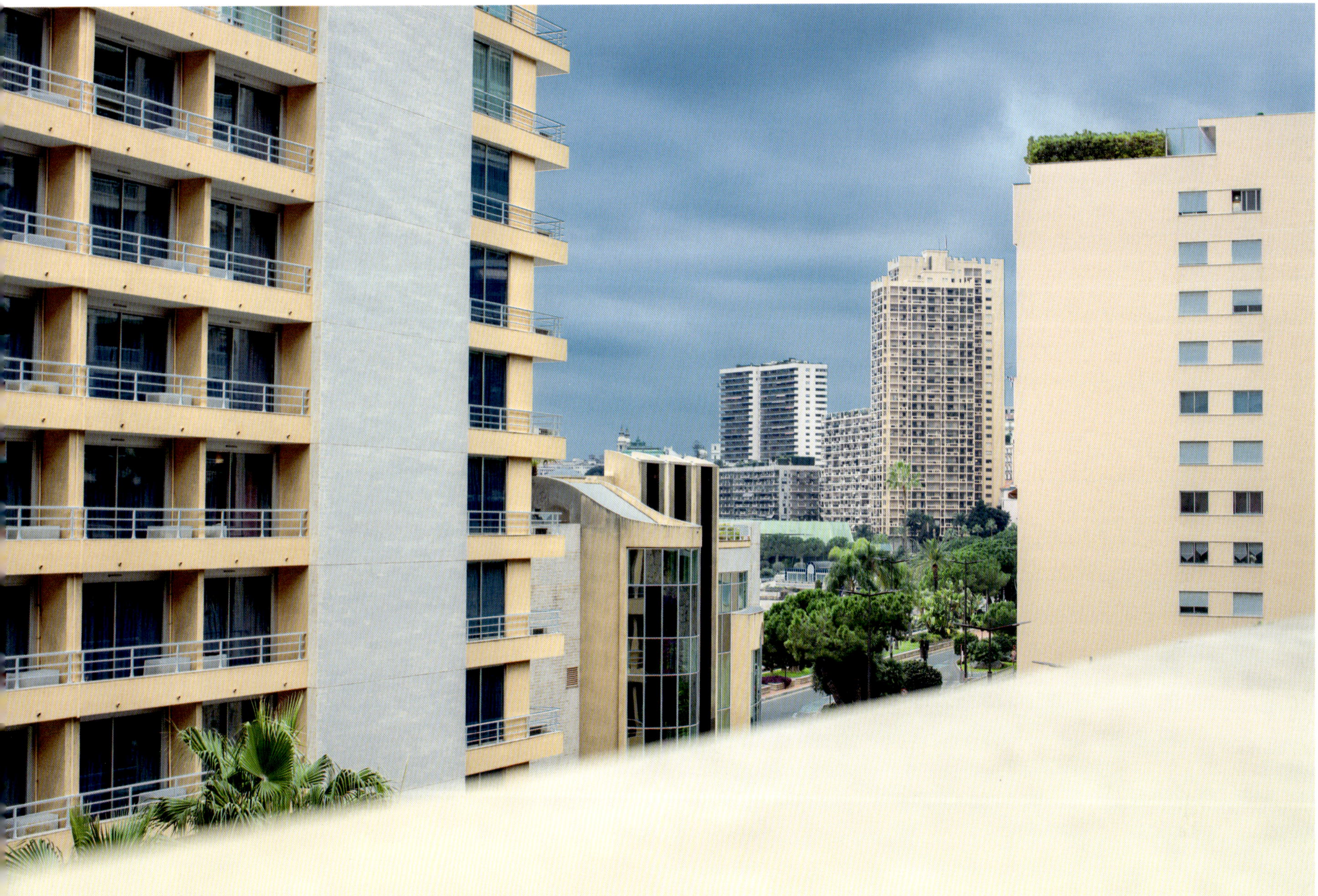

Looking over a balustrade on boulevard des Moulins, the interplay of lines and ingenuity of the vegetation can be fully appreciated. January 1, 2016, 10:48 a.m.

Left page. In a cul-de-sac on the edge of Larvotto Beach, the perspective created by side façades draws attention to a historical building. January 1, 2016, 9:38 a.m.

Following spread. The apposition of thriving vegetation and towering buildings creates an appealing harmony. Left, June 23, 2015, 5:12 p.m.; center, November 22, 2015, 12:55 p.m.; right, January 1, 2016, 10:36 a.m.

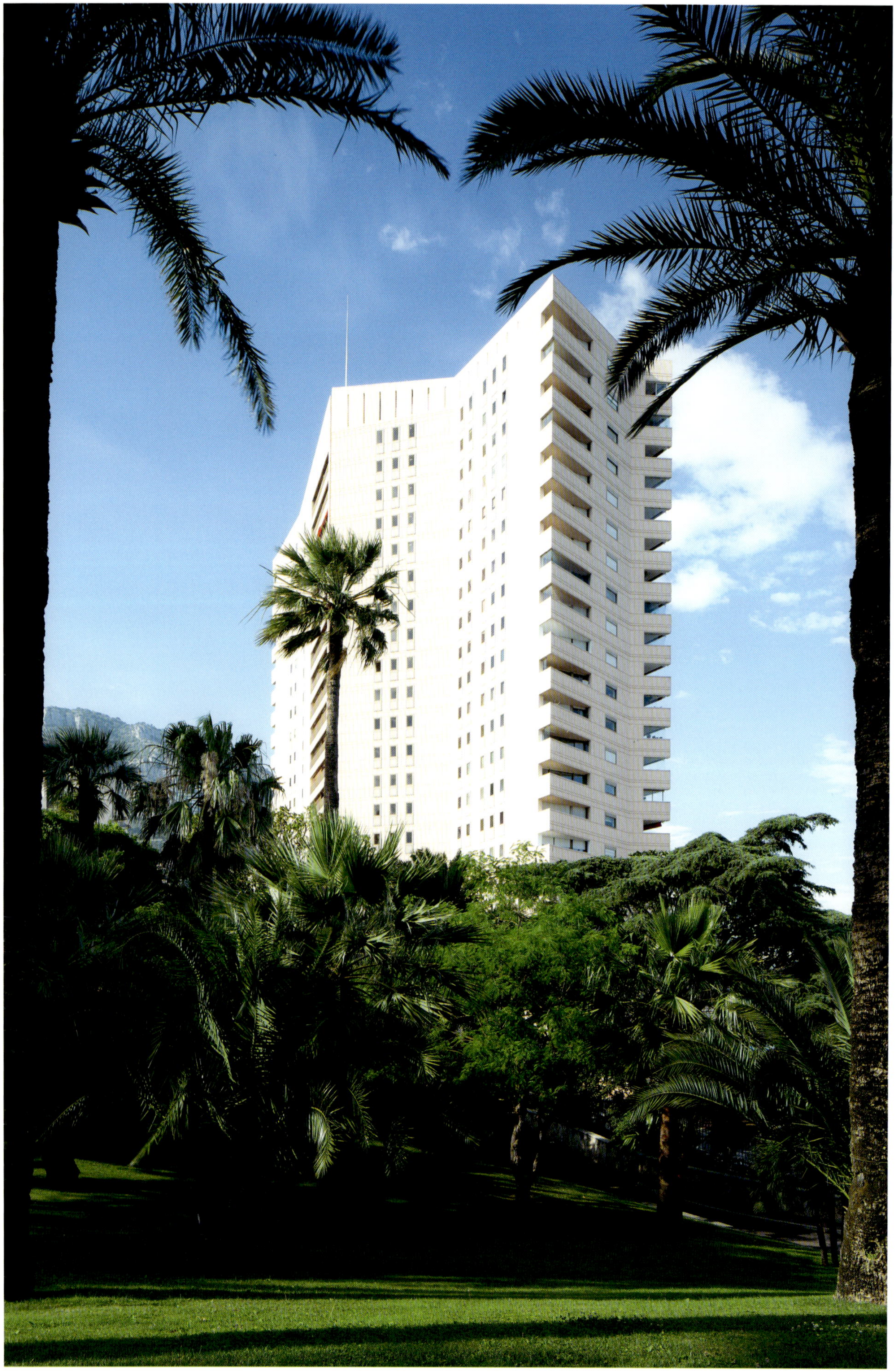

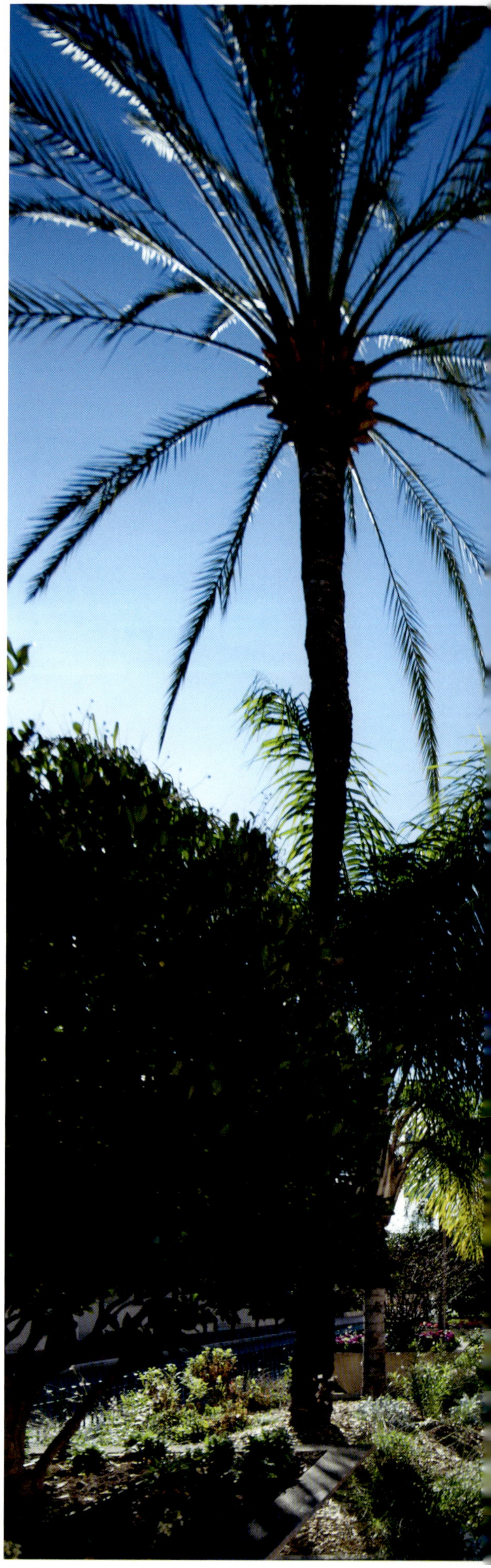

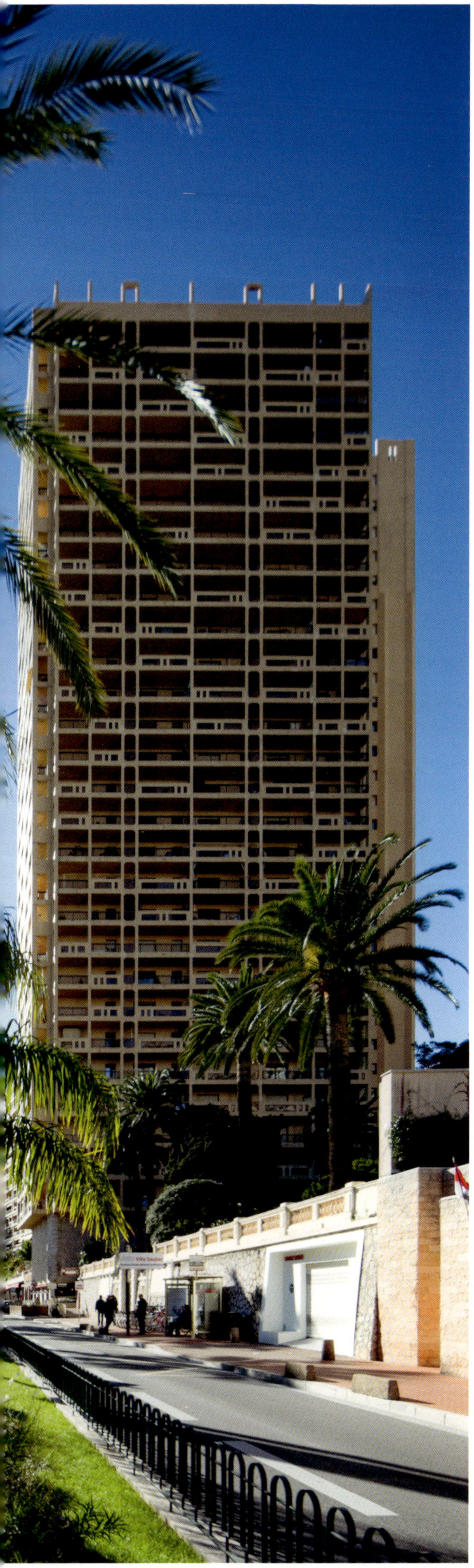

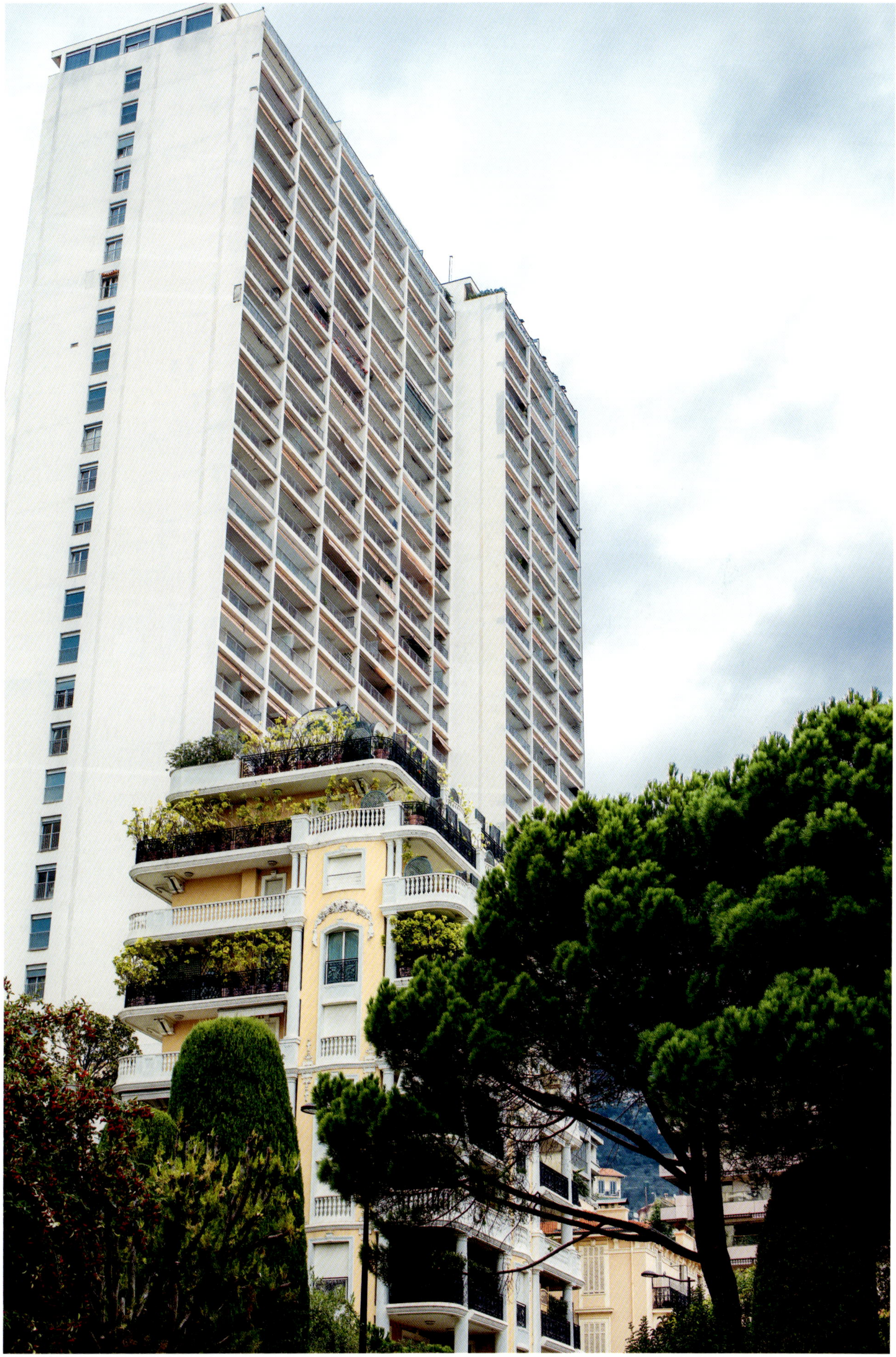

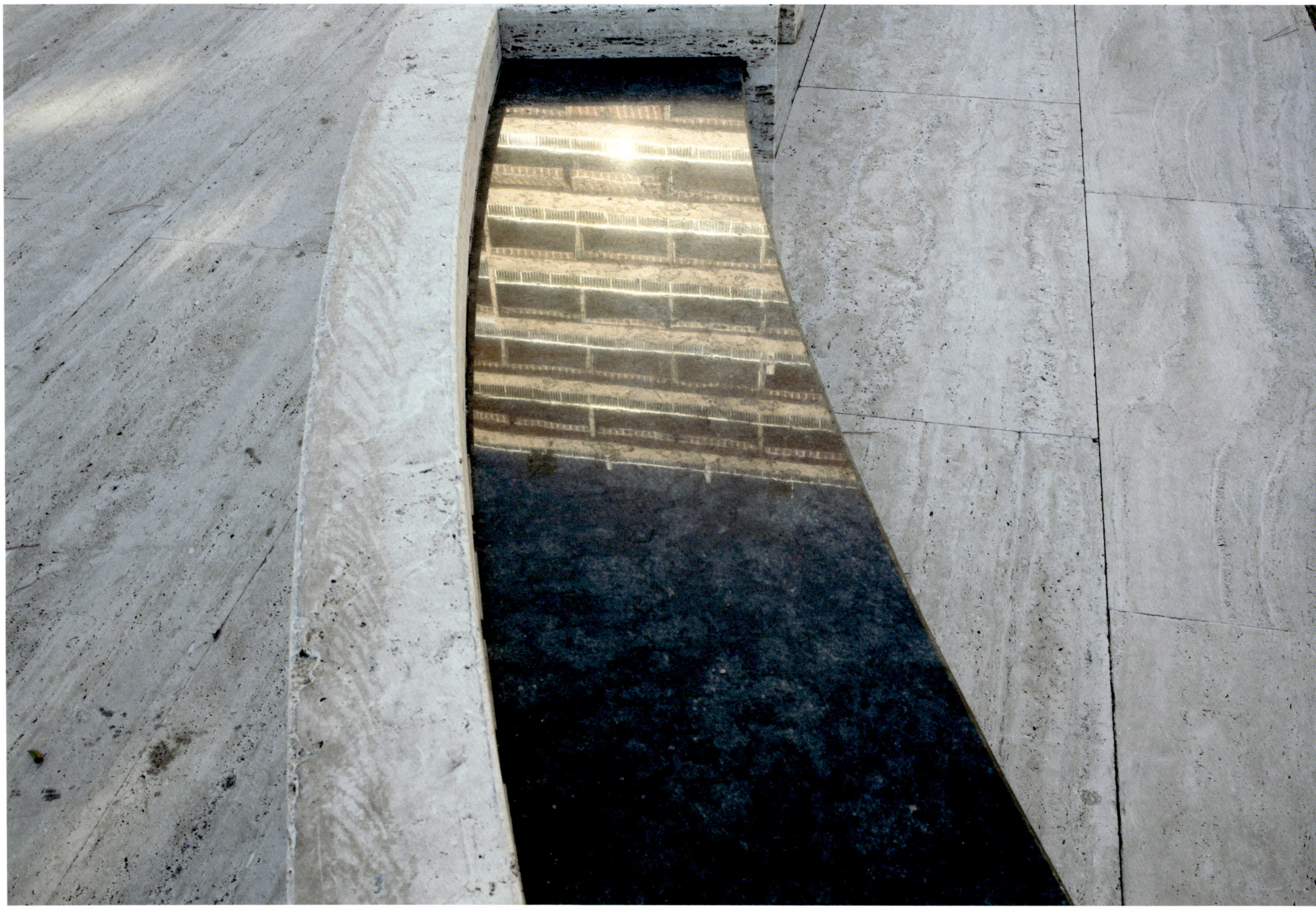

A building façade reflects the sun's light onto a bench over an hour.
November 22, 2015. Left page, 11:41 a.m.; right page, 3:48 p.m.

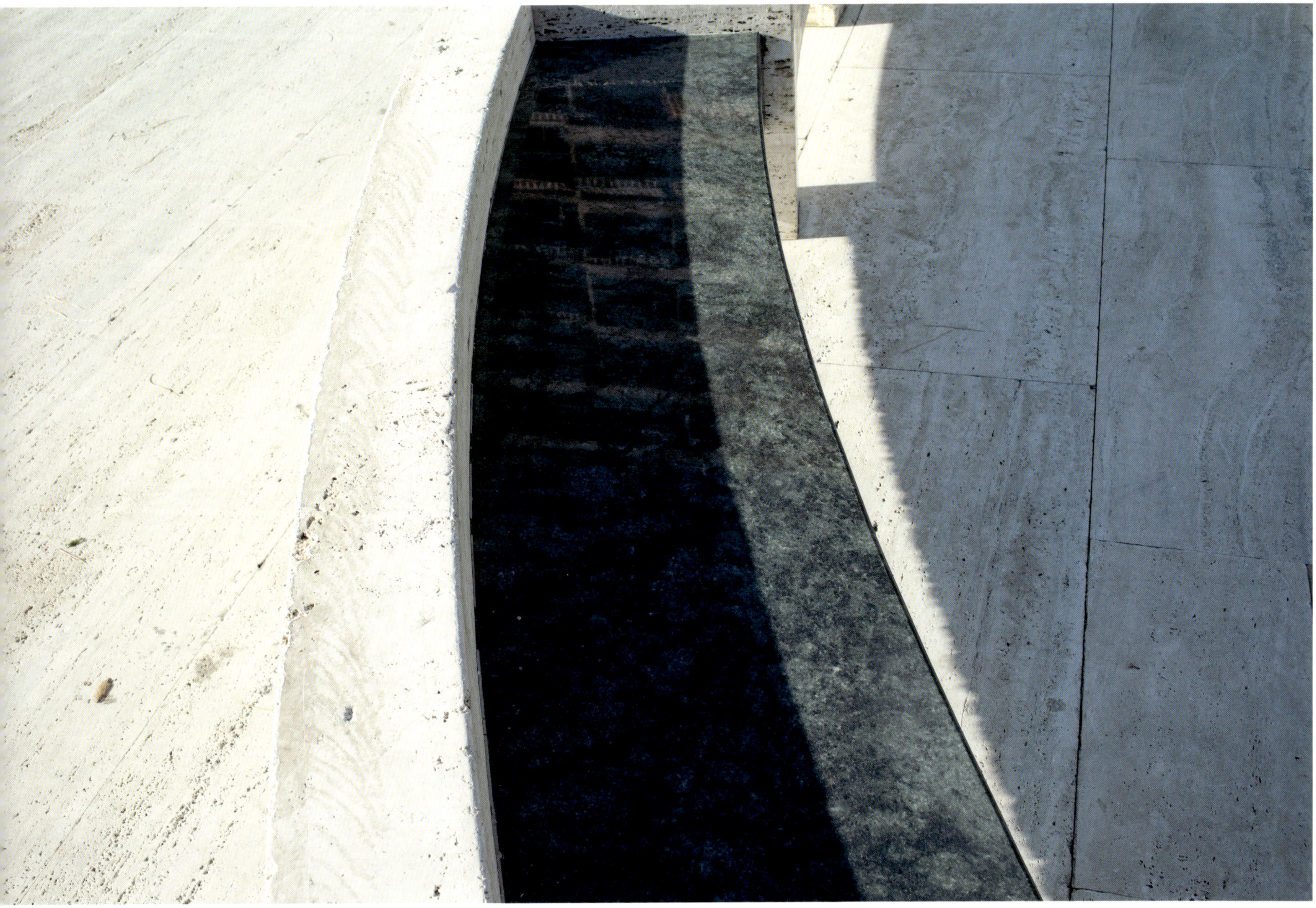

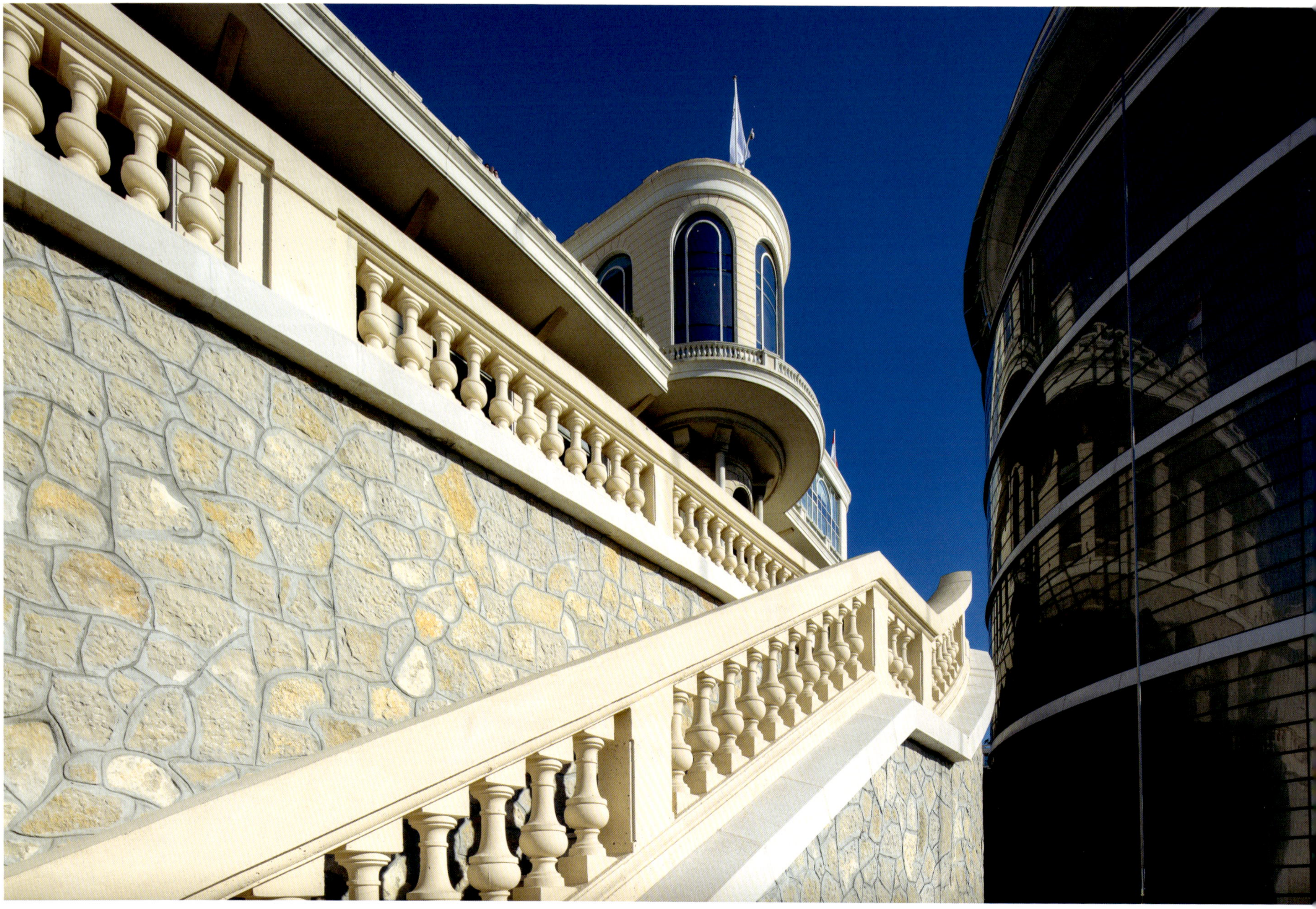

The steps linking Quai des États-Unis with boulevard Louis II are wedged between two different eras. The Yacht Club de Monaco and Thermes Marins come together in reflection. February 20, 2016. Left page, 10:12 a.m.; right page, 10:30 a.m.

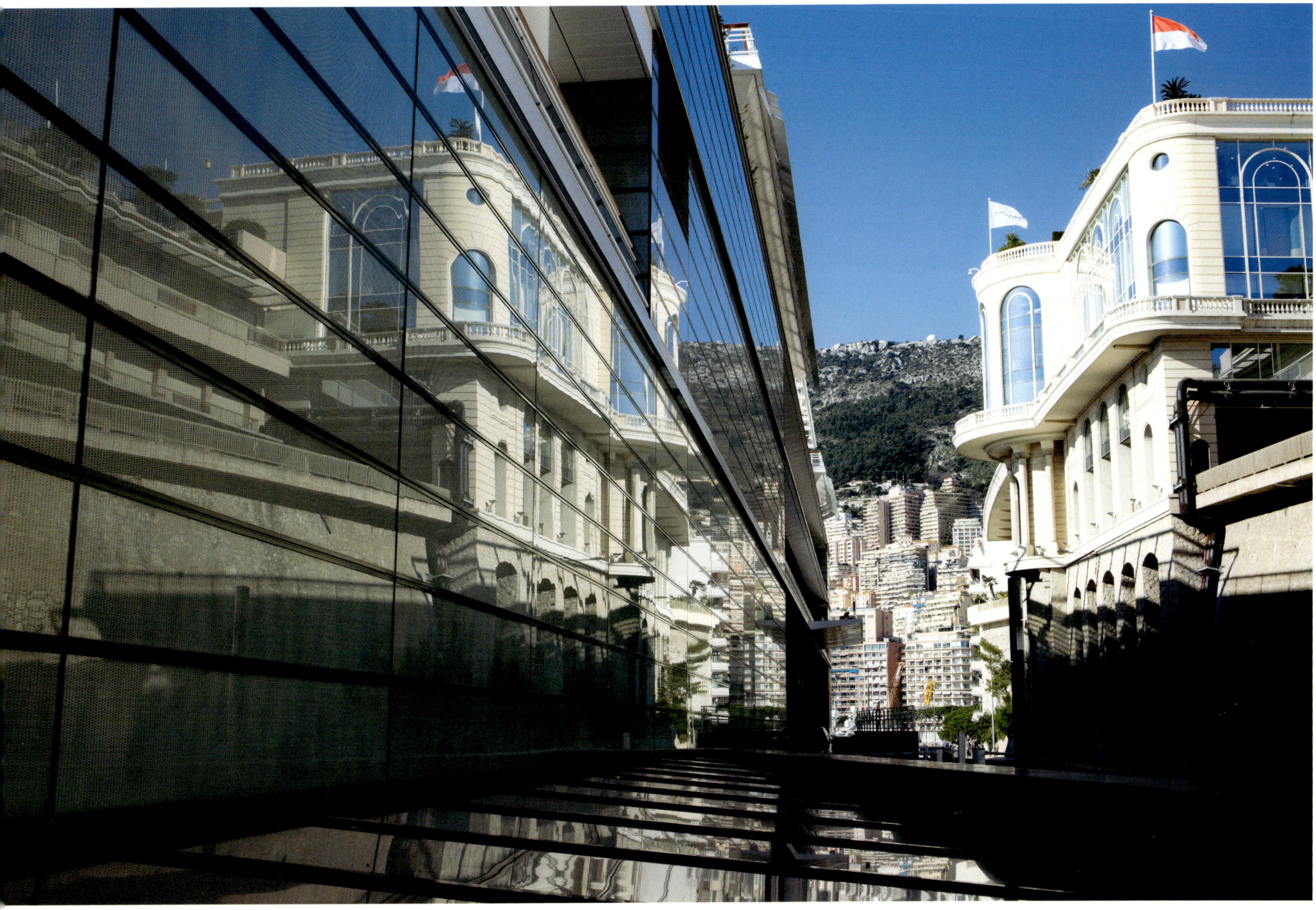

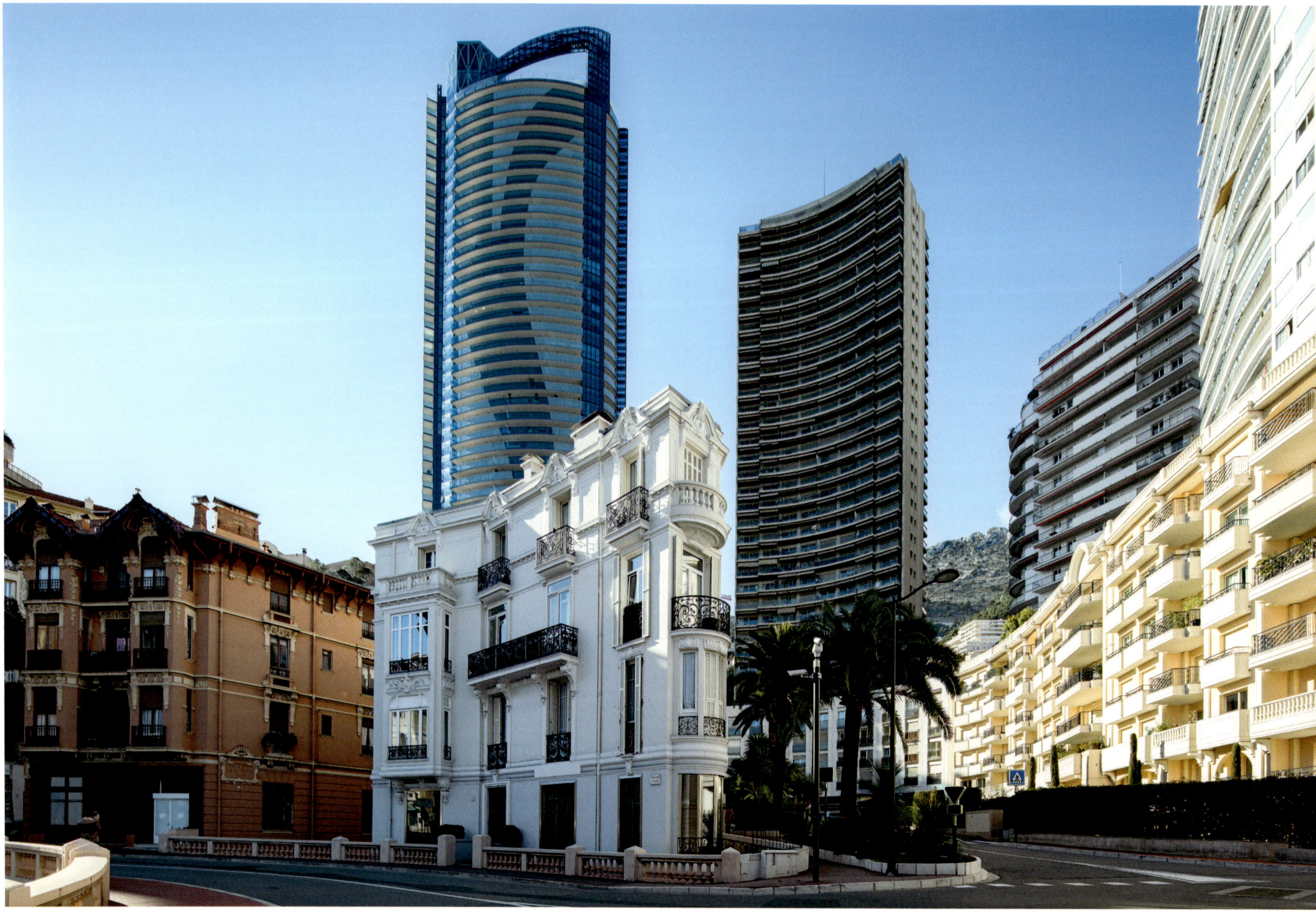

Looking out to sea from boulevard d'Italie, an island of heritage homes is surrounded by contemporary apartment buildings. March 5, 2016, 4:06 p.m.

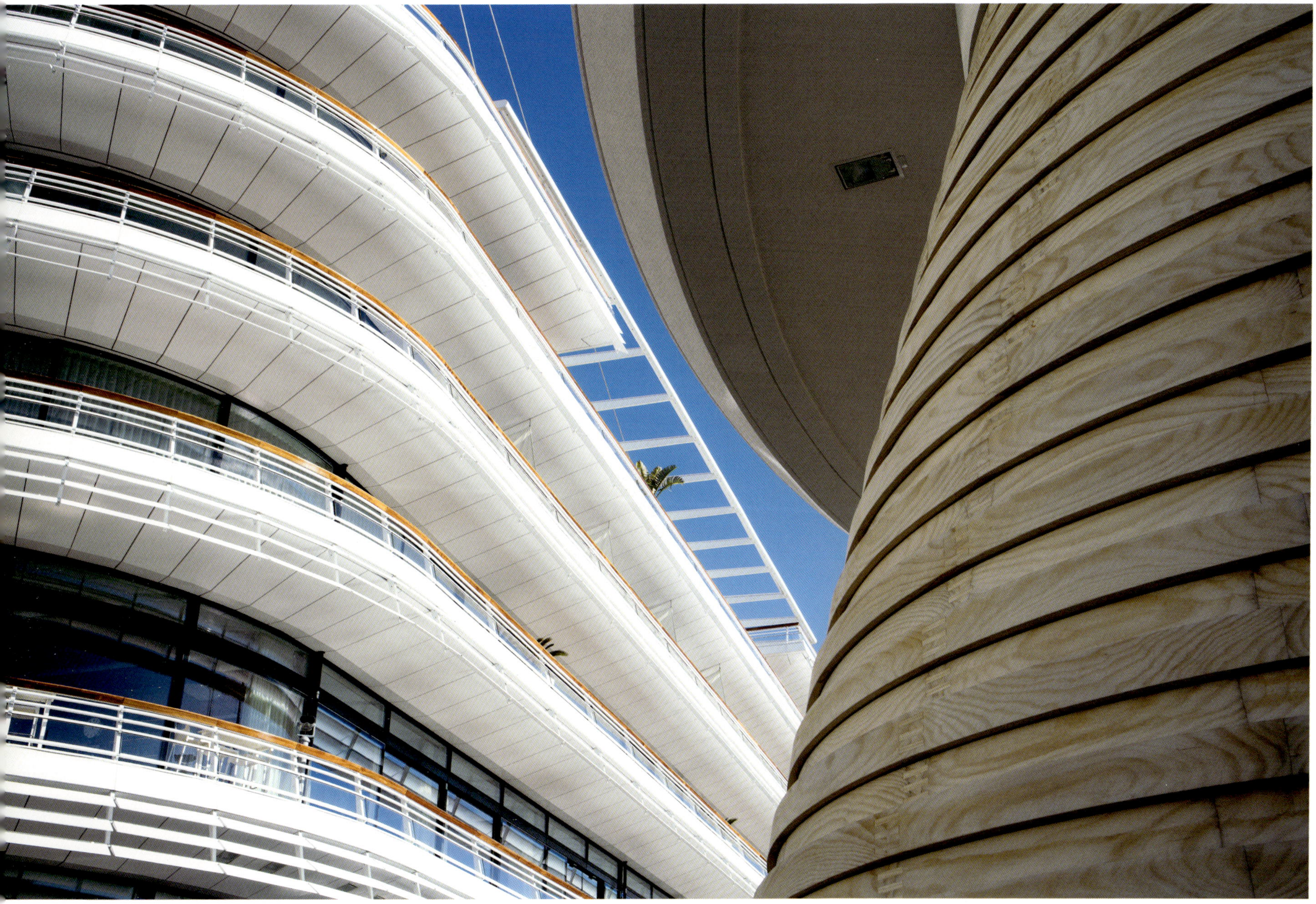

The Yacht Club de Monaco contributes to this interplay of textures and lines, like two boats moored side by side. February 20, 2016, 10:57 a.m.

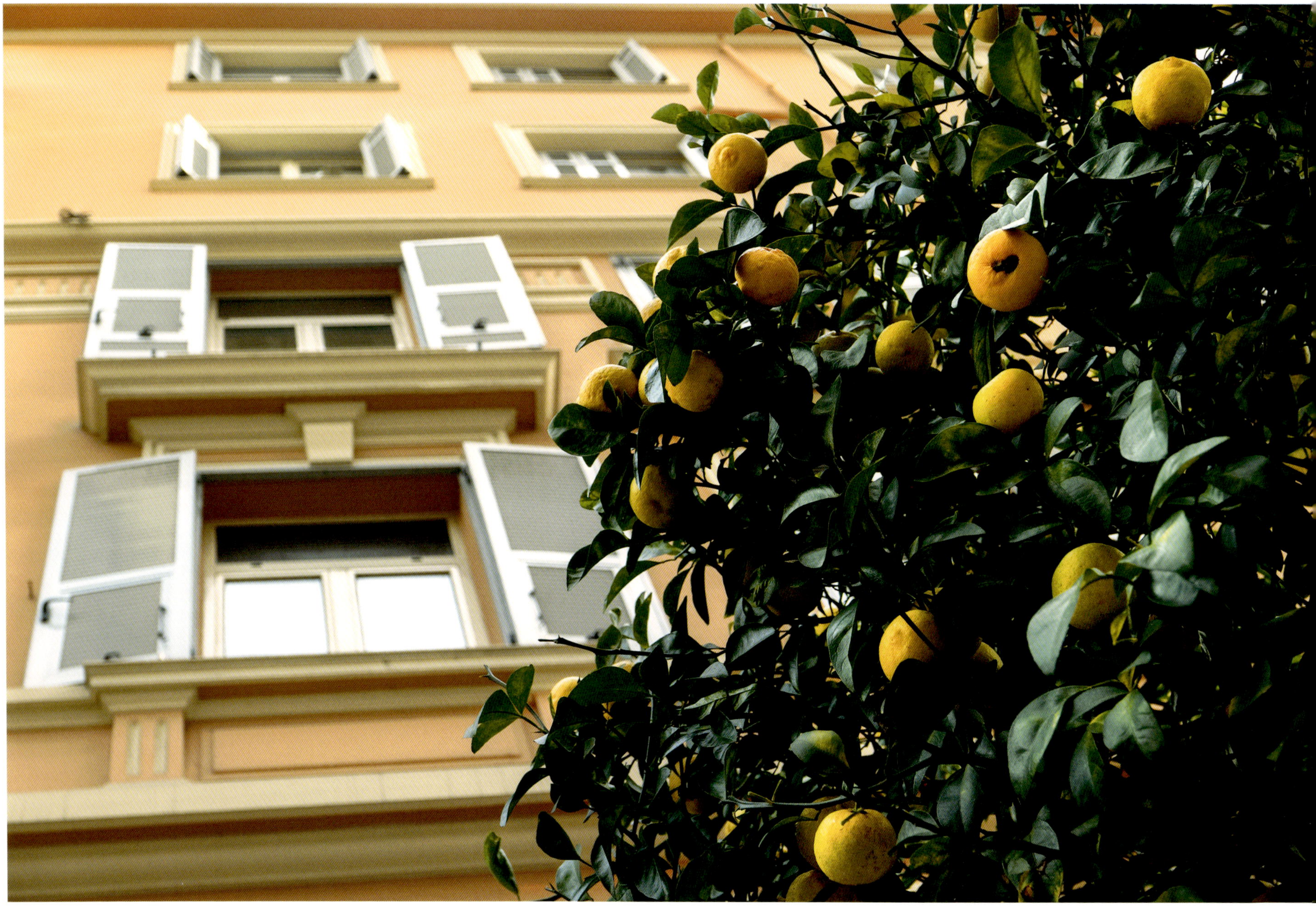

In the La Condamine district, the architecture has evolved over time, but we are still reminded of the cultures that came before urbanization.
Left page, November 29, 2015, 2:37 p.m. Right page, January 1, 2016, 10:39 a.m.

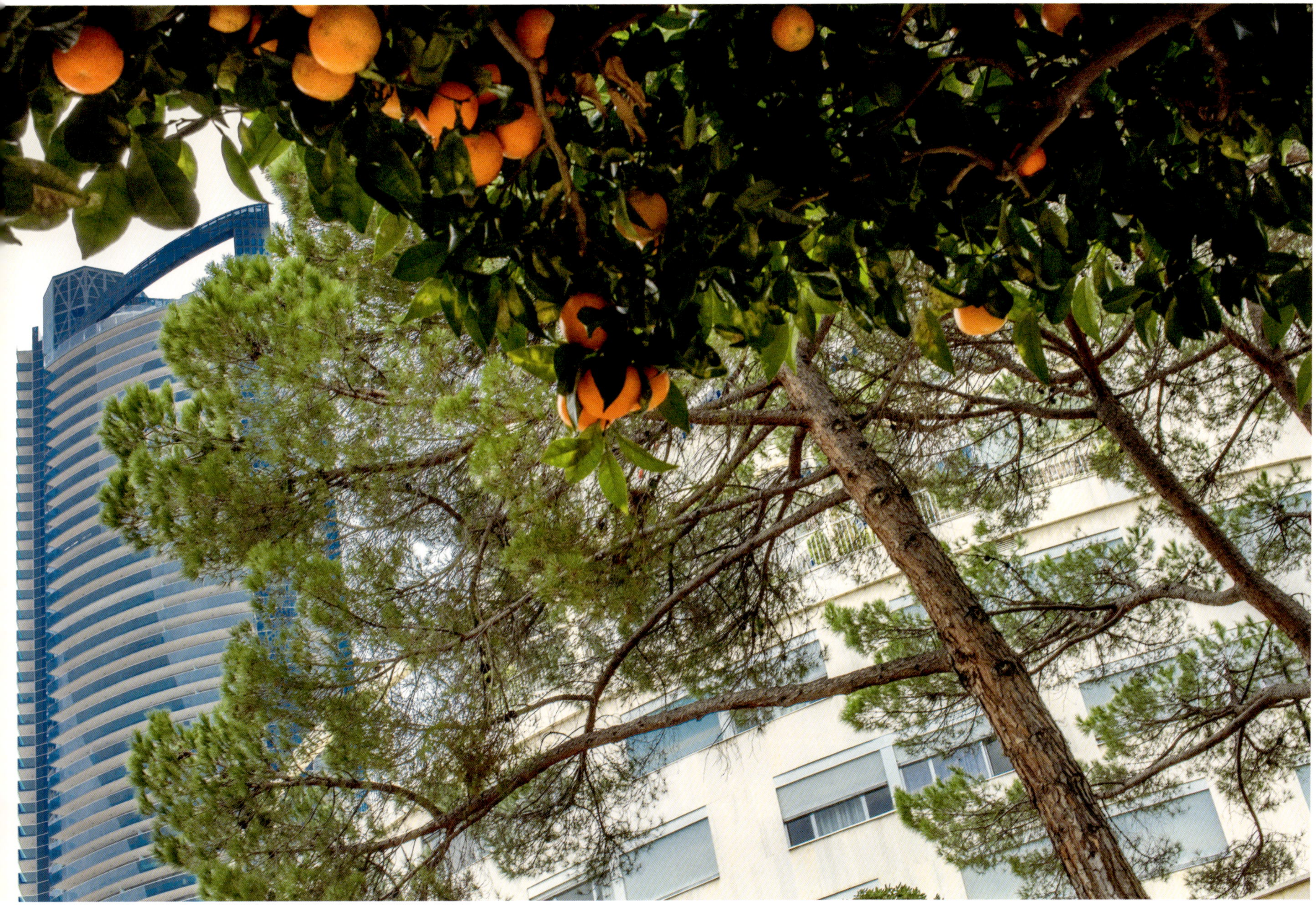

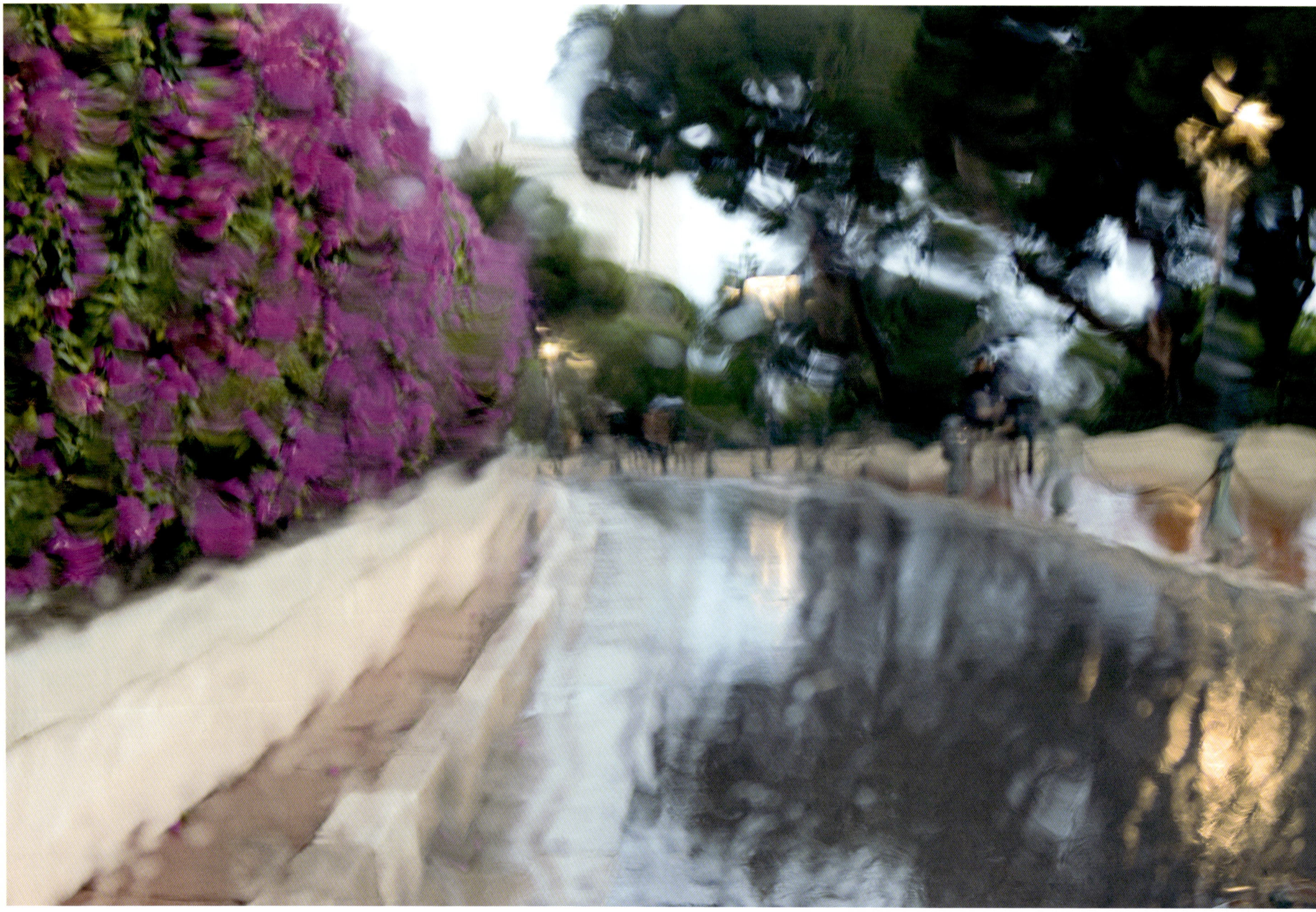

Near to the Oceanographic Museum, the sun returns after the rain.
Left page, February 7, 2016, 4:55 p.m. Right page, February 21, 2016, 2:54 p.m.

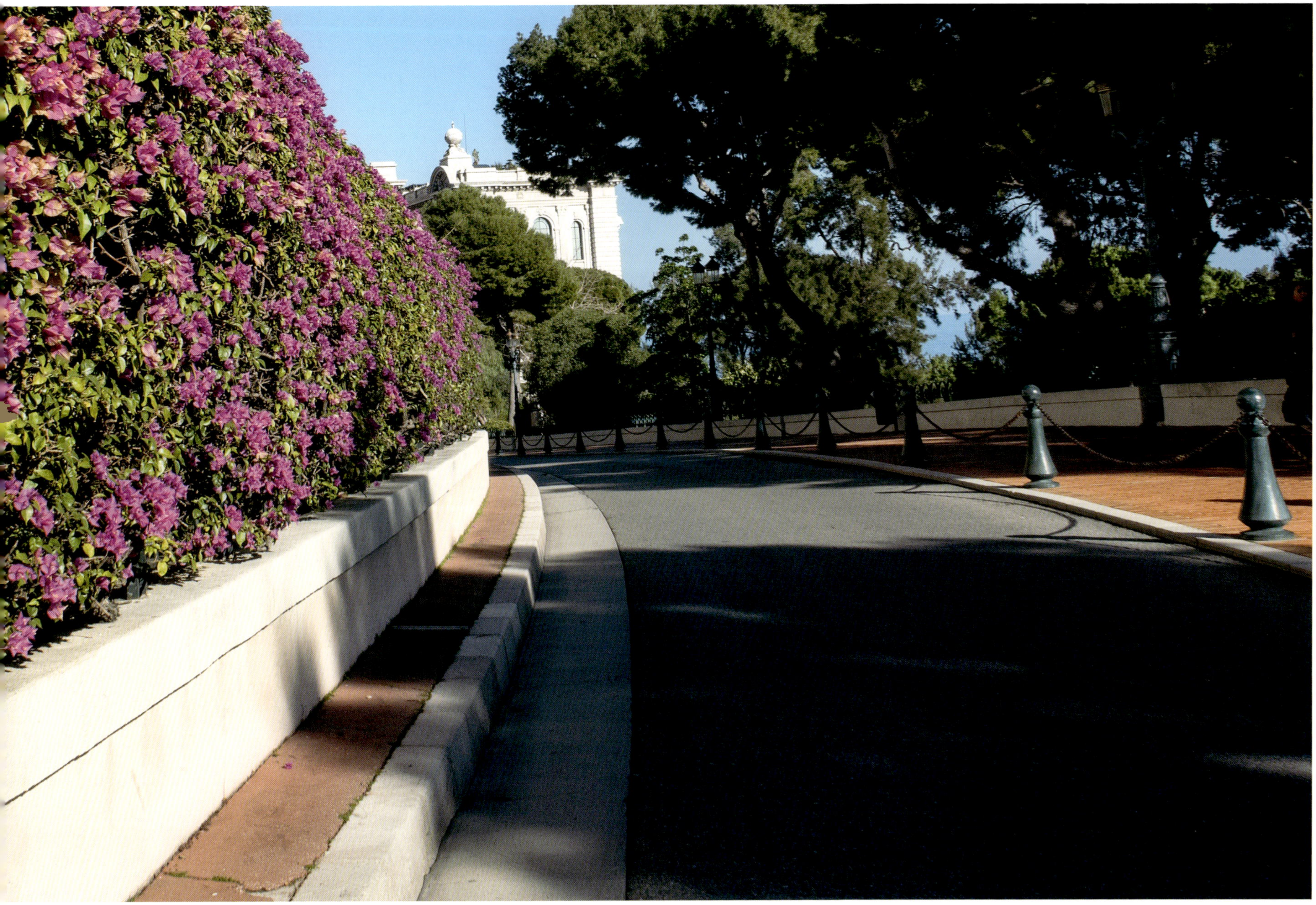

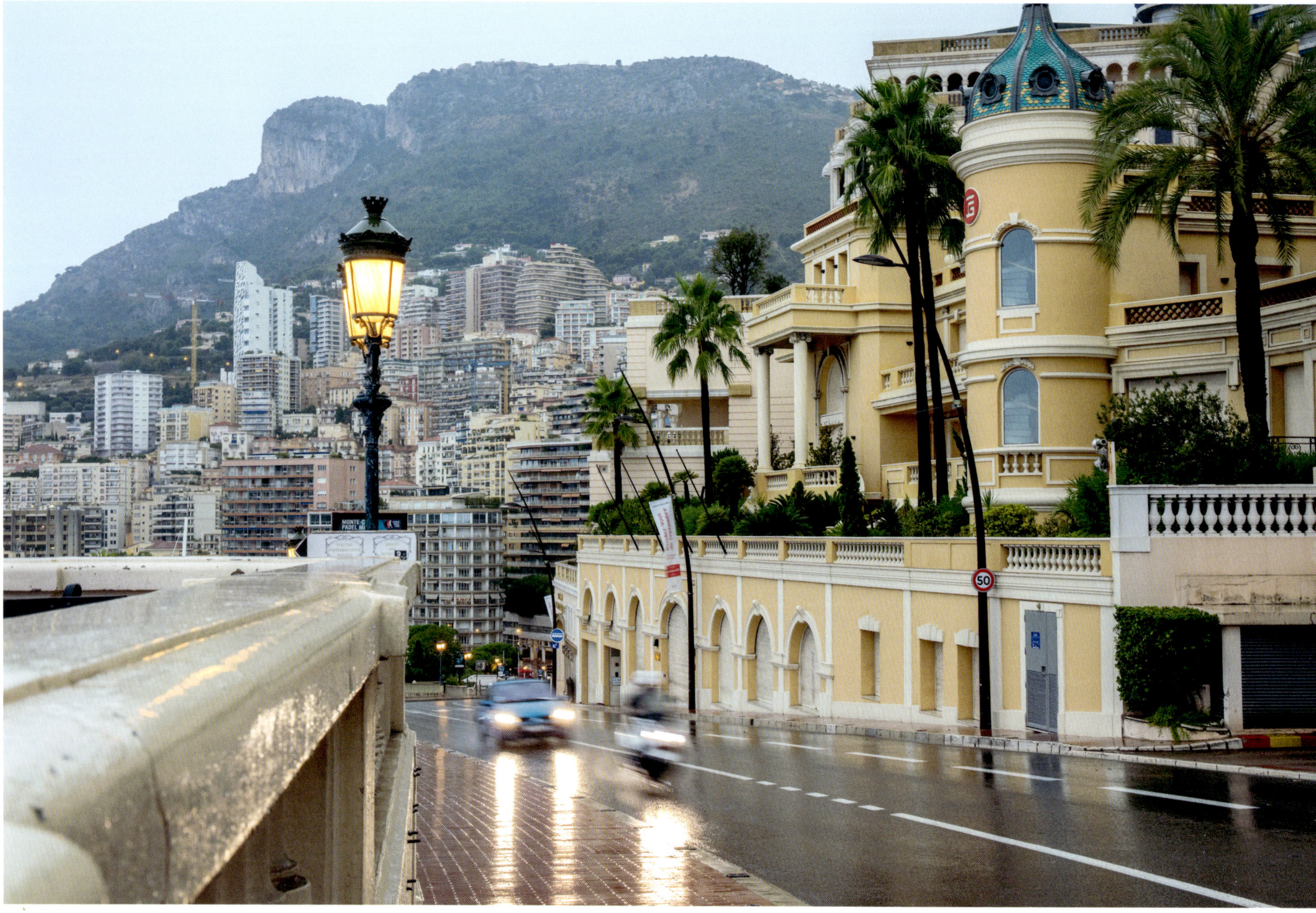
50

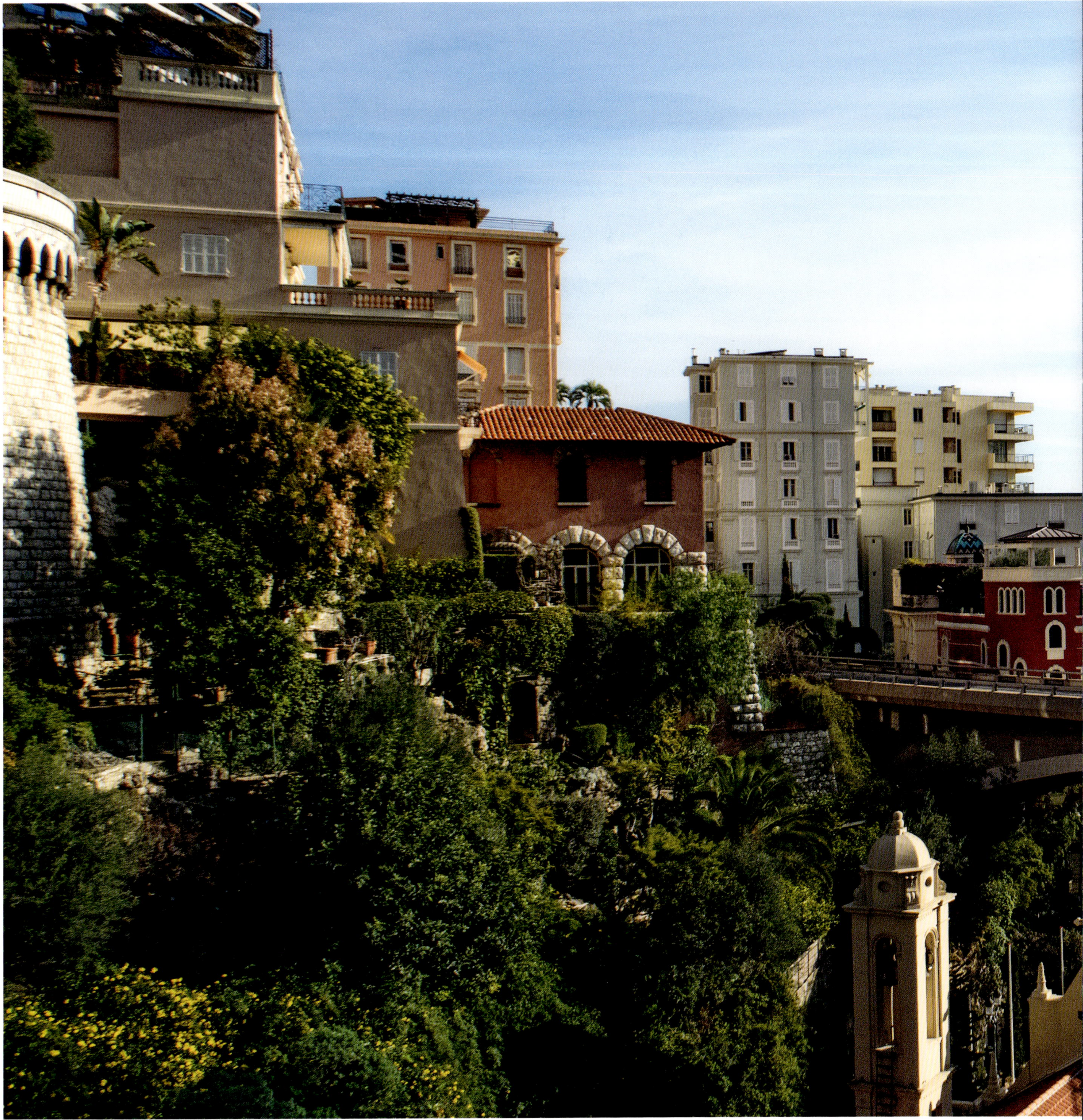

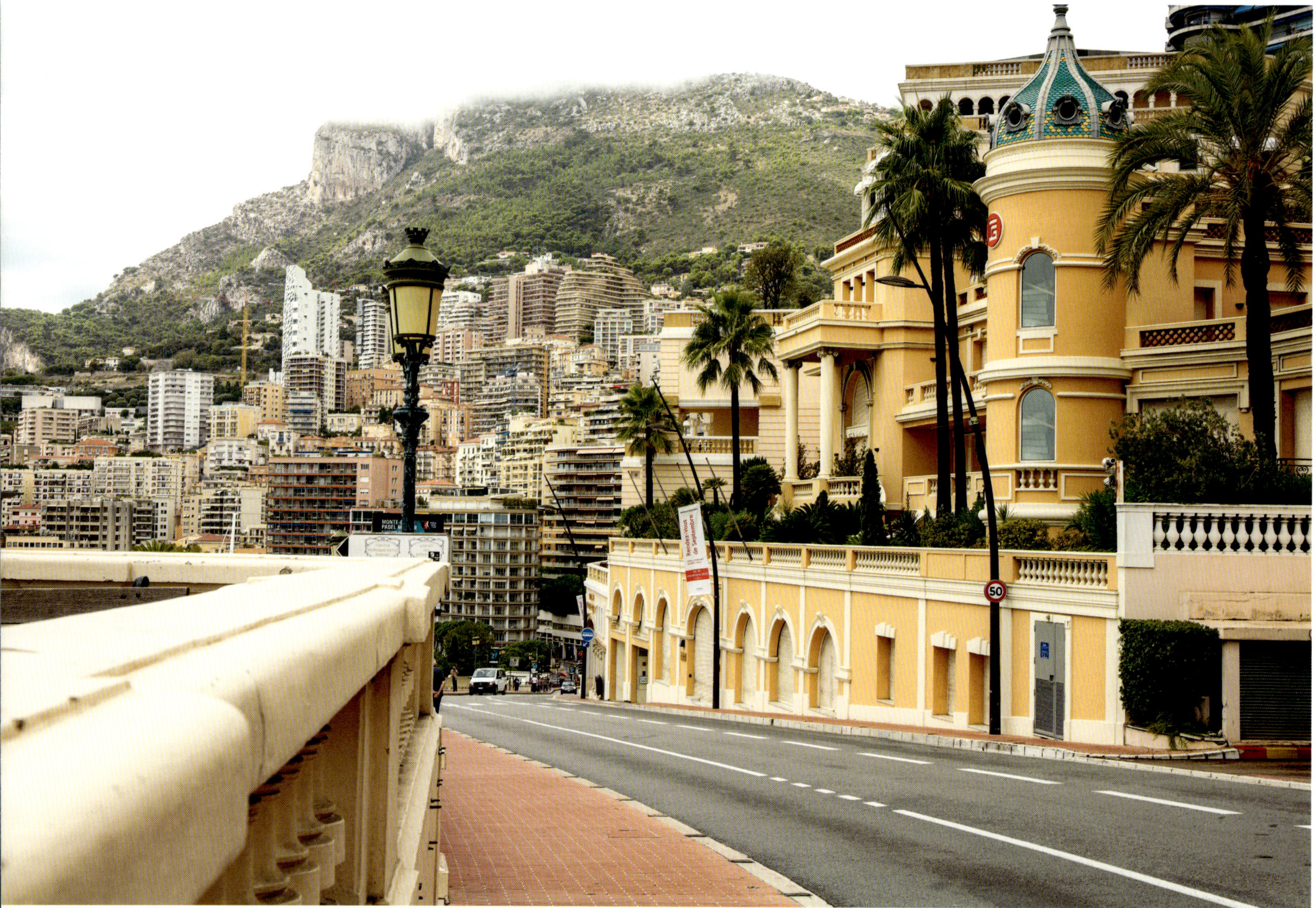
50

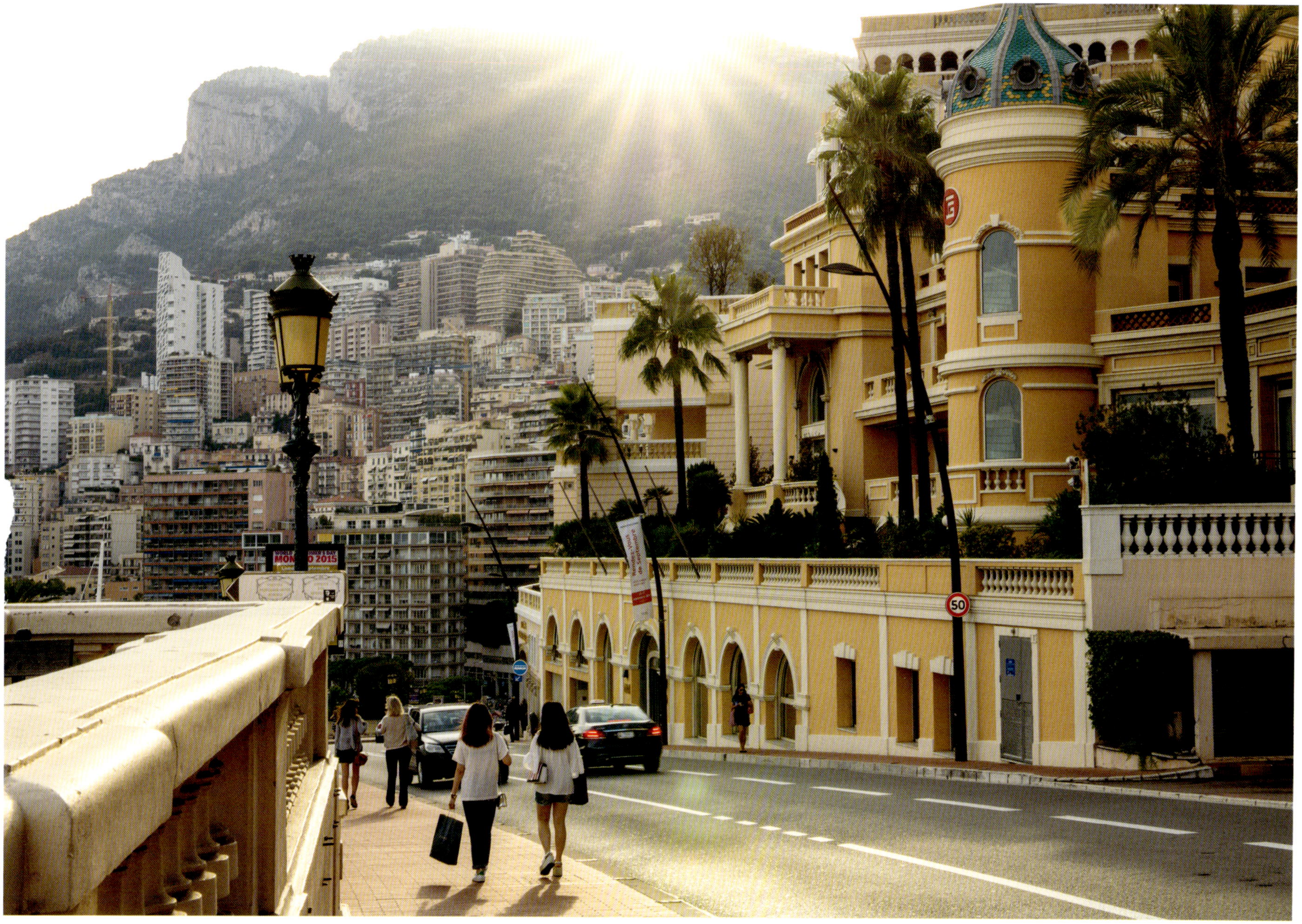
50

Previous triptych. Afternoon and early evening on the road leading from Monte Carlo to Port Hercules, as the weather goes from rain to cloud to sun. September 13, 2015, left page, 9:25 a.m.; center, 12:30 p.m.; right page, 6:12 p.m.

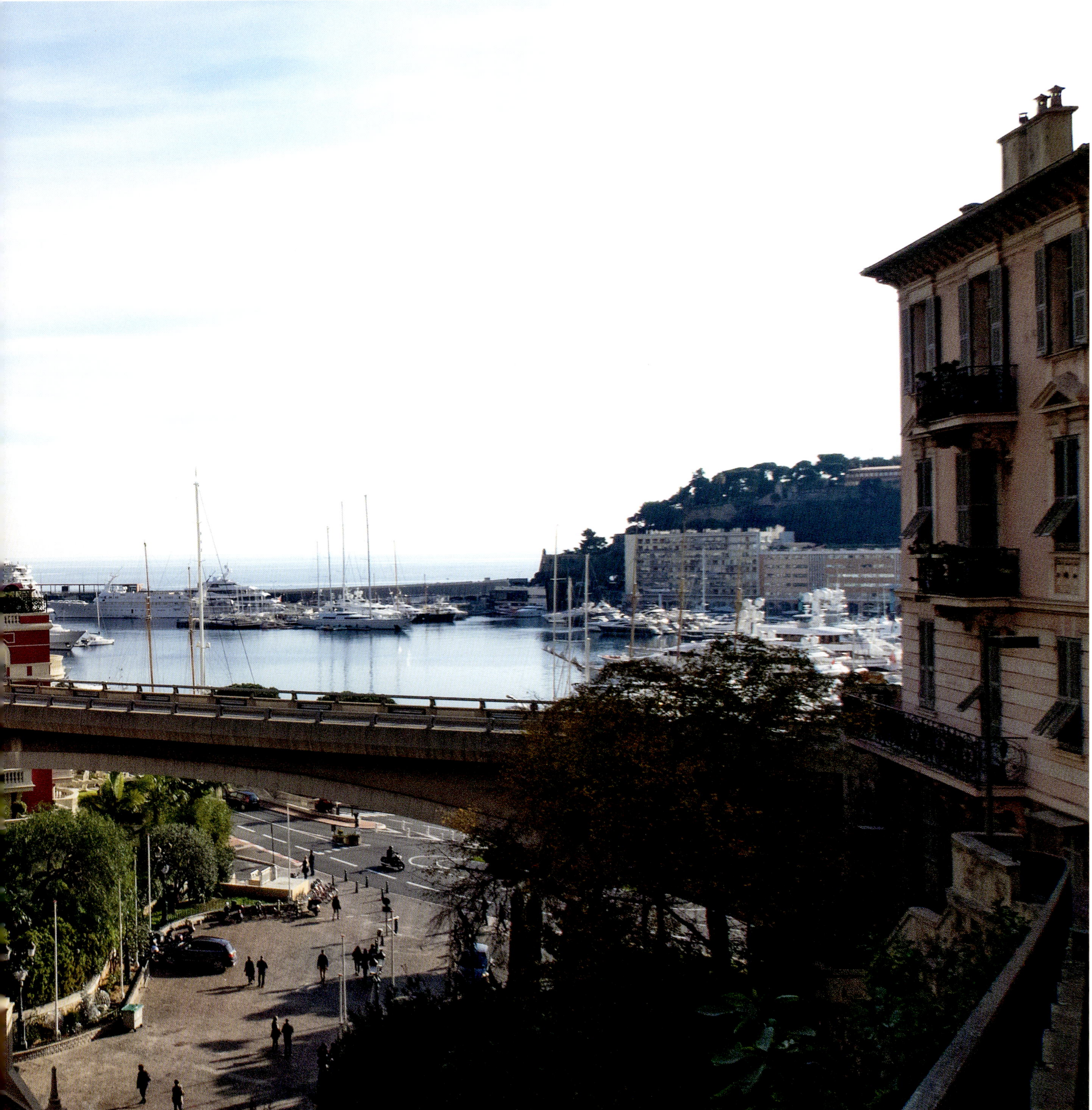

Previous spread. At midday, historic Sainte-Dévote Chapel has a clear view over Port Hercules and the Rock. November 26, 2015, 12:01 p.m.

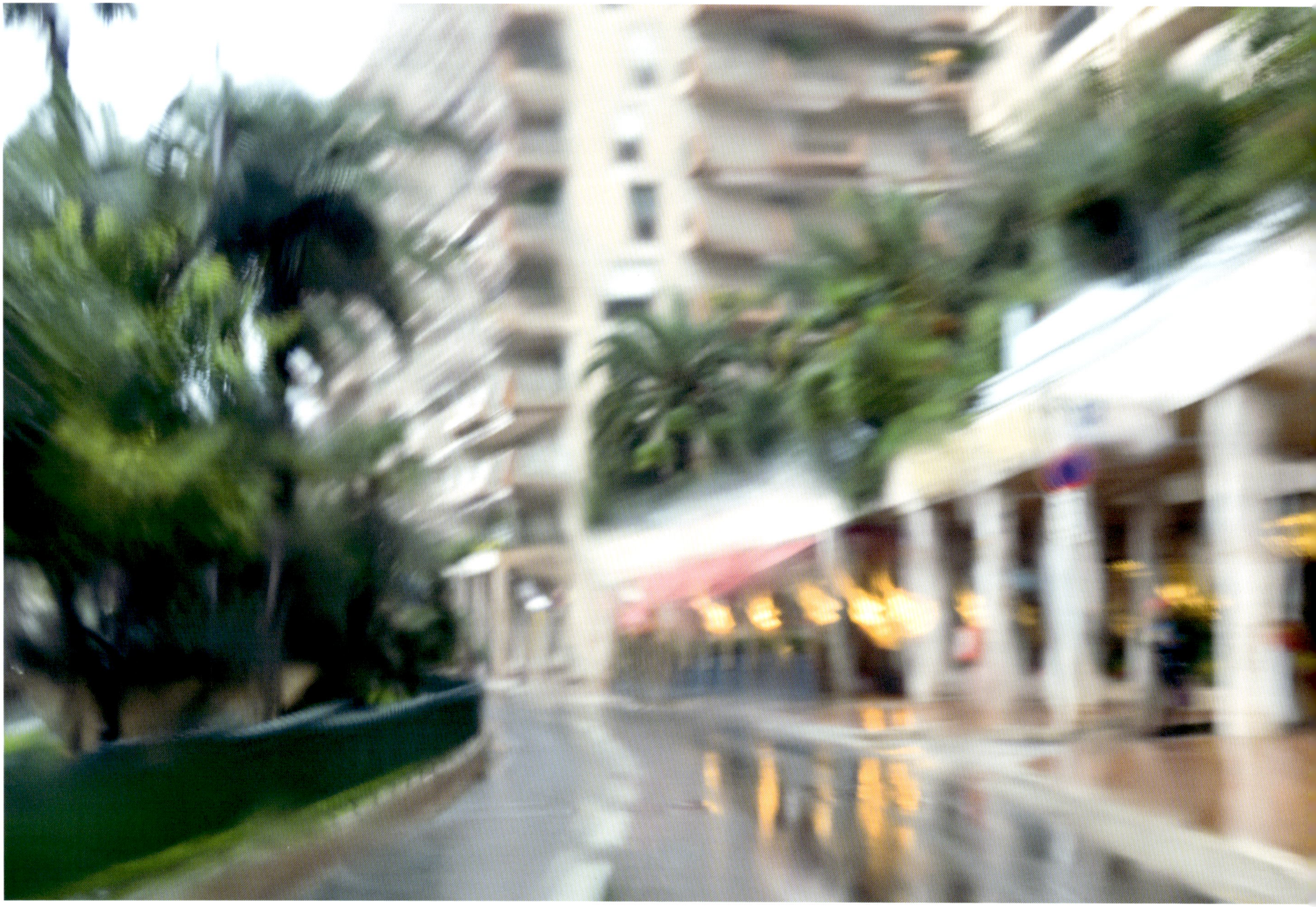

Unusual views of Monaco near the Japanese garden and the Prince's Palace, considering it enjoys three hundred days of sunshine every year. February 7, 2016. Left page, 4:27 p.m.; right page, 4:52 p.m.

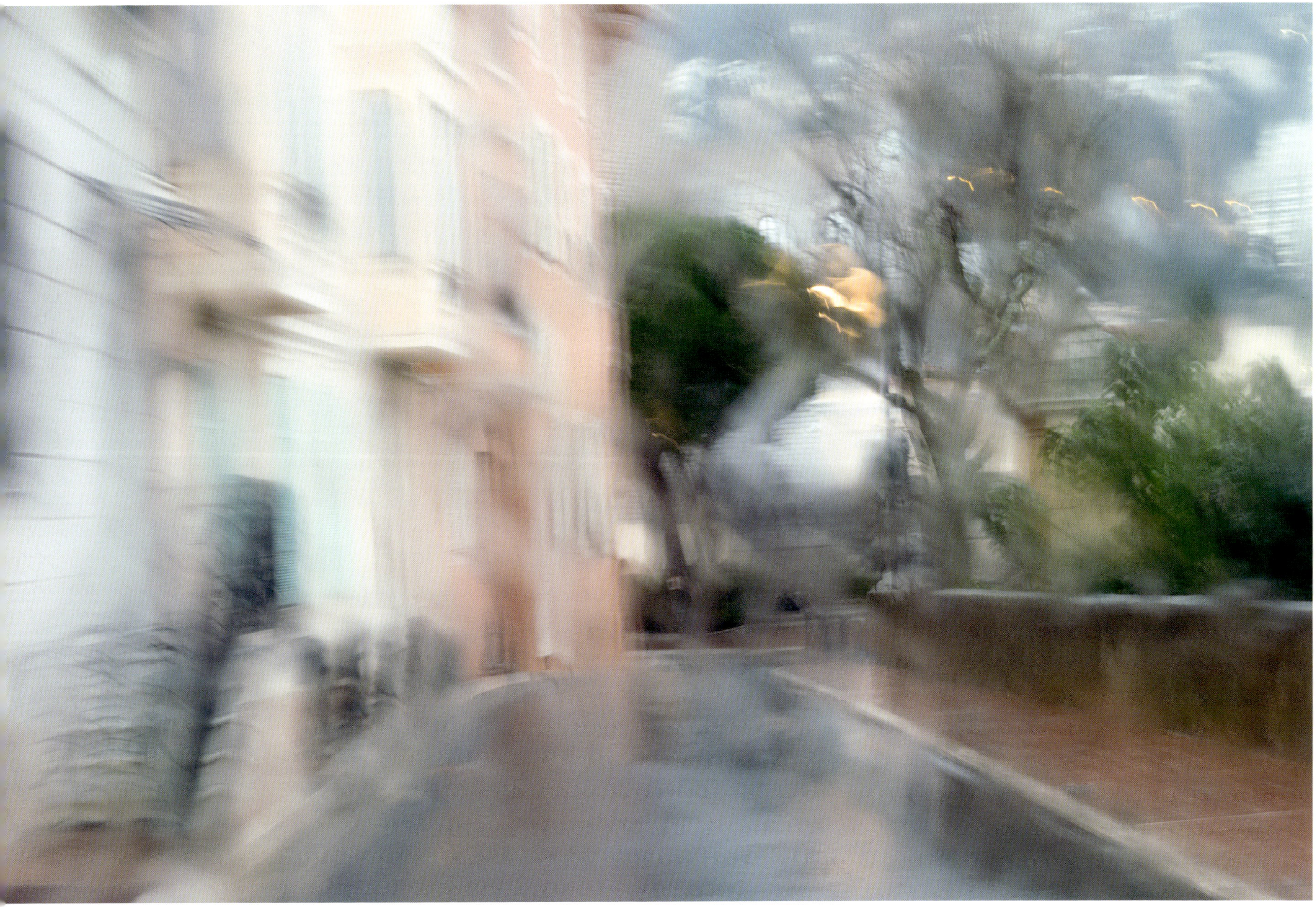

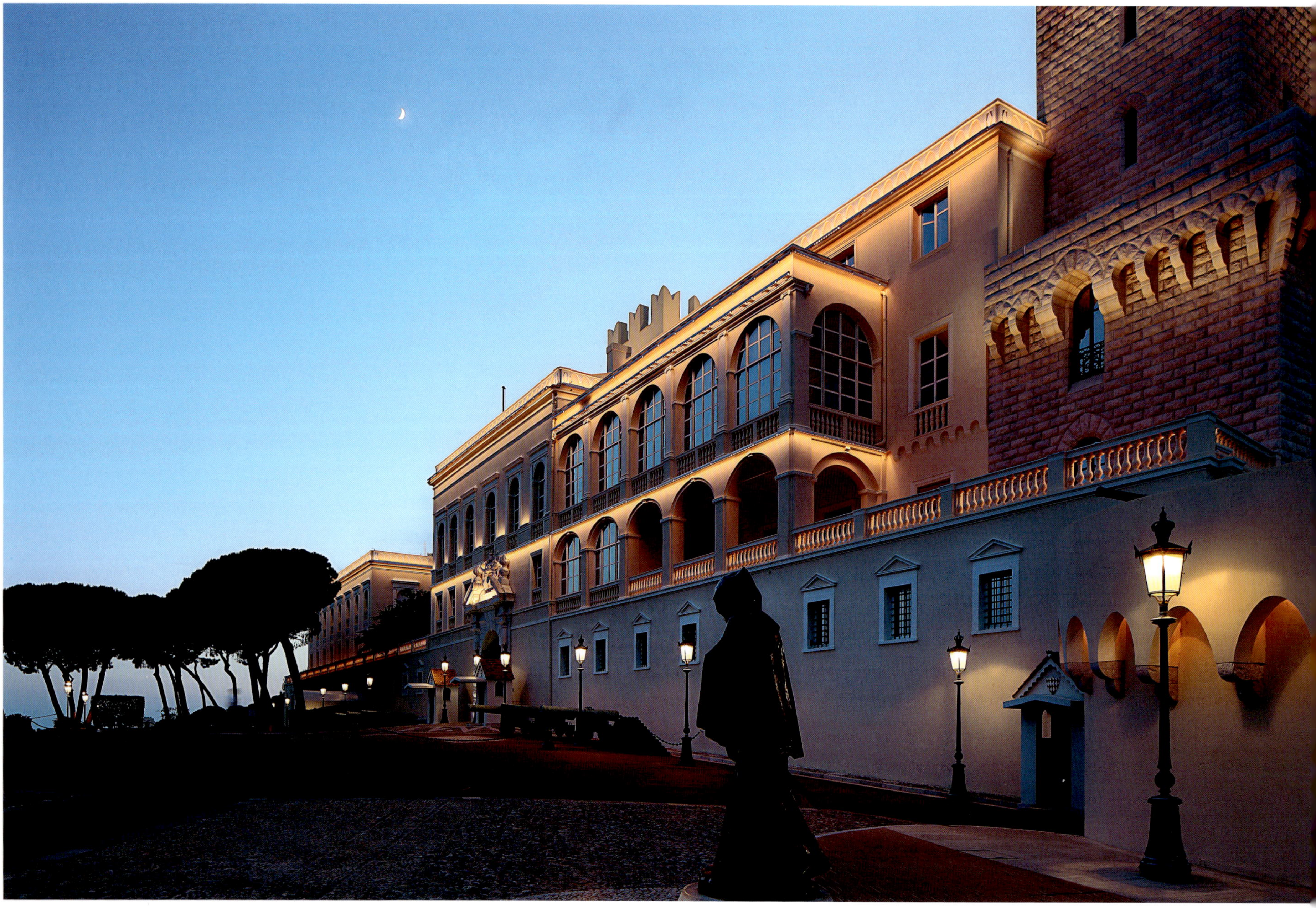

At dusk in front of the Prince's Palace, "Malizia" appears ready to try his deceit once more!
June 22, 2015. Left page, 8:24 p.m.; right page, 8:43 p.m.

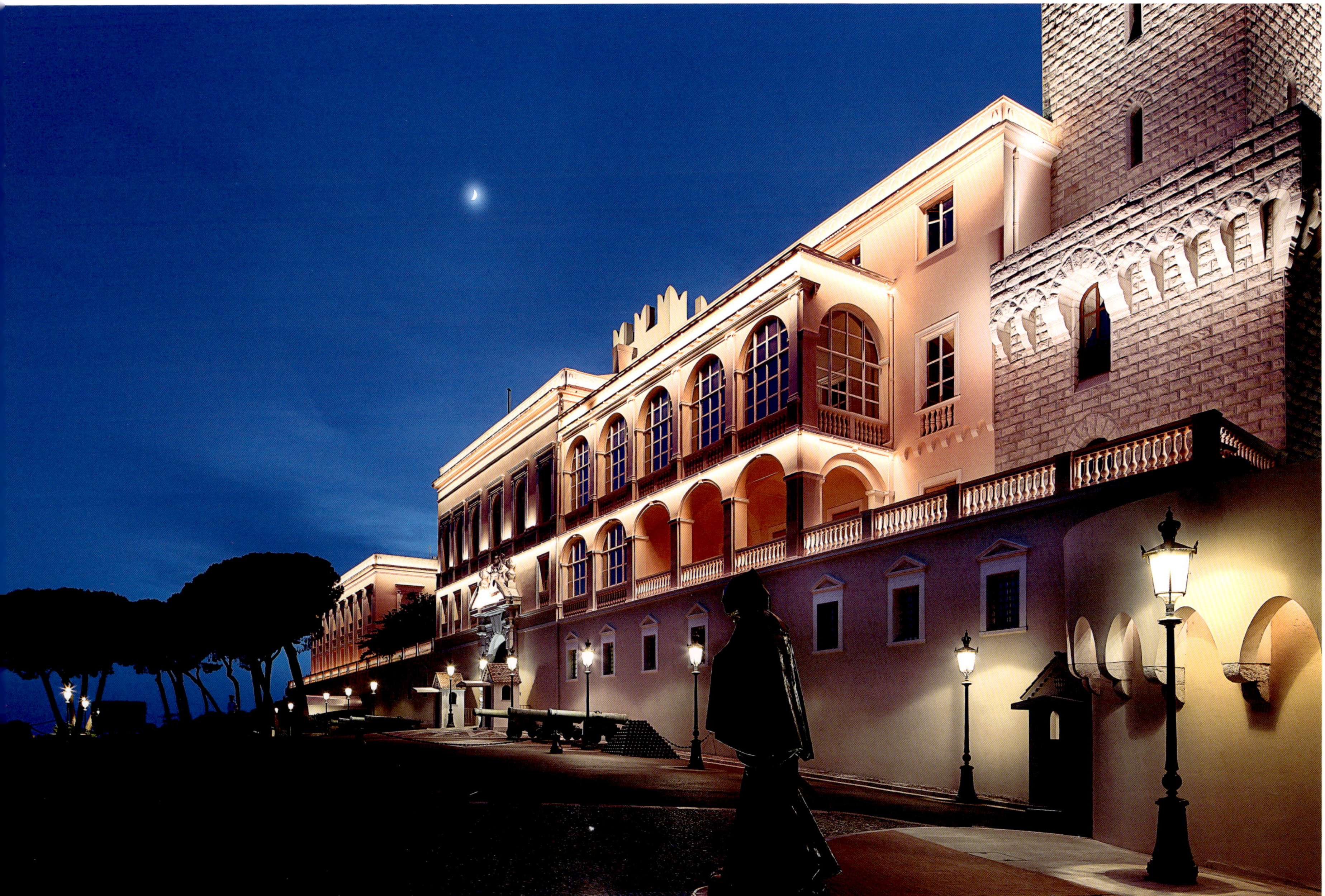

Early afternoon light accentuates the architecture and rampant vegetation.
December 10, 2015. Left page, 3:25 p.m.; right page, 3:13 p.m.

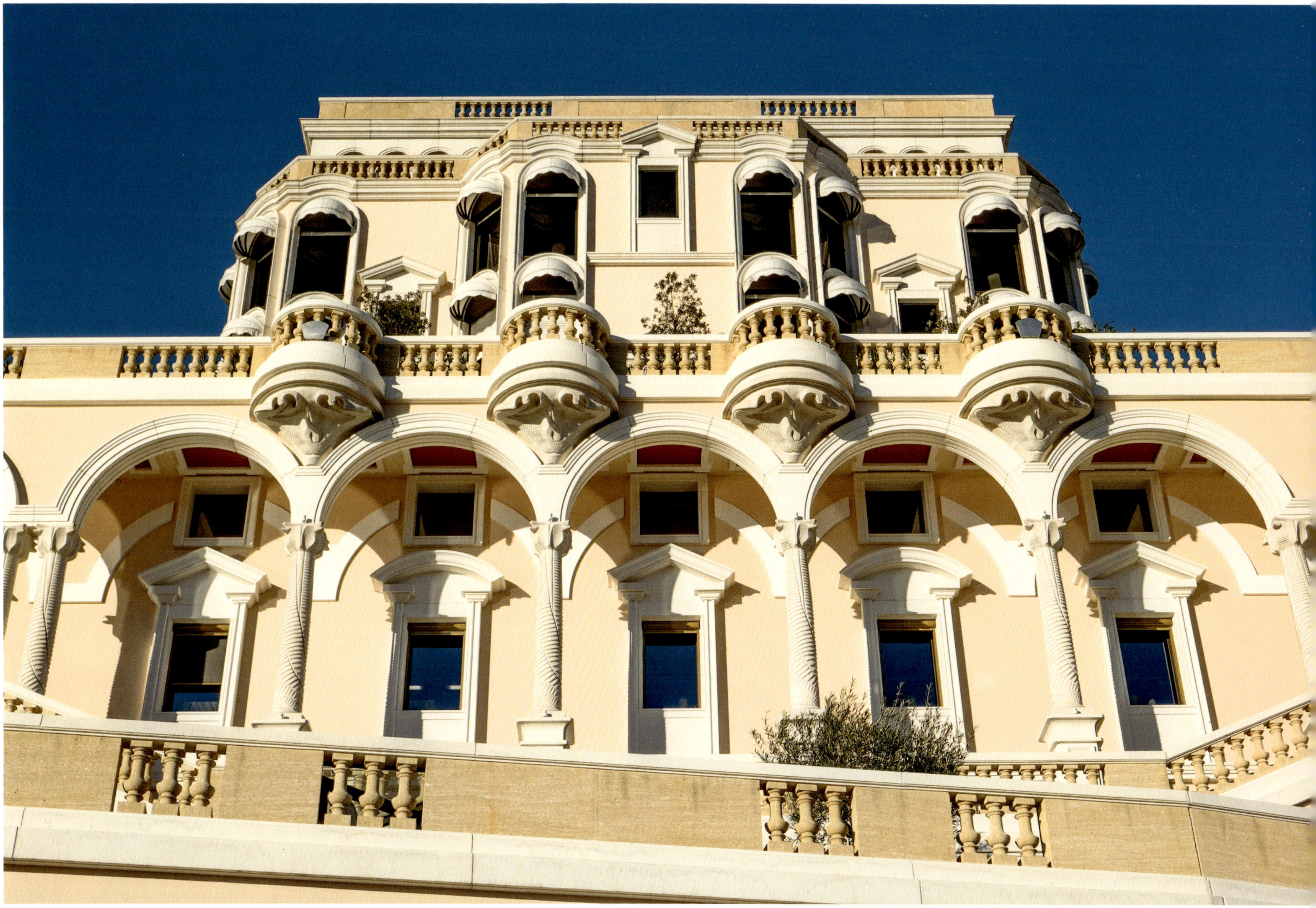

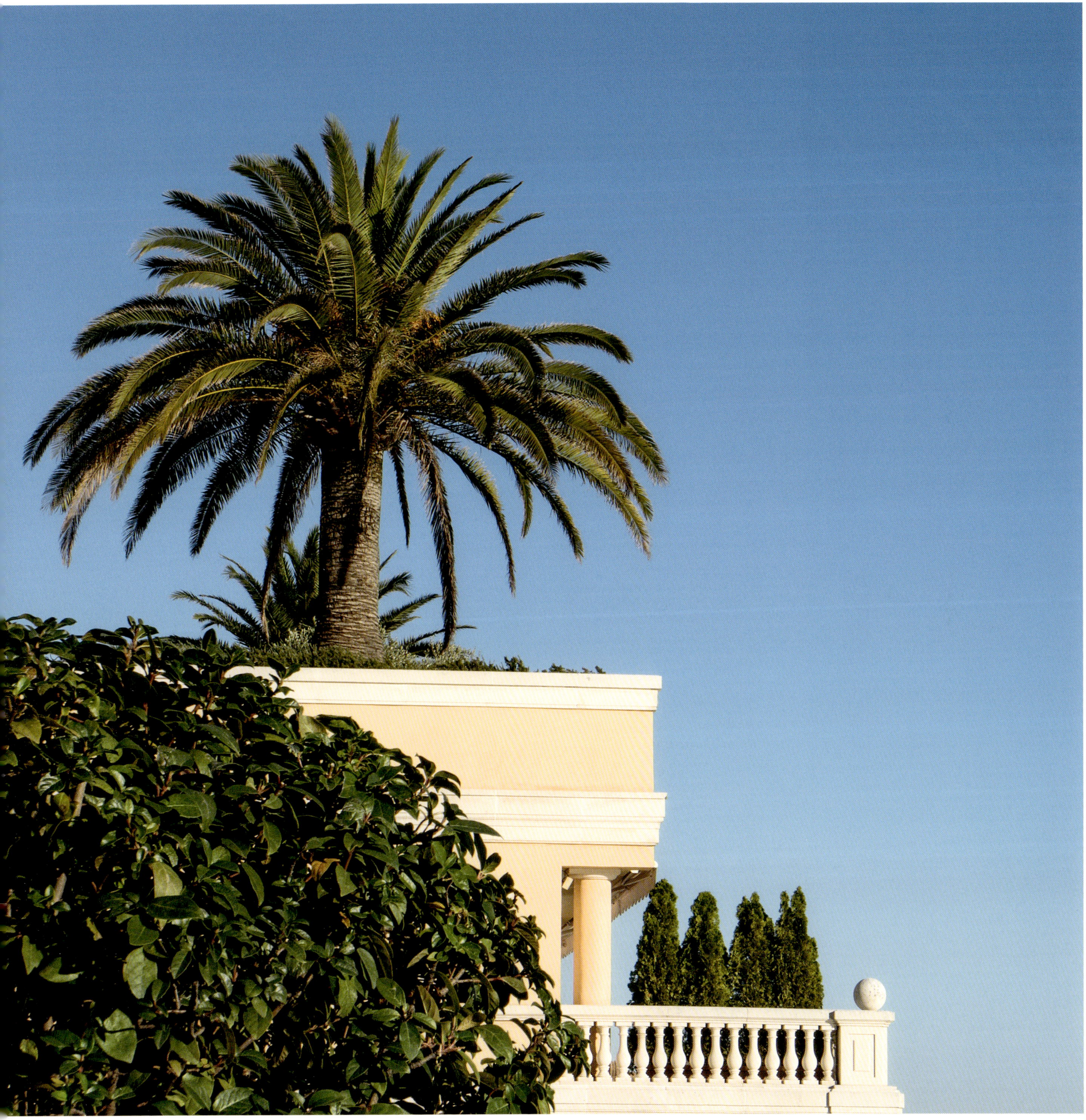

"An hour is not merely an hour, it is a vase full of scents and sounds and projects and climates."

Marcel Proust, *Time Regained*

Built in 1910, the Persian-style Villa Danichgah with its blue dome and bulbs sits on boulevard du Jardin Exotique in its new surroundings. January 26, 2016, 12:58 p.m.

Following spread. Avenue d'Ostende, series evoking the daily passage of time and authentic Monegasque colors. July 9, 2015. Left page, 10:24 a.m.; center, 14 seconds after 10:26 a.m.; right page, 21 seconds after 10:26 a.m.

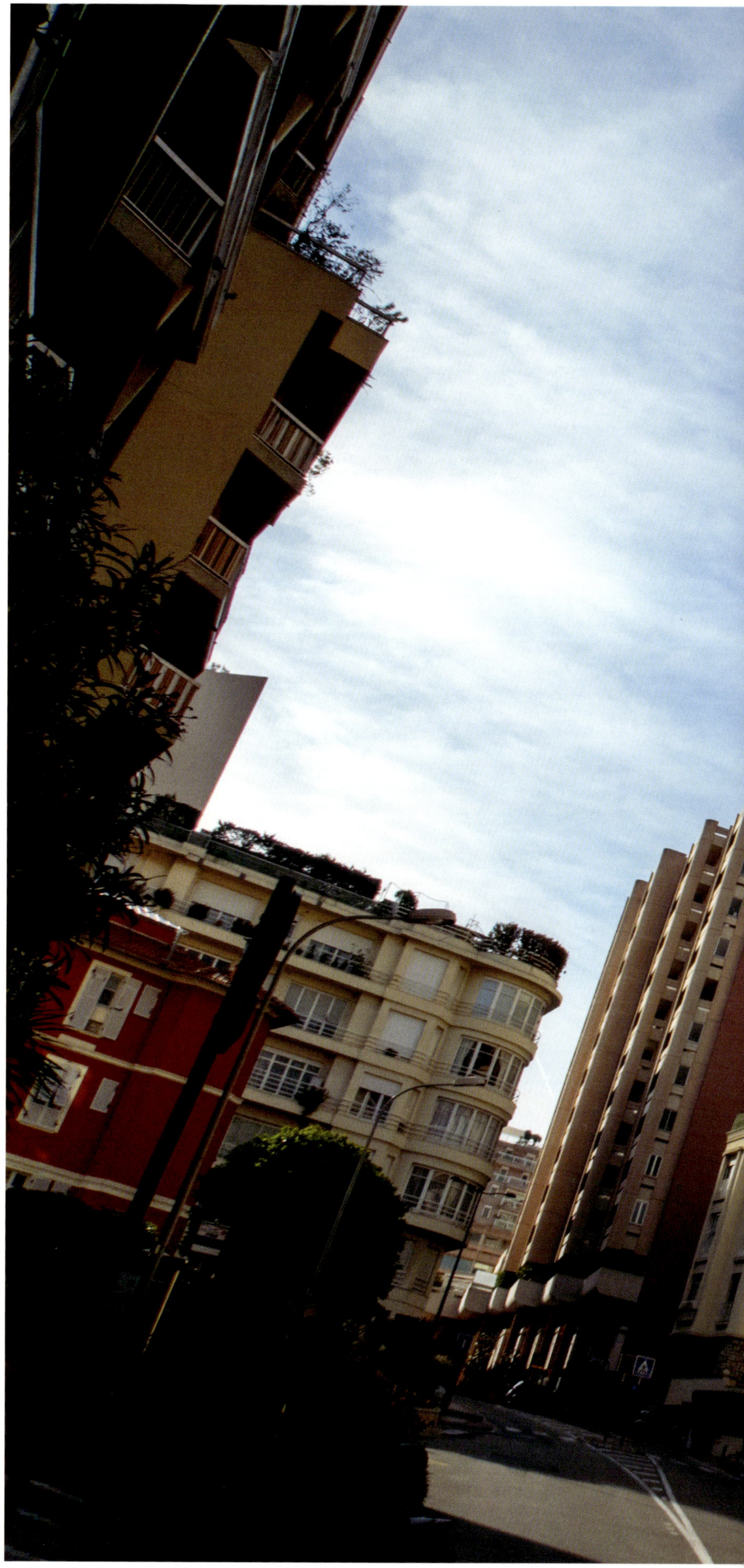

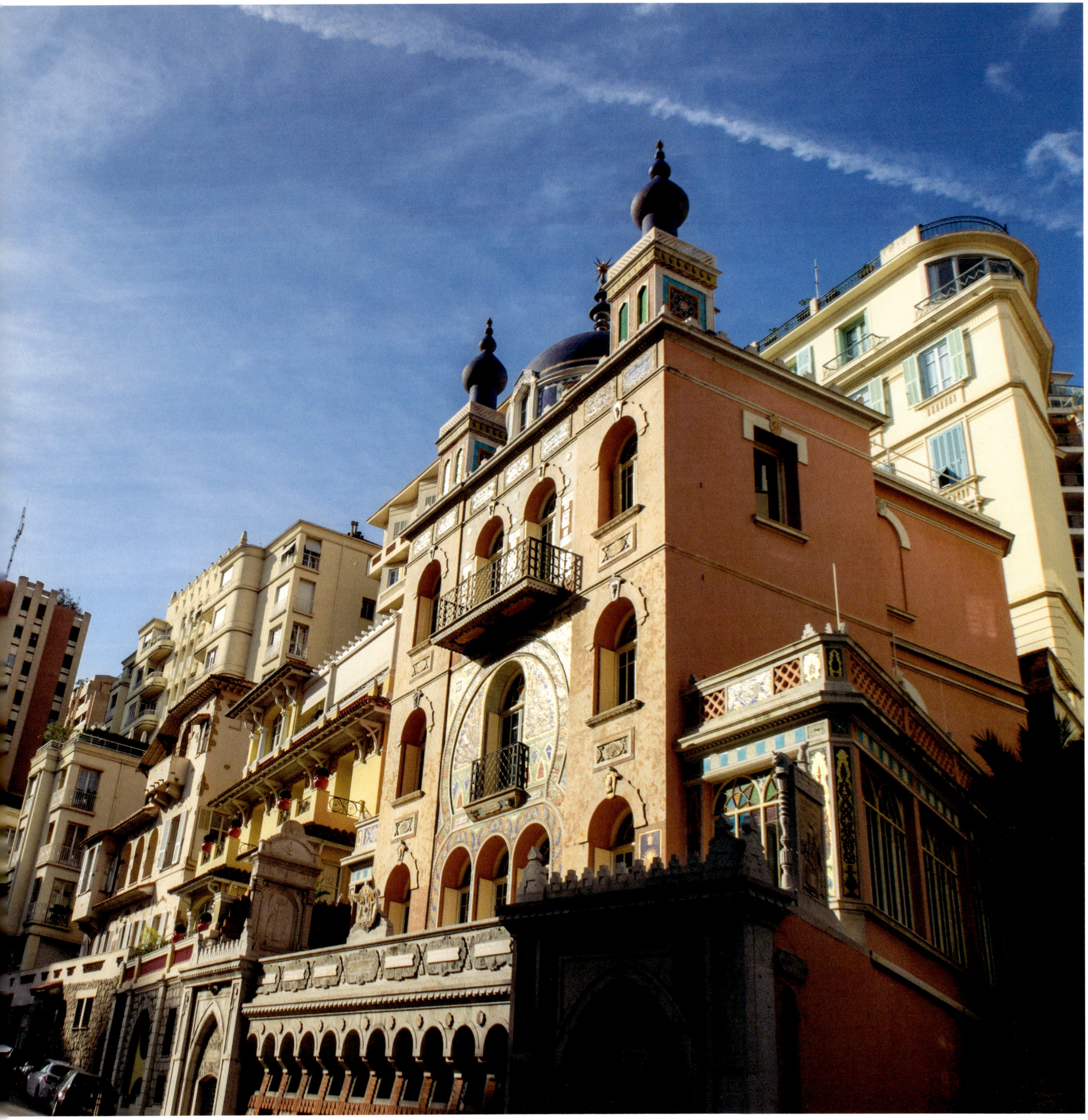

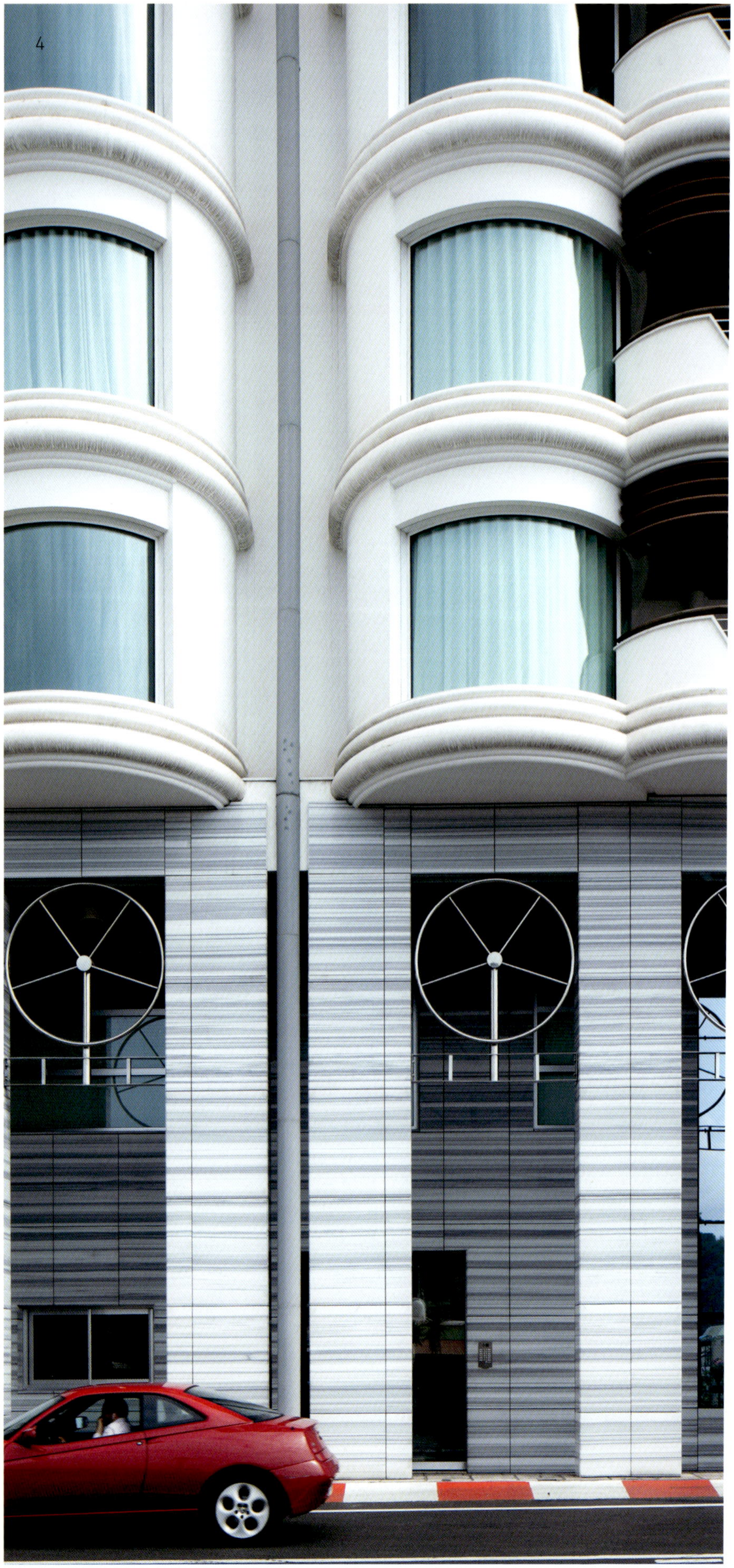

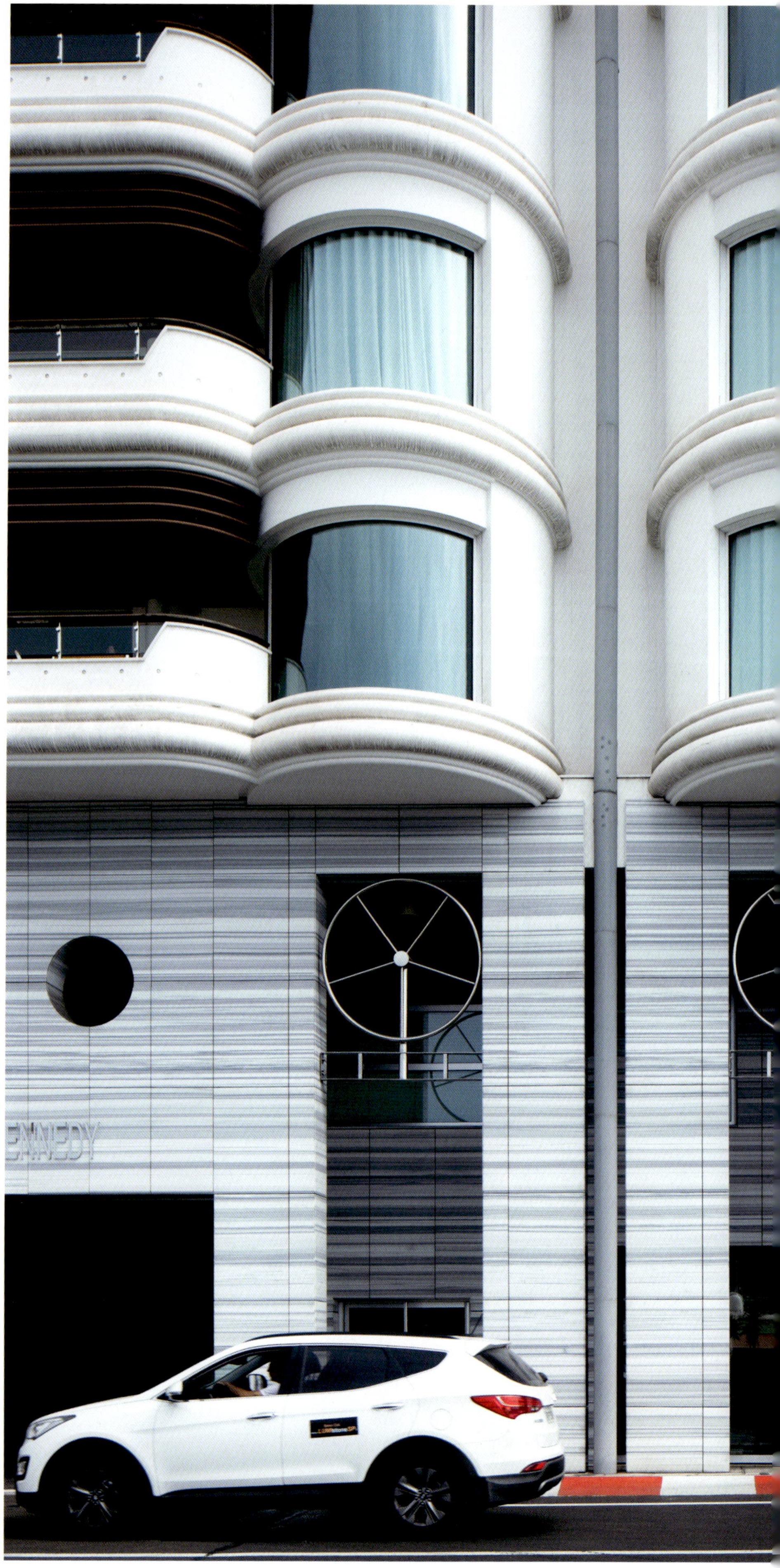

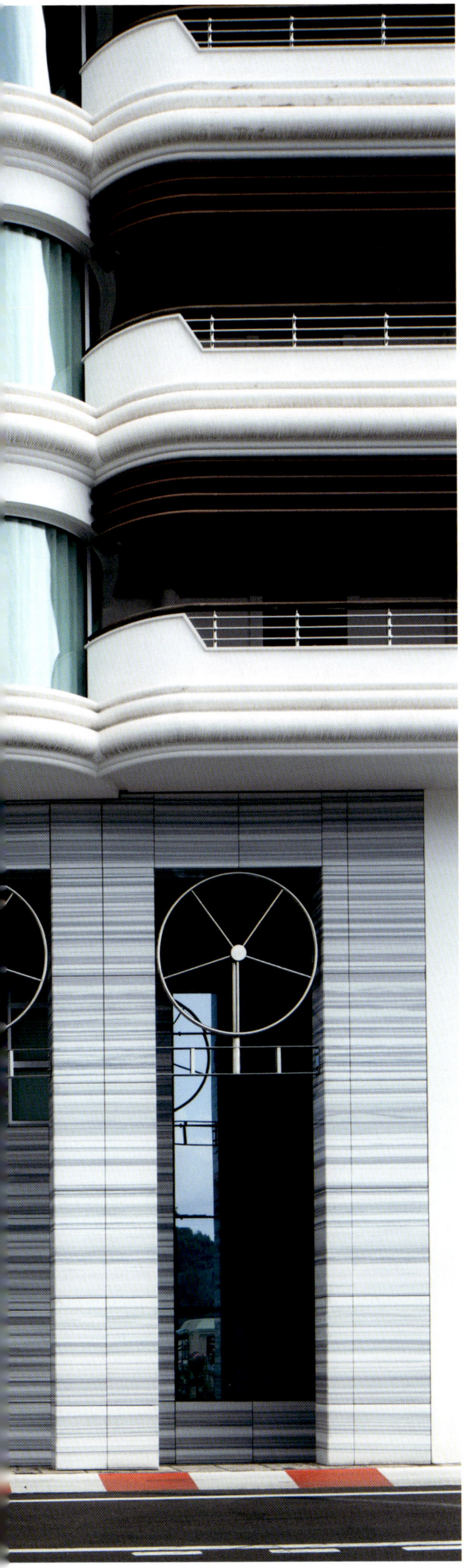

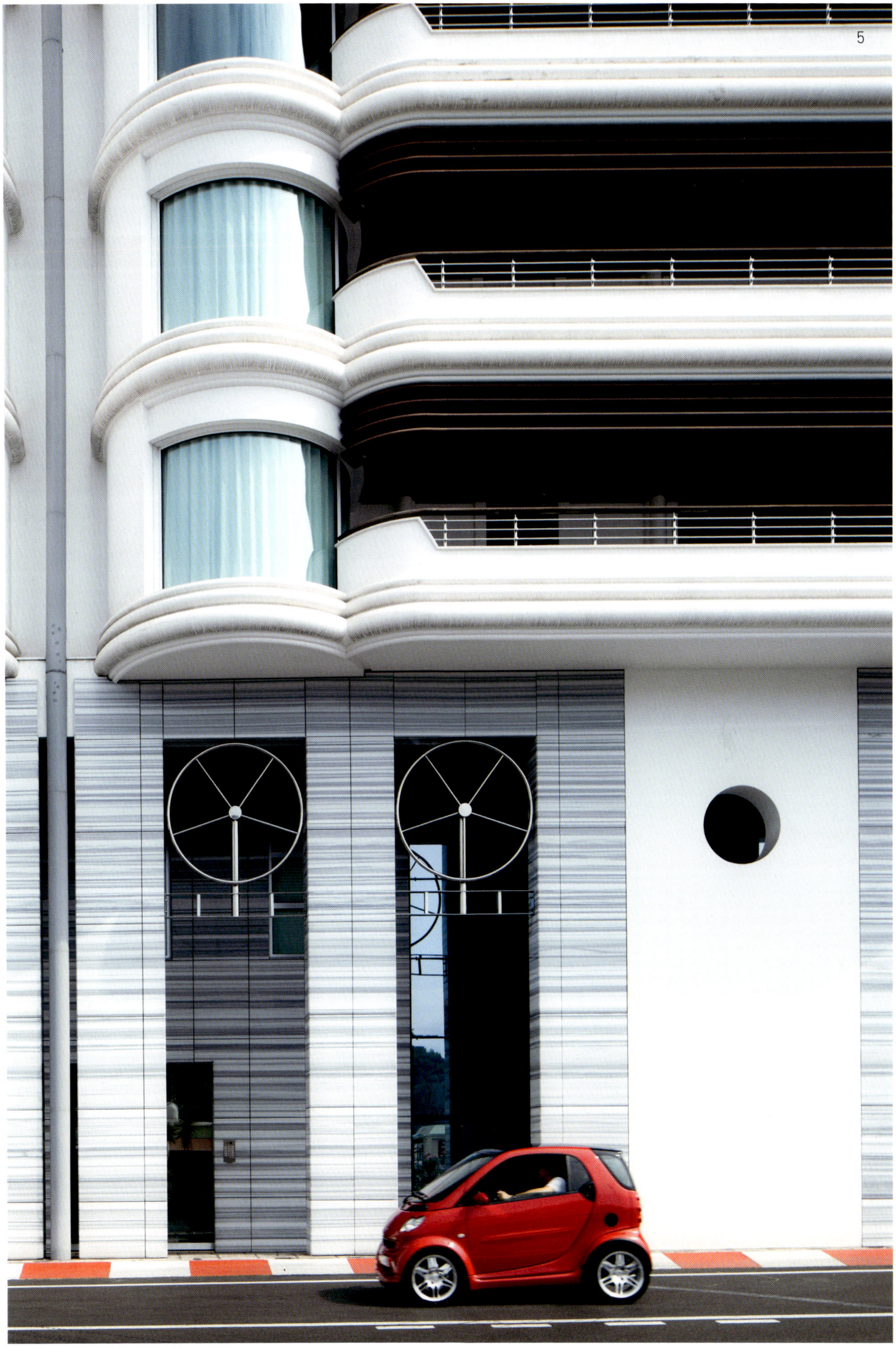

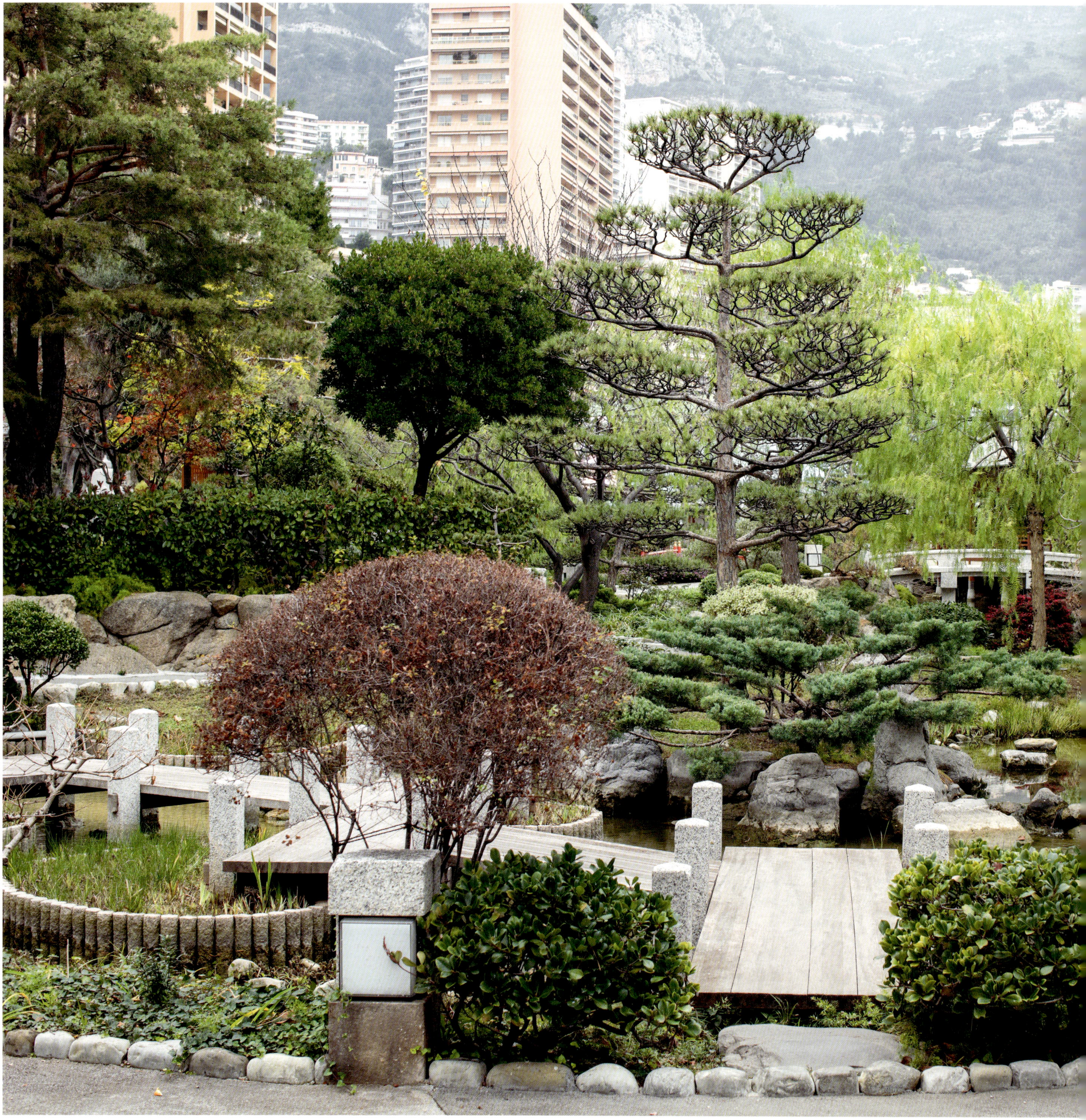

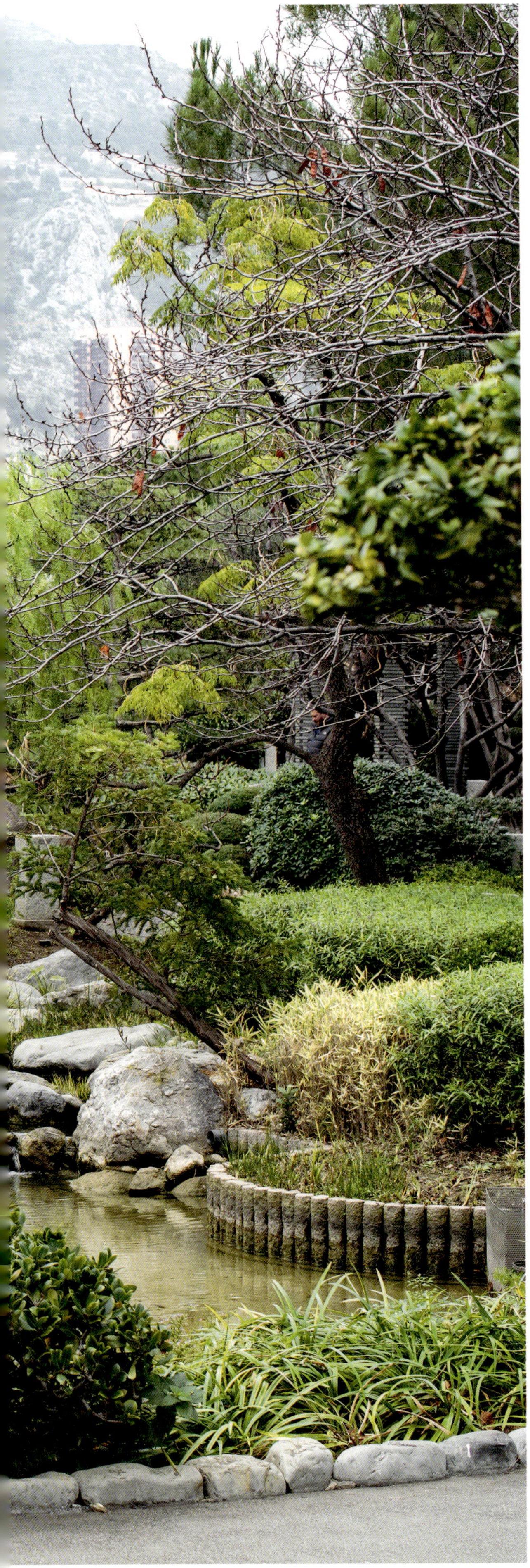

IV

NATURE REIMAGINED

Nature is around every corner in Monaco and ingeniously sets the stage for the city's architecture. Roofs are draped with hanging gardens, while every little patch of earth is home to a tree that soars upward to catch the light. Within a total area of 0.77 square miles, the Principality offers its residents 562,000 square yards of greenery, nearly 20 percent of its territory. This is the result of a sustained effort by Prince Albert II, who is fiercely committed to protecting the environment and promoting sustainable development through his eponymous foundation. One example is the Prince Albert II of Monaco Foundation's study on plant biodiversity in Monaco's five habitats of heritage interest, including the banks of the Rock, where conservation is high on the agenda. Among the eighteen listed heritage species, six endemic species have been identified, including *Limonium cordatum,* a type of sea lavender with pinkish violet flowers; *Allium acutiflorum* with umbel pink flowers; *Acis nicaeensis* with white flowers; and *Campanula macrorhiza,* a type of blue bellflower. This fragile ecosystem is a keen area of study for the Principality's scientists.

The heritage of Monaco's parks is itself quite extraordinary considering the size of the territory. Between the cathedral and the Oceanographic Museum, the beautiful Saint-Martin Gardens tumble down the sides of the Rock to the sea. Its fragrant paths run through a verdant patchwork of shade and light reflecting off the sea. Sights to discover include a watchtower built into the walls and overlooking the port of Fontvieille, statues telling of the journey taken by those commemorated, and exotic trees providing botany lessons on their plaques. Created out of a pine forest by Prince Honoré VI in 1816, the gardens were originally planted with oaks, myrtles, and pistachio trees before being redesigned in the early eighties. Paths were added with grass embankments, while camellias, azaleas, and rhododendrons were planted for their delicate petals.

In front of the casino, the gardens of La Petite Afrique offer a chance to travel afar. This park was created as a large outdoor winter garden in the new district of Monte Carlo around 1879 by the Société des bains de mer to satisfy the tourists' appetite for the exotic. It was designed by the landscape architect Édouard André and planted with rare evergreen trees from all over the world. A river snakes through it, providing an oasis for birds to bathe before hopping onto the lawns. As in English gardens, roses climb the trunks of palms, adding their luxurious colors to the lush trees. This haven of tranquility can also be educational as the rarest species are all identified and named.

At 420 feet above sea level, the Jardin Exotique features footbridges, arches, pergolas, a wealth of succulents, and steep, winding paths. The gardens, which were twenty years in the making, also attract those who just want to look out to sea and take in spectacular views of Monaco and the French and Italian Rivieras. Looking closer to the ground, over a thousand species of cacti, agaves, euphorbias, and stonecrops from the world's deserts put on a flamboyant display of curious shapes and blooms. The gardens are also used for conservation, and its greenhouses are home to species destined to preserve biodiversity. This was already one of the goals set by Prince Albert I when the garden was created in 1913 by the engineer Louis Notari. Prince Albert's first collection of eighteen thousand succulents had been planted near the Oceanographic Museum by the gardener Augustin Gastaud.

Dedicated primarily to children's recreation, Princess Antoinette Park, created in 1916 by Prince Albert I, features stone terraces and staircases, and has been planted with 157 olive trees that date back to the ancient Monegasque culture that stretched from the Moyenne Corniche to the shoreline. At the bottom of the park stands a thousand-year-old olive tree. One of the oldest trees on the French Riviera, it boasts a circumference of nearly sixteen feet.

Built by Prince Rainier III as a tribute to Princess Grace who loved roses, the Princess Grace Rose Garden has added color to the Fontvieille district since 1984 with its 8,000 elegant roses. Surrounded by high-rises and facing the imposing rock escarpment known as the Tête de Chien, it is the jewel of Fontvieille and features sculptures, a lake, palm trees, and an olive grove. Expanded to over 16,000 square feet in 2014 to accommodate 2,500 new roses, it includes special rose varieties dedicated to the Grimaldi family near a statue of the princess.

Opened in 1994, the Japanese garden by the Grimaldi Forum is a place where time no longer matters. This green space was designed by a Shinto landscape architect who met Princess Grace at the international floral competition of the garden club she founded in 1968. This magical 75,000-square-foot space of self-reflection is bordered by the sea and a row of pine trees on one side and cherry trees on the other. Through the gate, connecting trails take visitors through diverse environments and past a covered terrace, a gazebo, a pergola, a tea house, and a little red bridge. Here, a waterfall flows into a river, which settles in a pool before trickling away into the ground, representing the passage from youth to adulthood to old age, and finally the end of life's journey. However, the red bridge can also be used to reach the Isle of the Immortals according to Taoist philosophy!

Outside the gardens, several streets recall the old plantations from when Monaco was still a countryside: the sidewalks of rue Grimaldi, rue Princess Caroline, boulevard de Belgium in the neighborhood of La Condamine, and avenue de Grande-Bretagne in Monte Carlo are lined with deliciously tempting orange trees. The fruit is picked by gardeners and given to residents for making jams and jellies. Elsewhere, on boulevard Albert I, pine trees are on show all year round. Both Mediterranean and imported species make up the varied Monegasque landscape. All trees are subject to a sovereign ordinance dating from March 2011 to protect and care for them. They are all individually cataloged so that their diversity, age, distribution, health, and role in Monaco's natural history are all recorded. A heritage tree trail is also offered to visitors. Starting from the gardens of La Petite Afrique where it lists eight exceptional trees among some sixty identified, it continues on to Saint-Charles Church, Marcel Pagnol Square, Villa Sauber, the Grimaldi Forum, the Japanese garden, and the casino gardens. It is a unique way to discover the Principality while also admiring such treasures as *Oreopanax nymphaeifolius,* the desert fan palm, the umbrella tree, and the baobab.

Previous spread. Soft light over the Japanese garden promises a haven in which to meditate in peace and tranquility. January 1, 2016, 12:22 p.m.

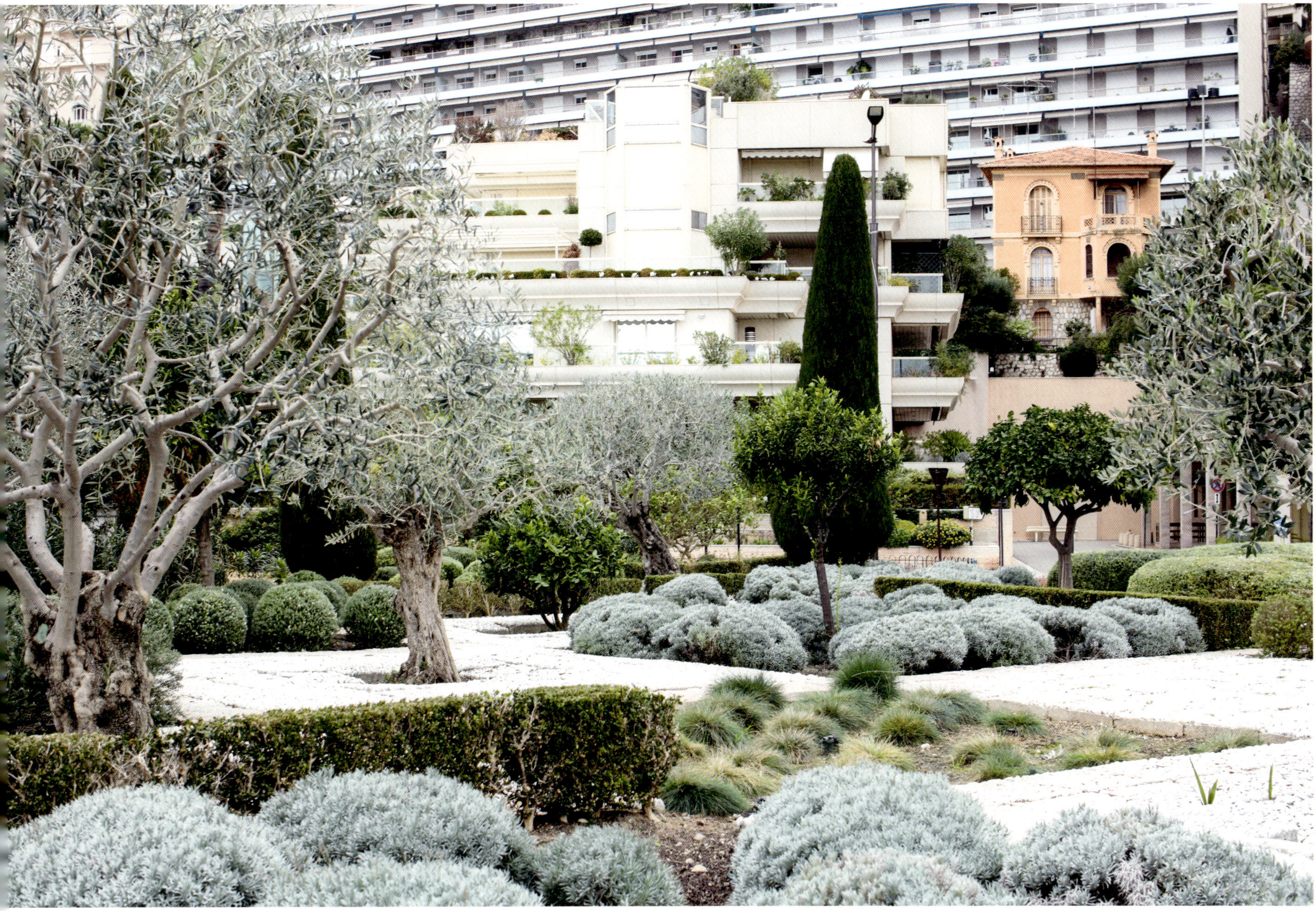

Plants and stone in perfect harmony between the Japanese garden and Grimaldi Forum.
January 1, 2016, 11:16 a.m.

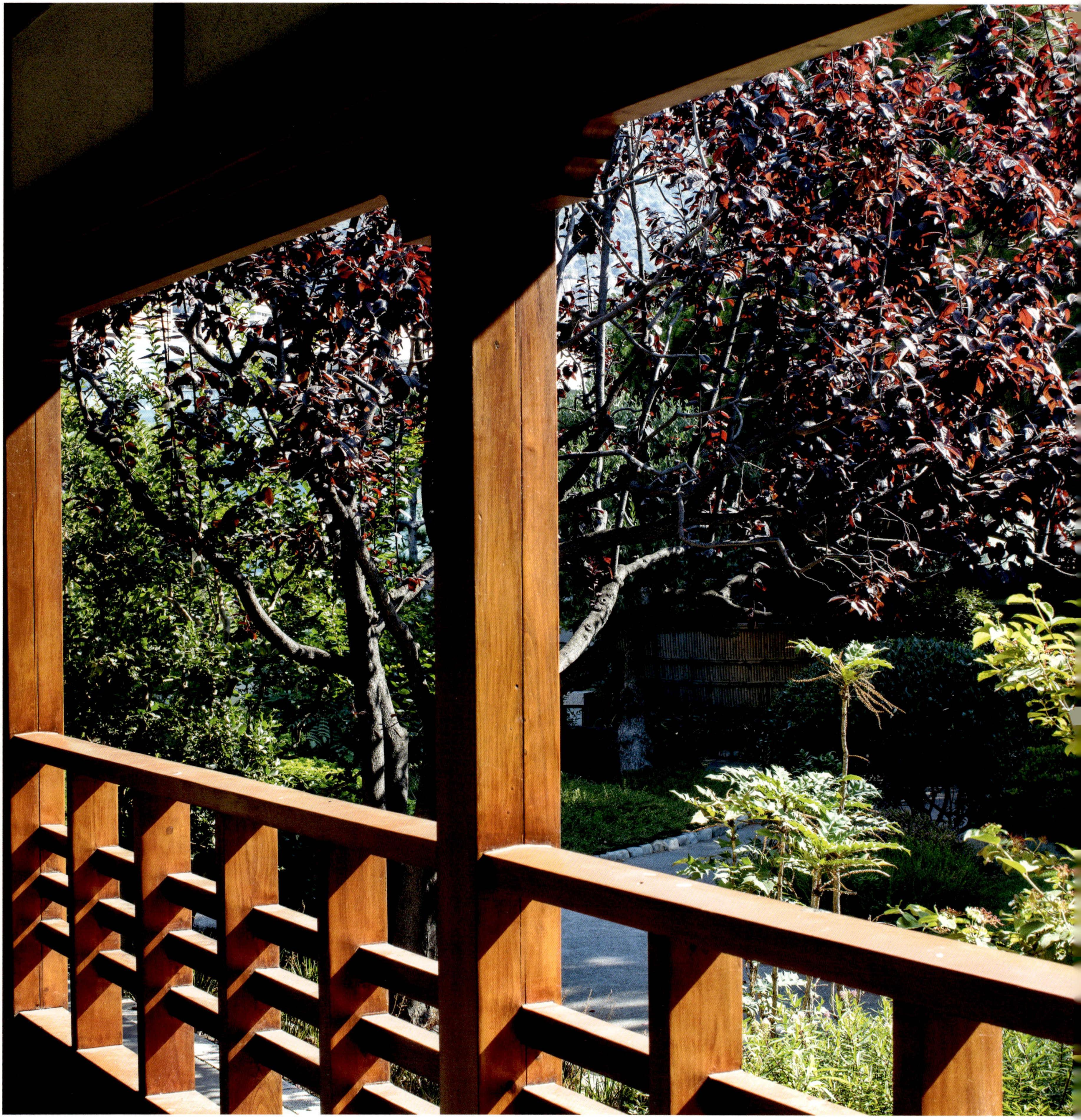

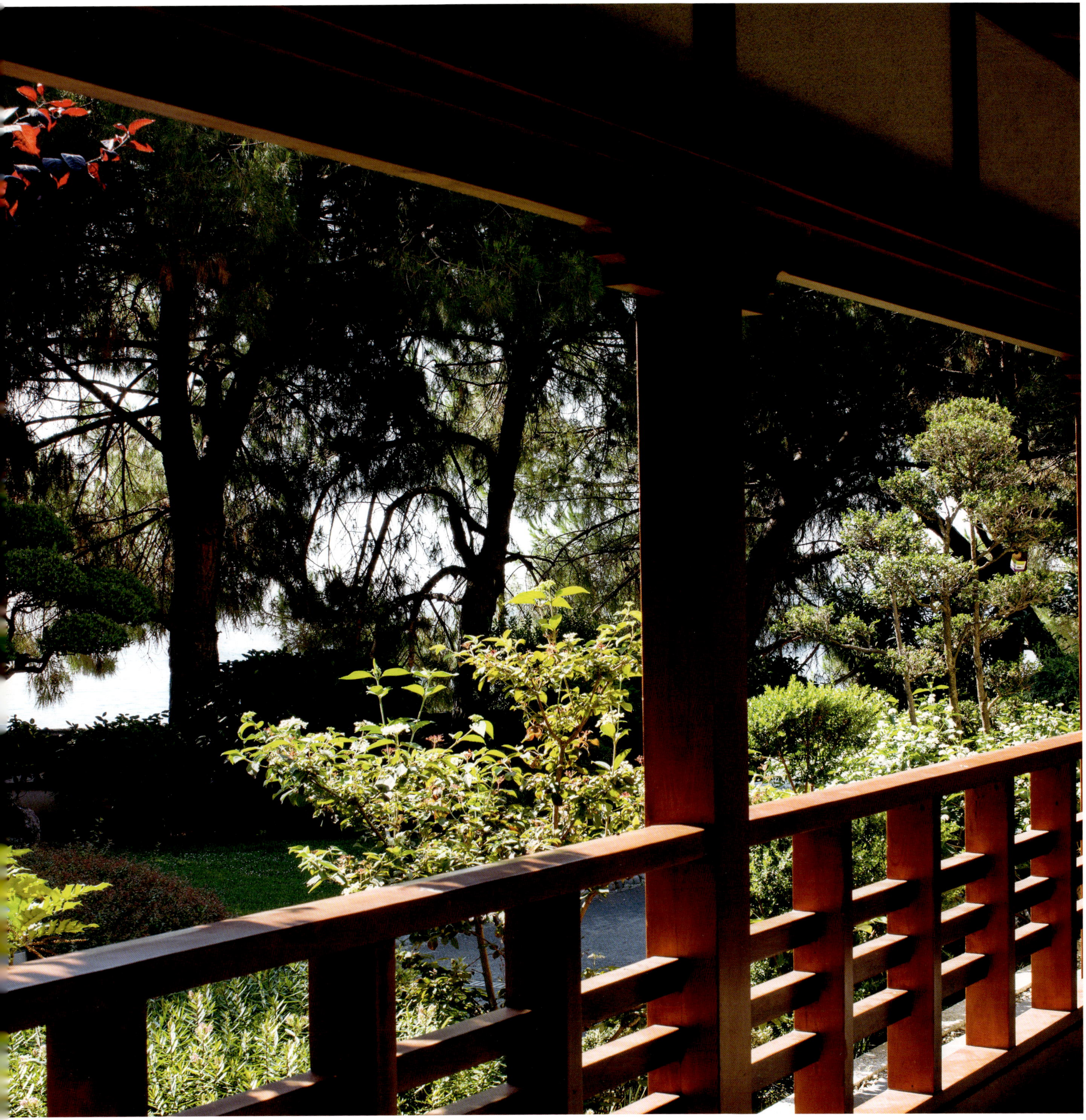

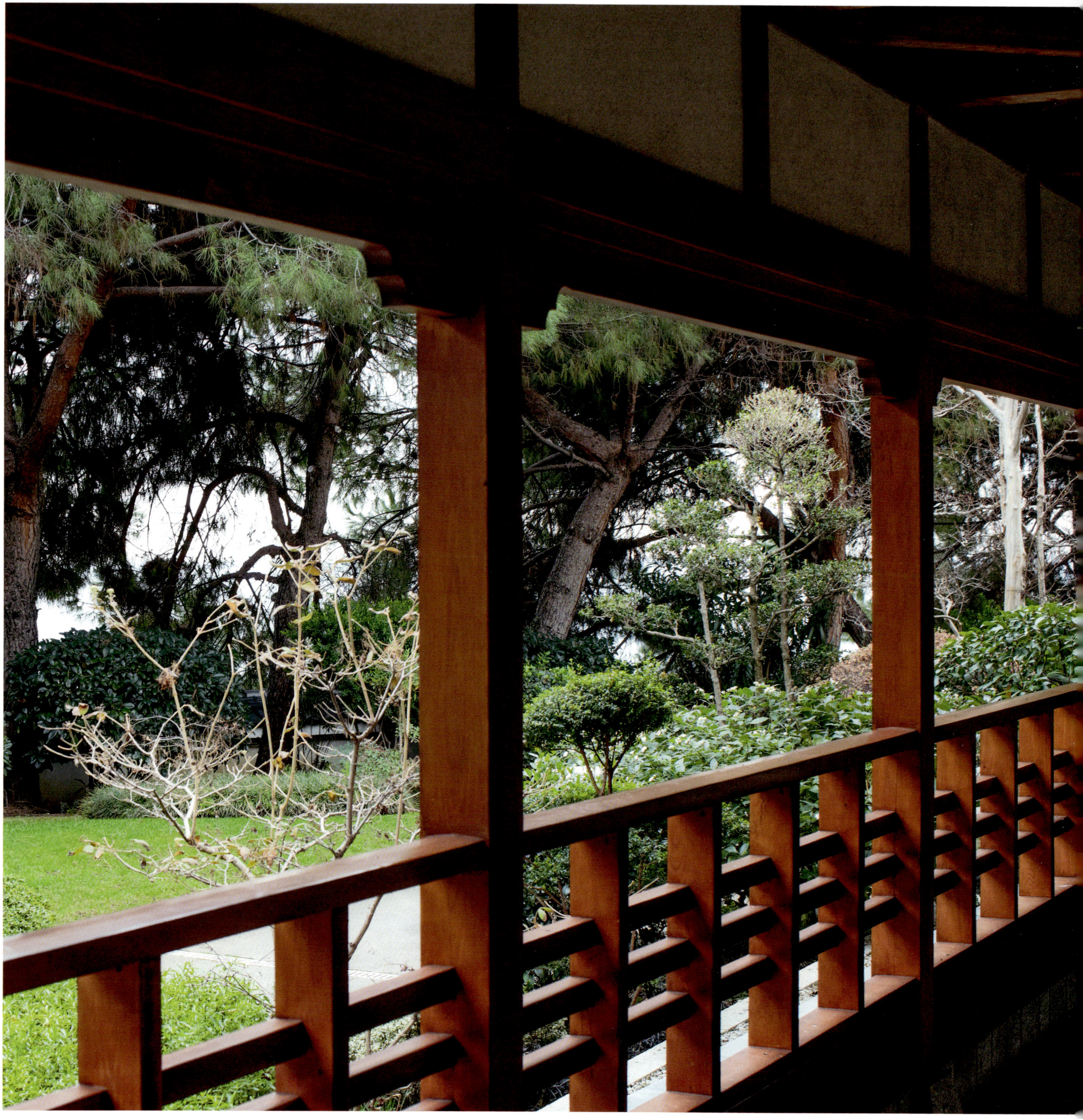

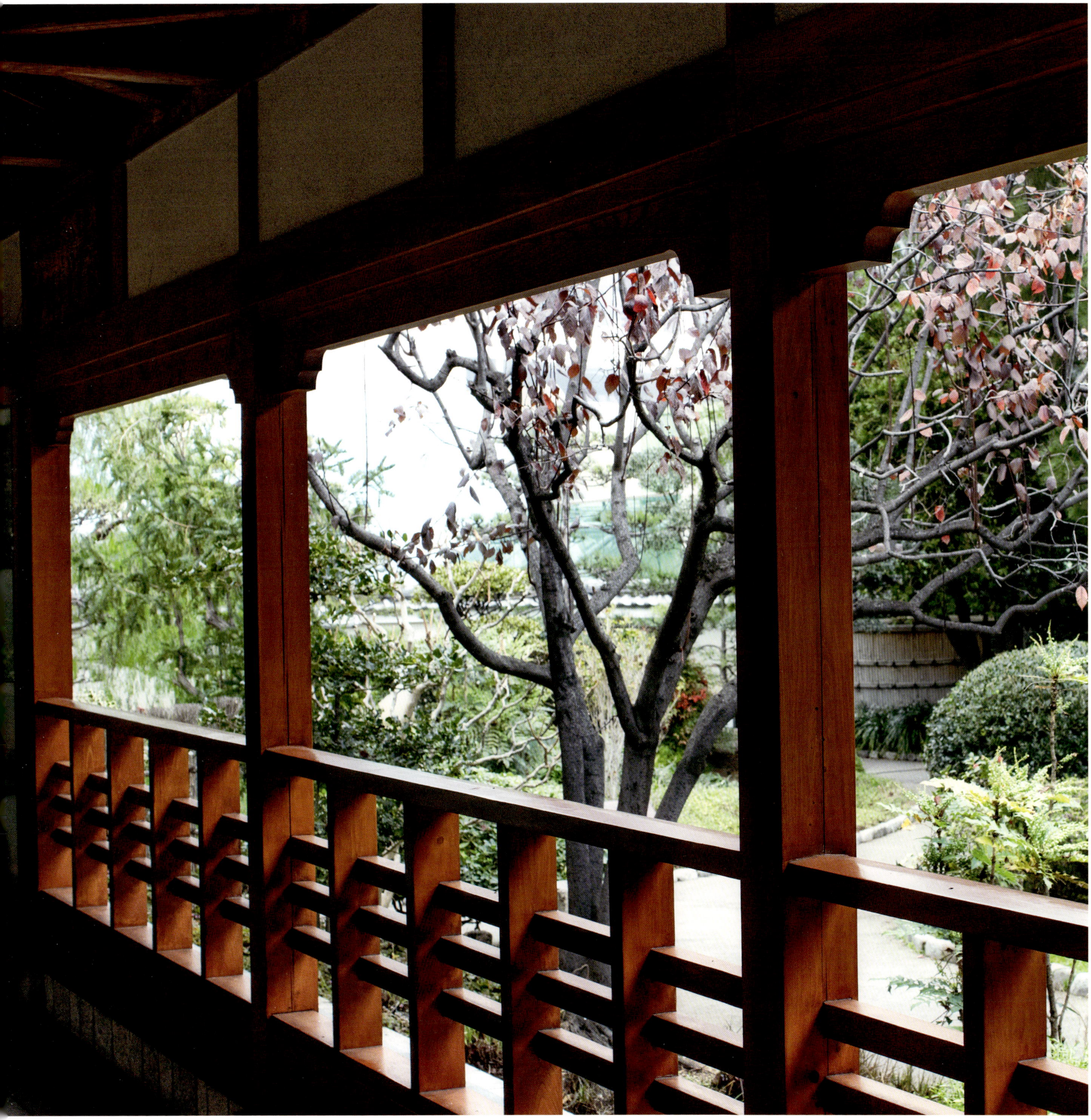

Previous spreads. Perspectives of opposite seasons from the Pavillon de Contemplation in the Japanese garden. First spread page, July 11, 2015. Left page 9:57 a.m.; right page, 9:59 a.m. Second spread, January 1, 2016. Left page 11:30 a.m.; right page, 11:32 a.m.

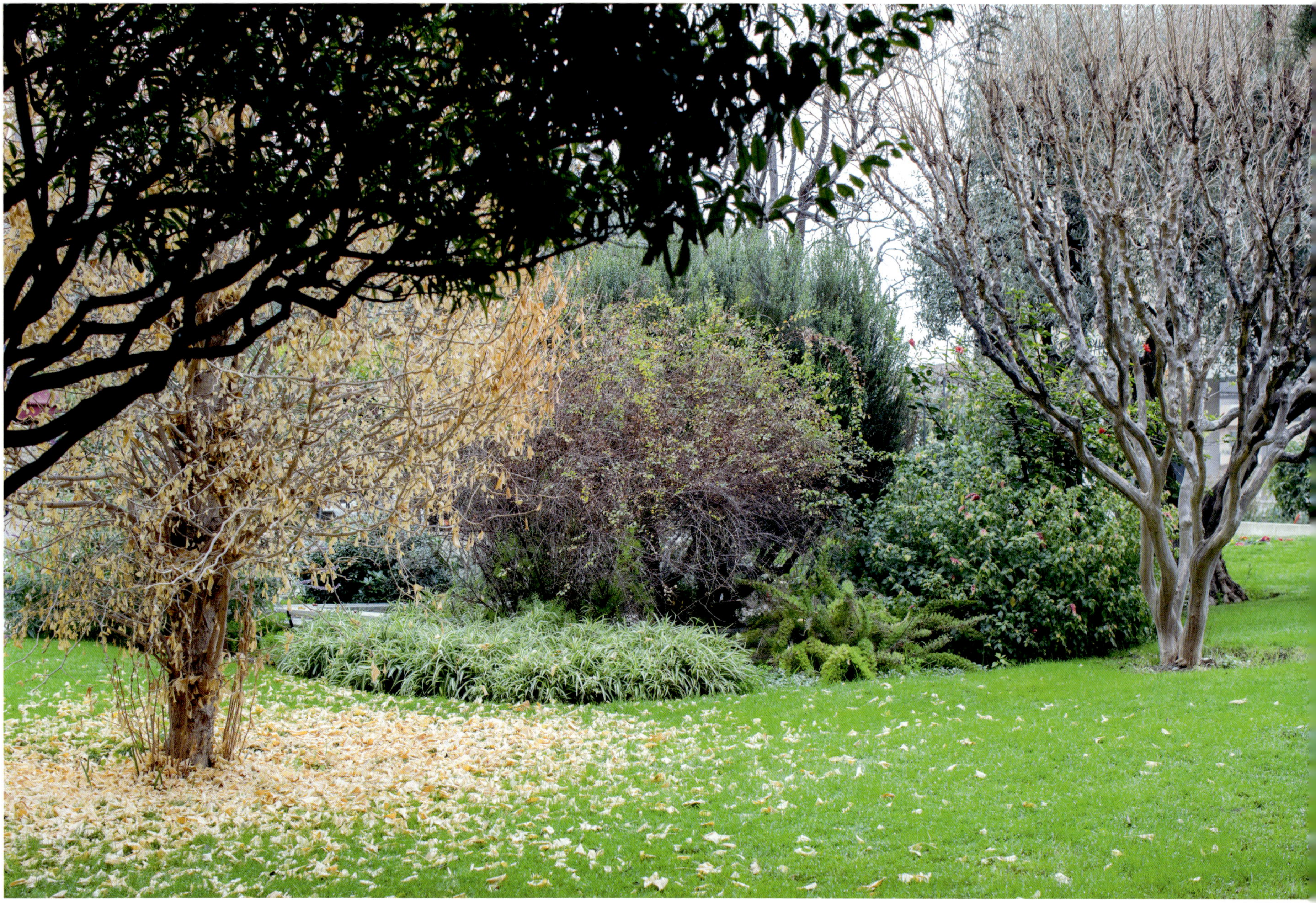

The ideal place to muse over "childhood memories" in Marcel Pagnol Square. January 1, 2016. Left page, 10:02 a.m.; right page, 10:06 a.m.

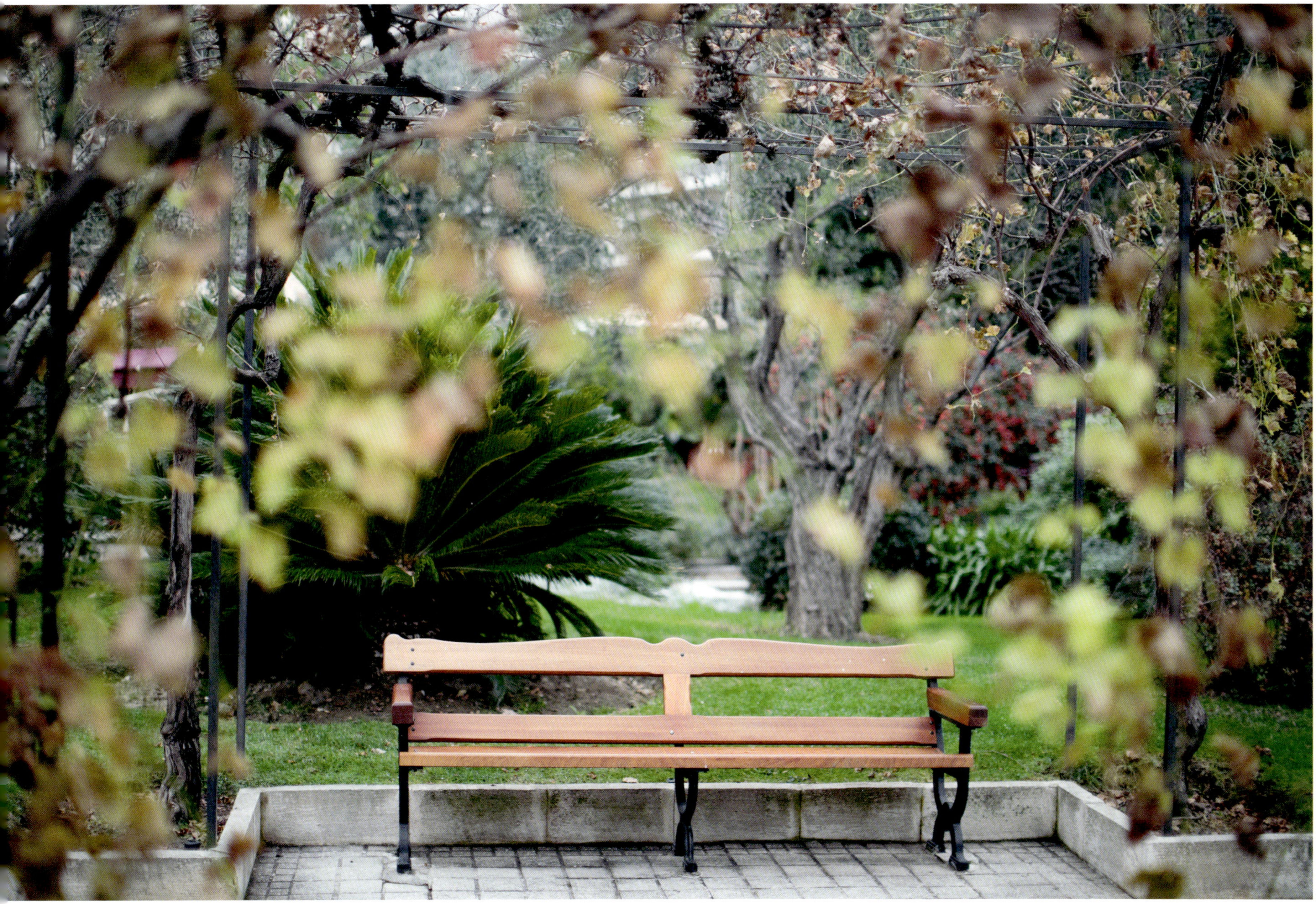

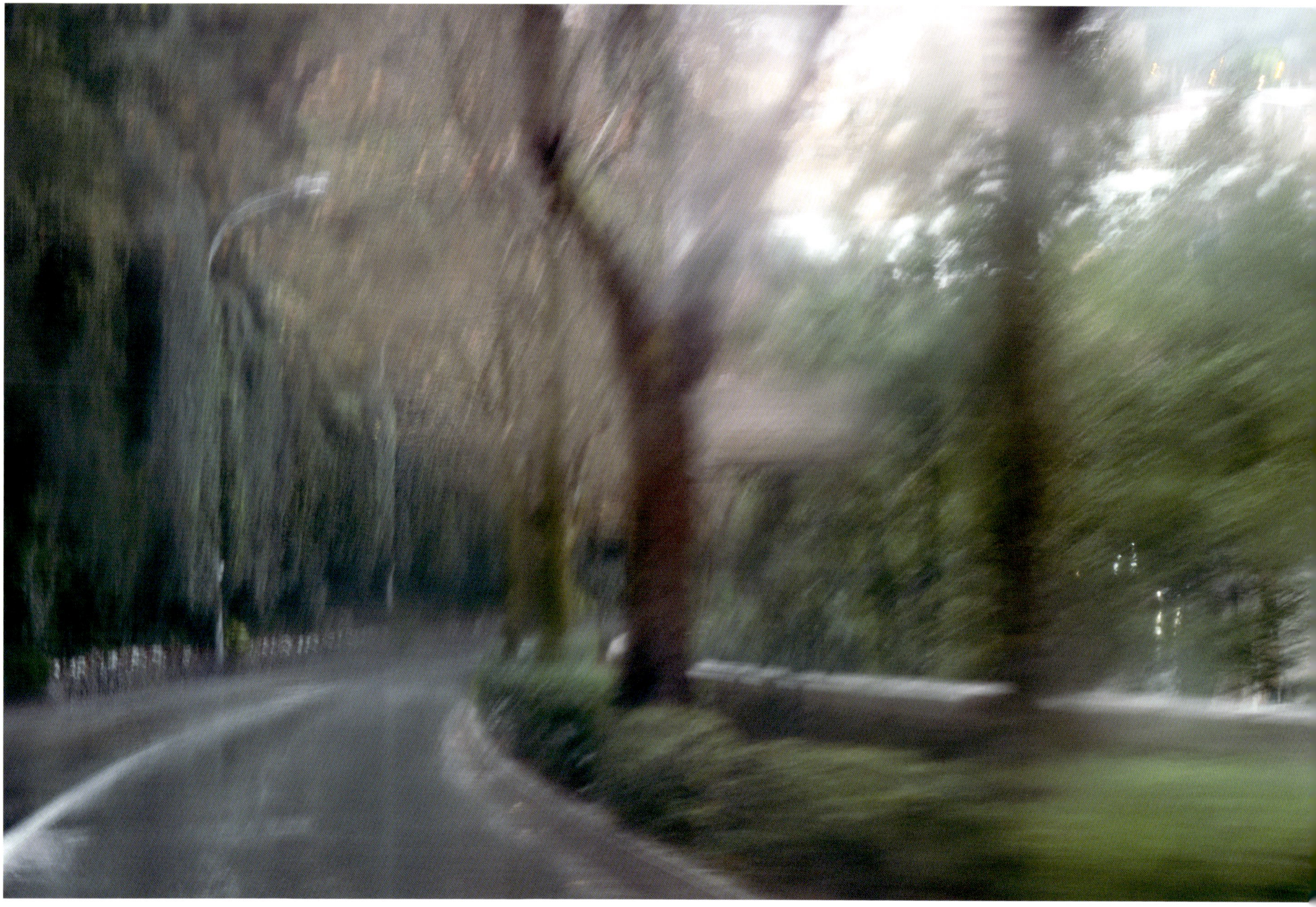

Down avenue de la Porte-Neuve, a splash of color from an umbrella suggests the painter van Dongen's *Rainy Day in Monte Carlo*. February 7, 2016.
Left page, 29 seconds past 4:58 p.m.; right page, 31 seconds past 4:58 p.m.

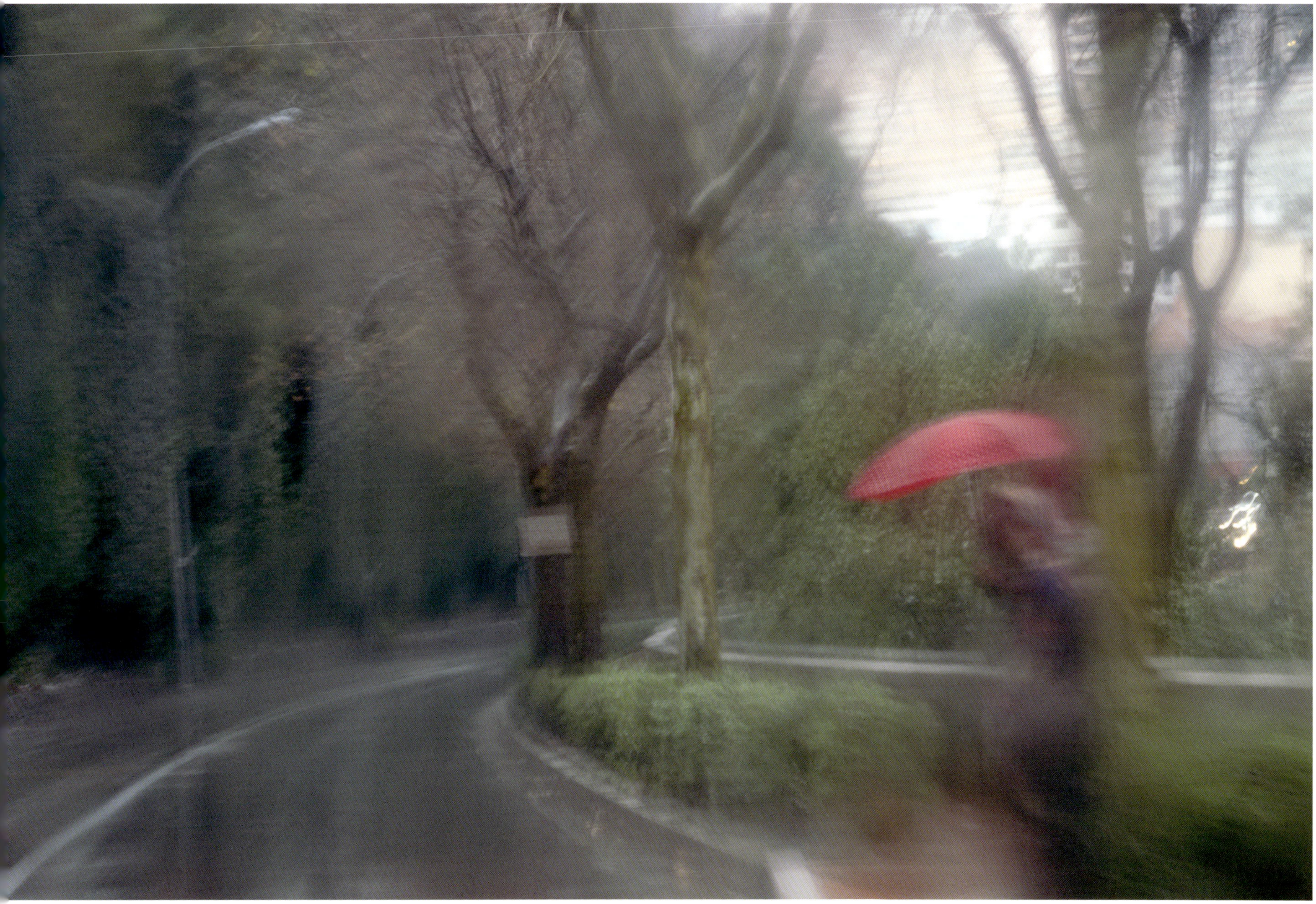

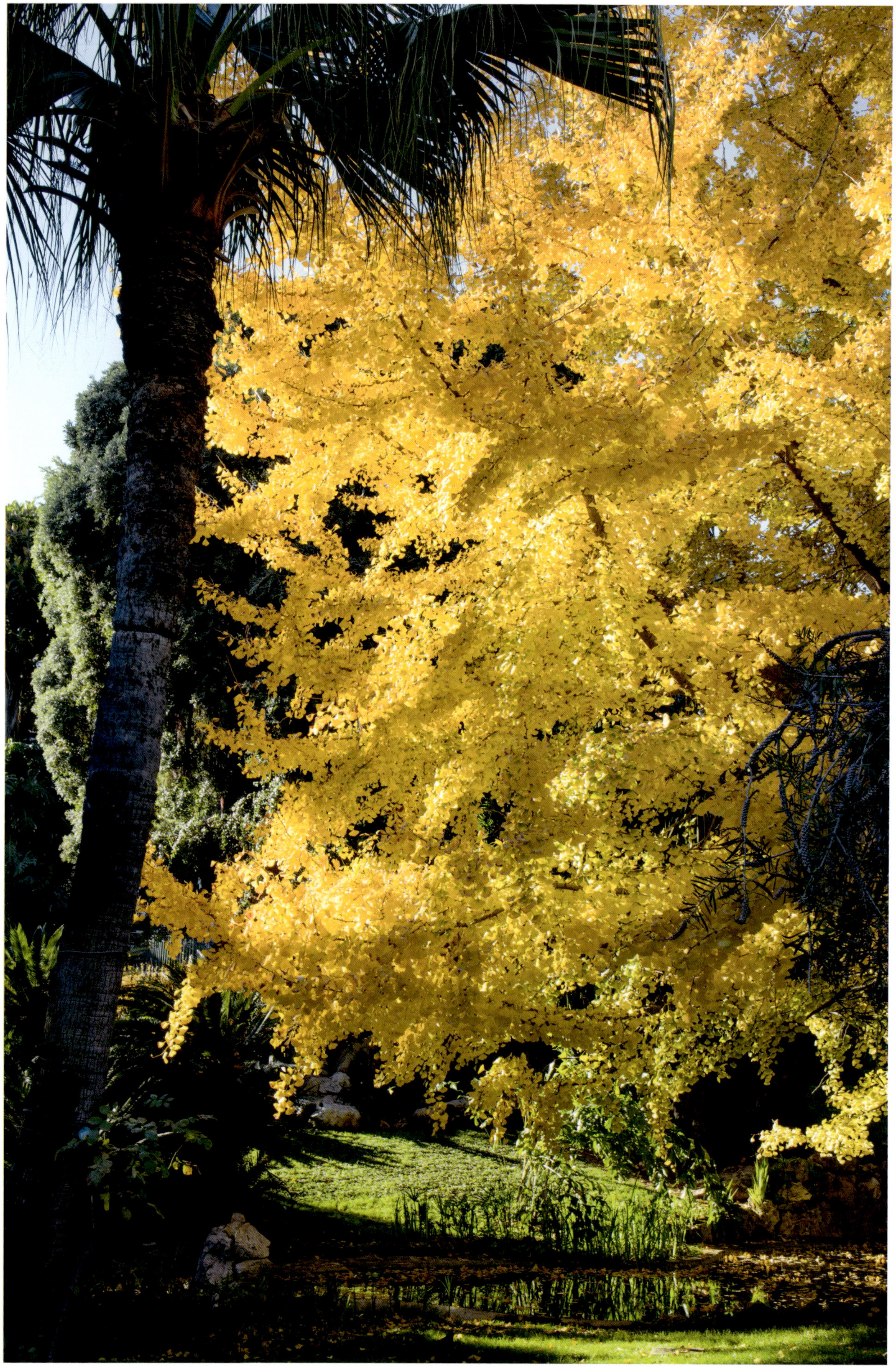

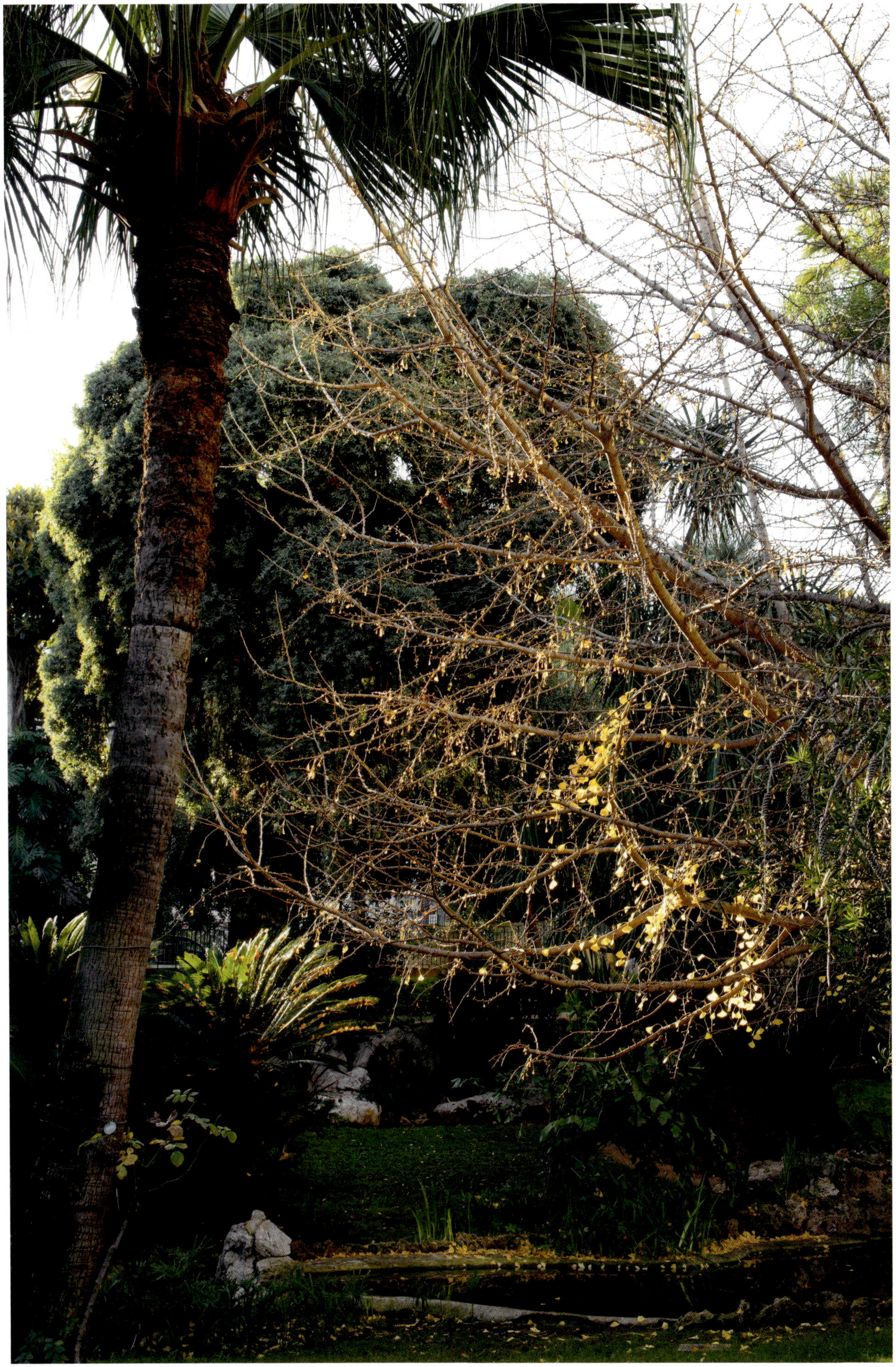

In the gardens of La Petite Afrique, a gingko biloba tree displays its splendid gold crown, which it loses just a few days later.
Left page, December 10, 2015, 1:01 p.m.
Right page, December 26, 2015, 2:56 p.m.

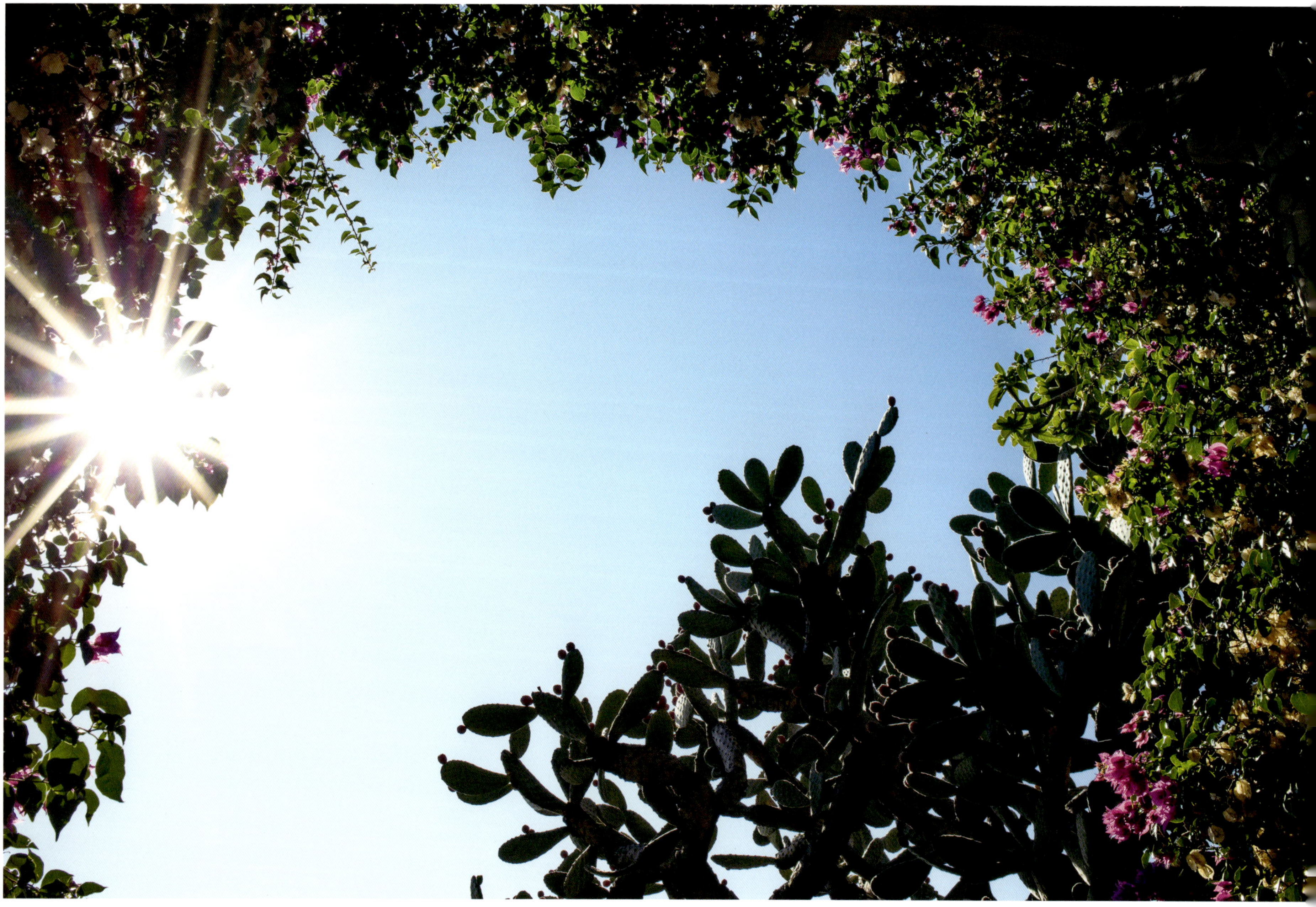

The effect produced by the sun's path creates characteristic silhouettes out of the foliage and flowers in the Jardin Exotique. October 31, 2015. Left page, 12:52 p.m.; right page, 5:59 p.m.

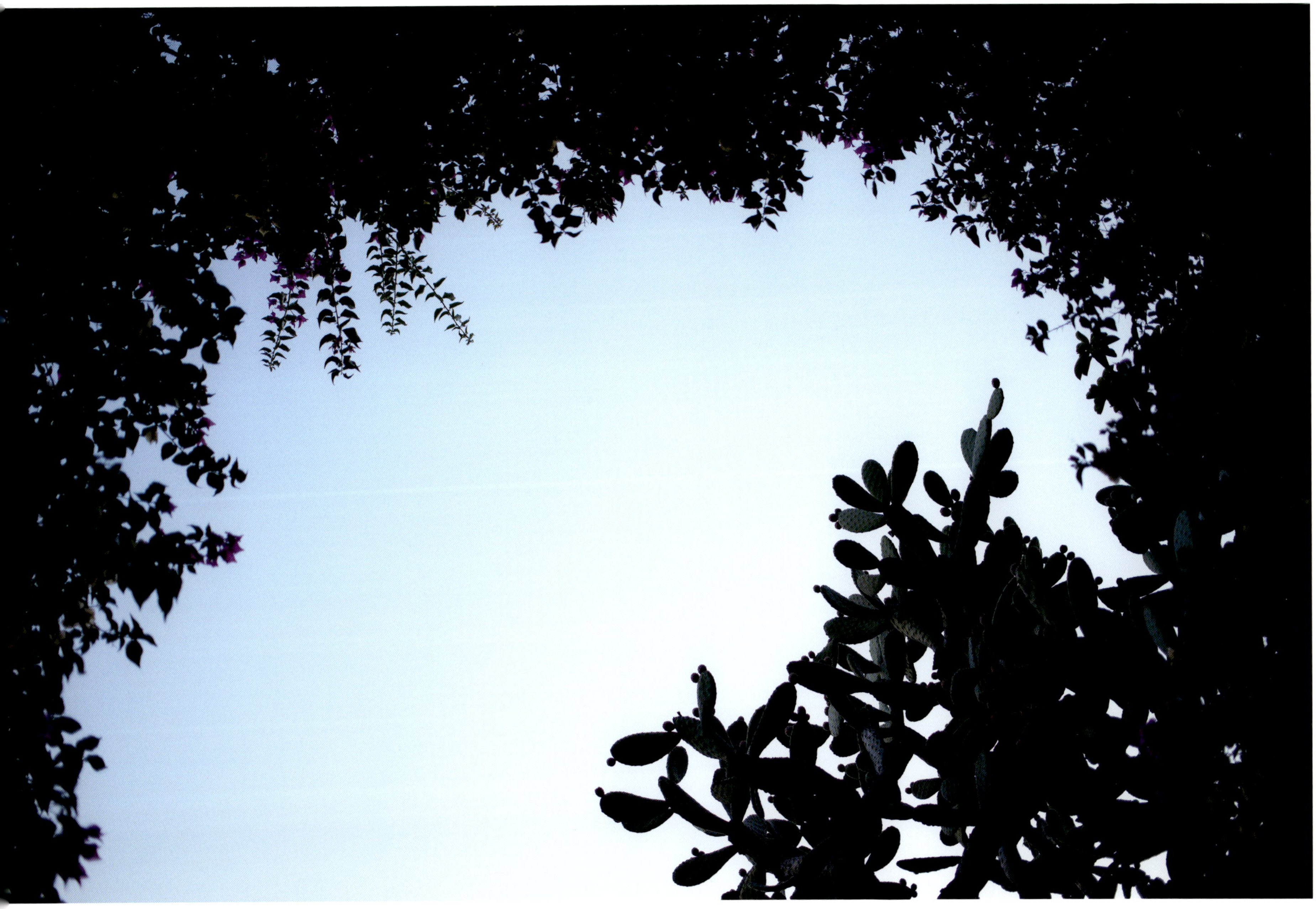

Following spread. The dynamic branches of a ficus radiate with spectacular energy on the terraces of the casino. December 28, 2015, 11:08 a.m.

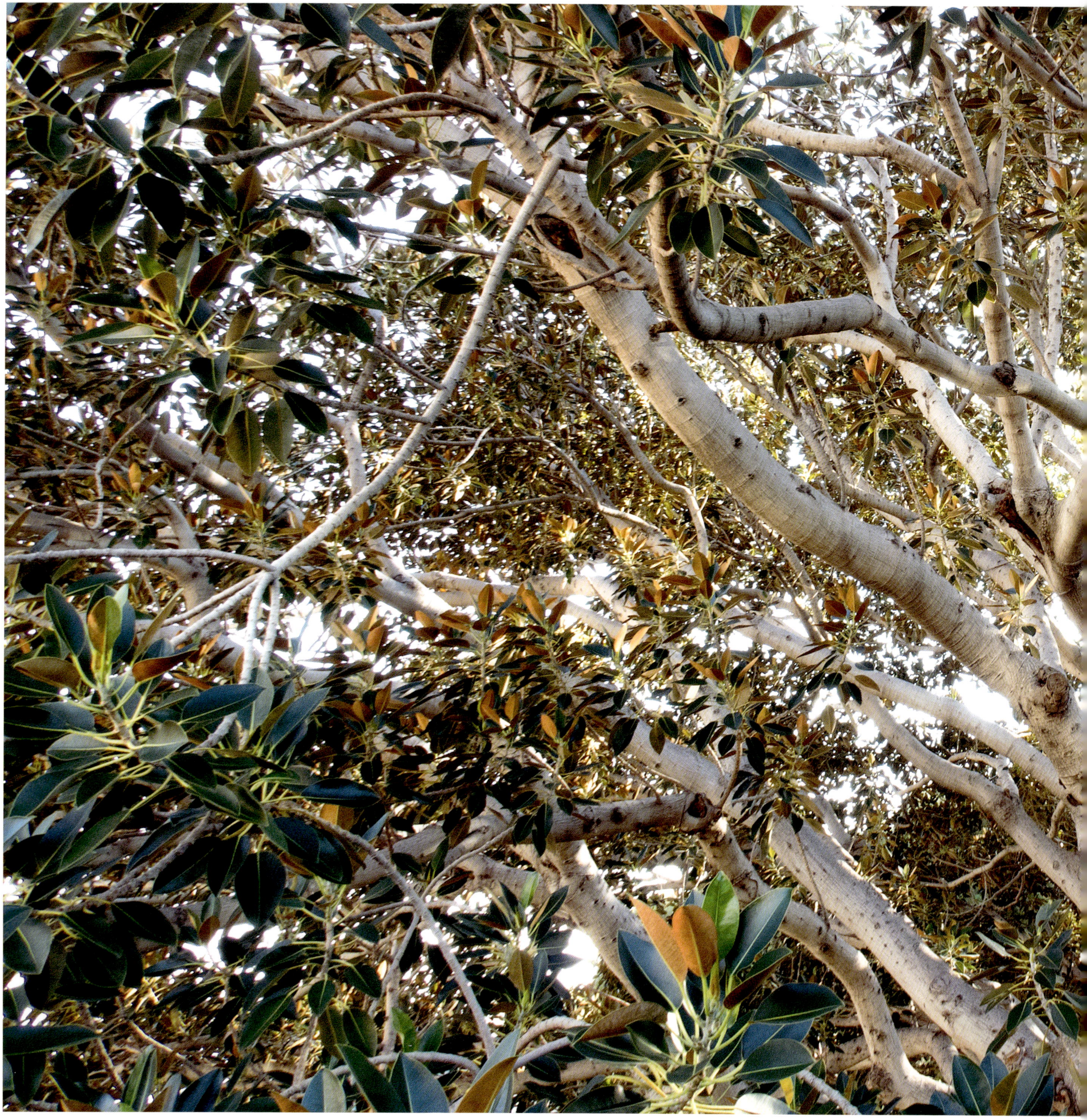

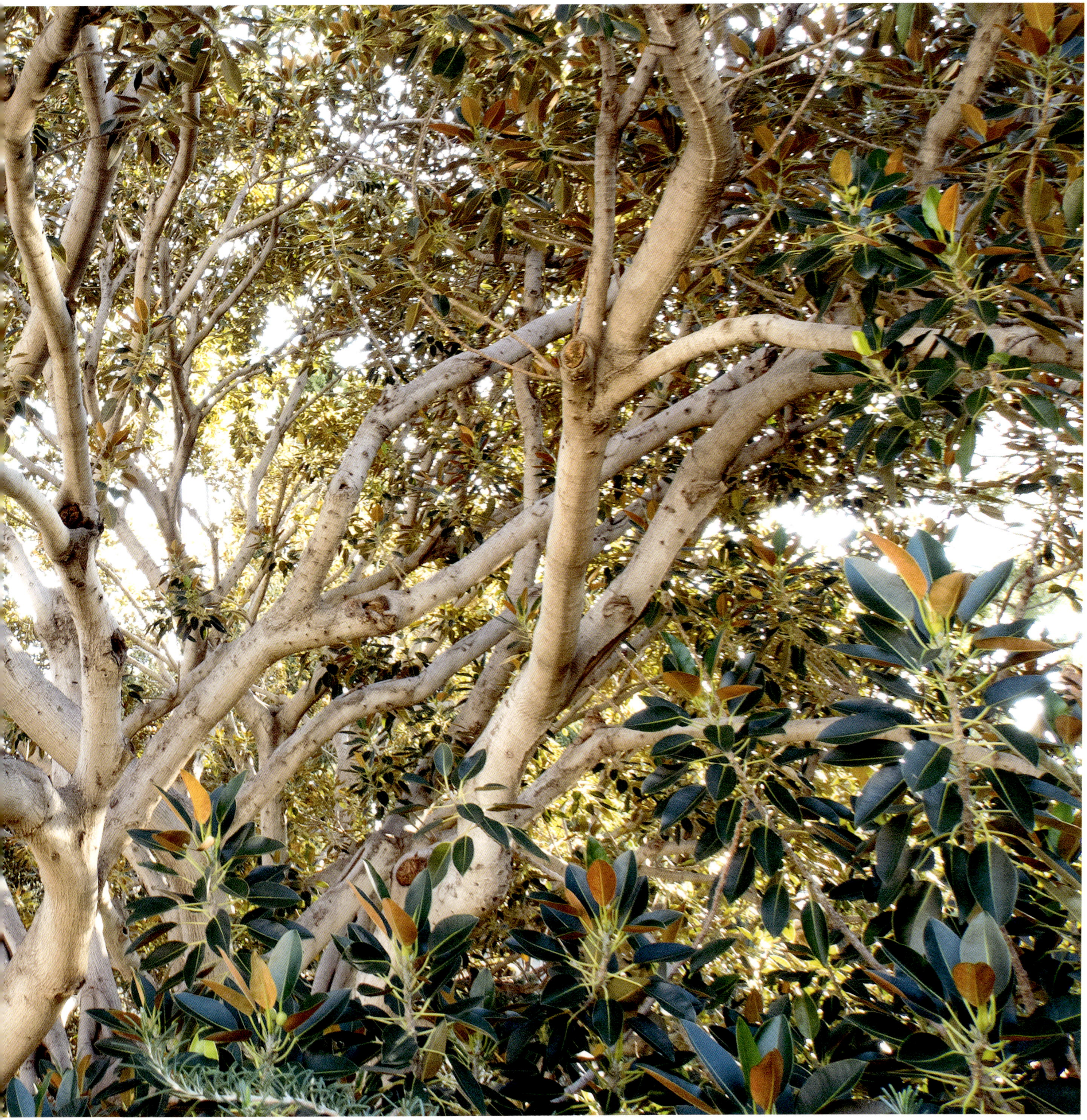

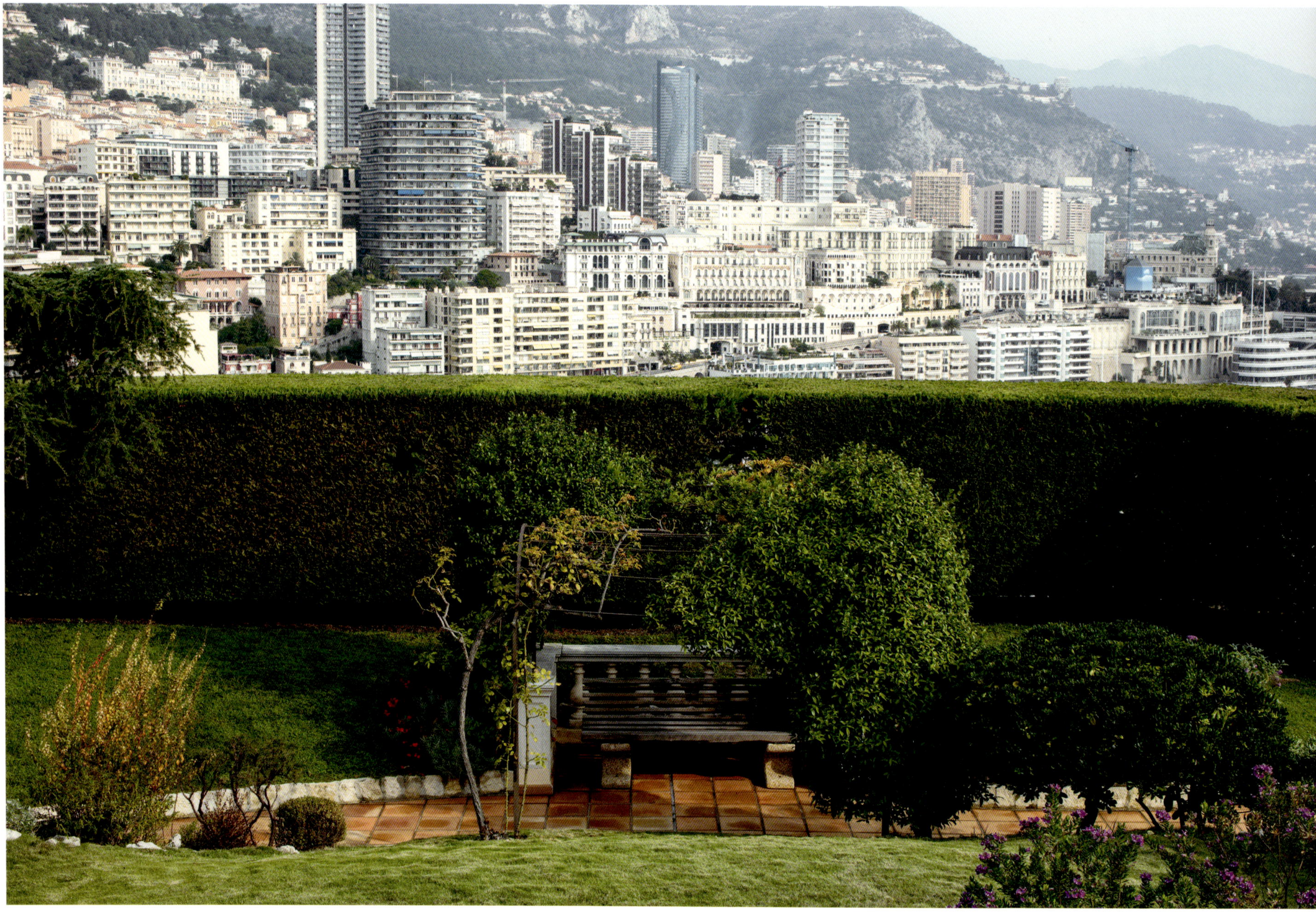

A balcony of green overlooks Port Hercules as autumn turns to winter in the palace gardens.
Left page, October 26, 2015, 11:16 a.m. Right page, December 28, 2015, 9:24 a.m.

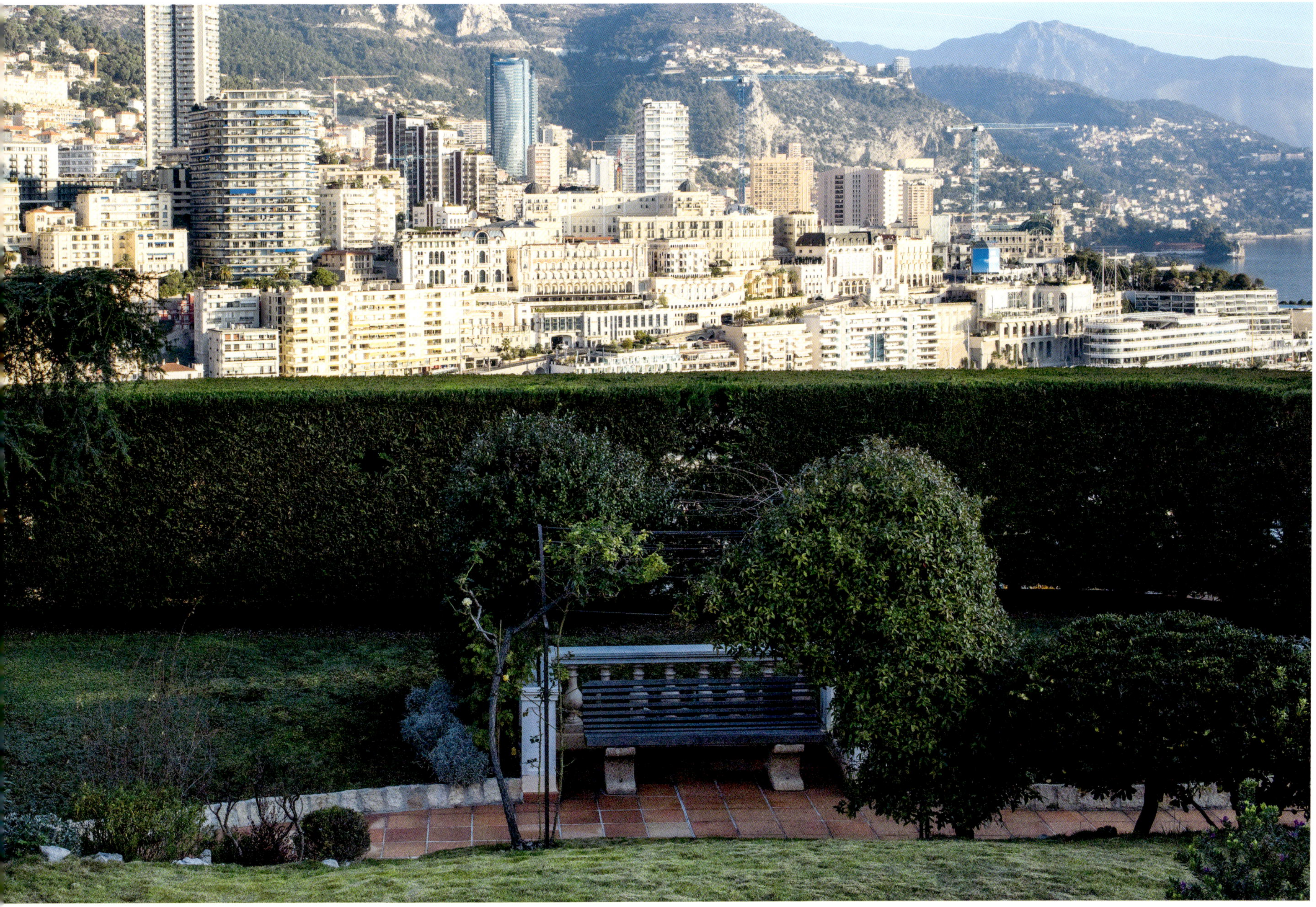

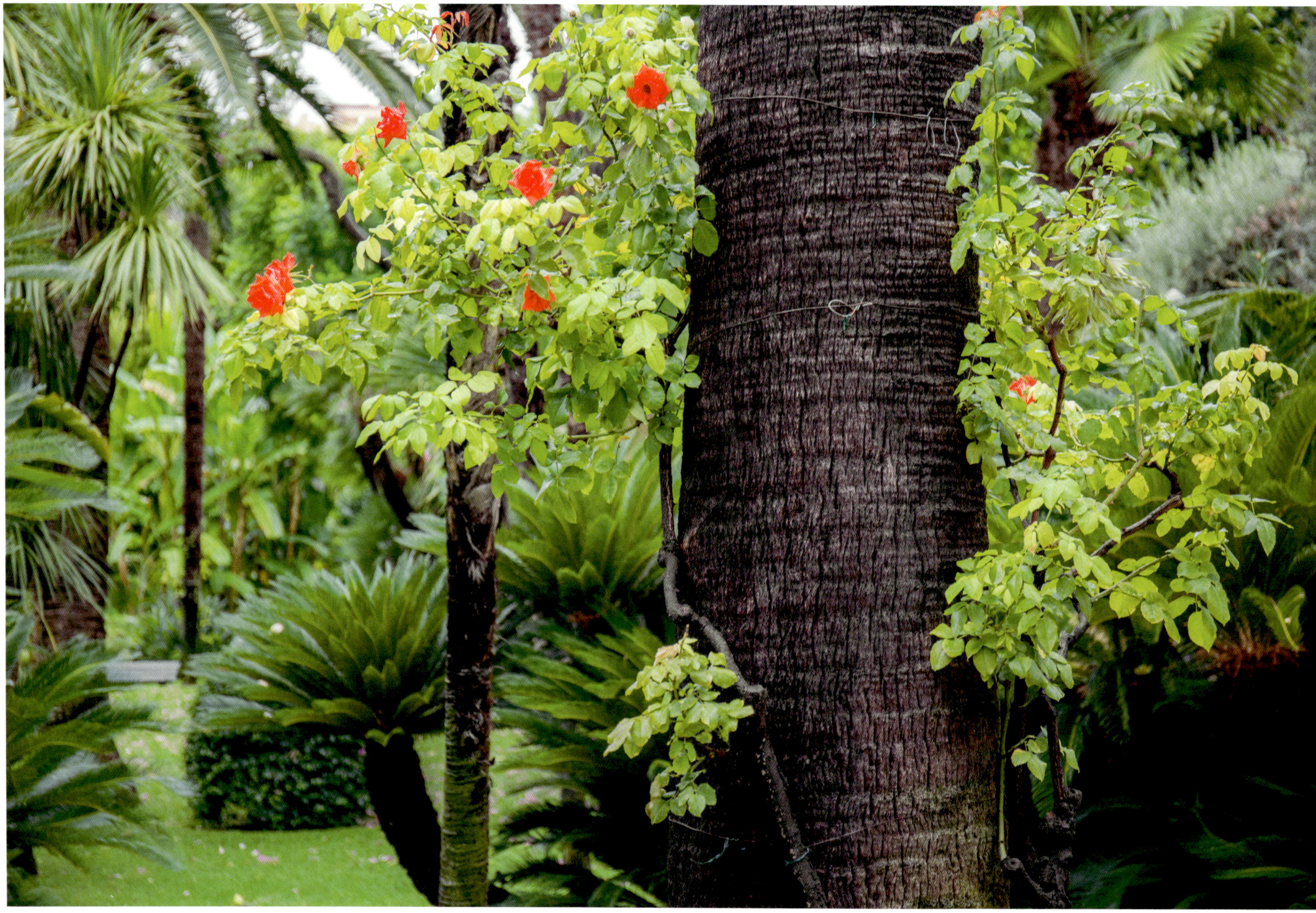

A climbing rose advances through the seasons as well as up palm trunks
in the gardens of La Petite Afrique.
Left page, September 13, 2015, 9:55 a.m. Right page, December 26, 2015, 10:27 a.m.

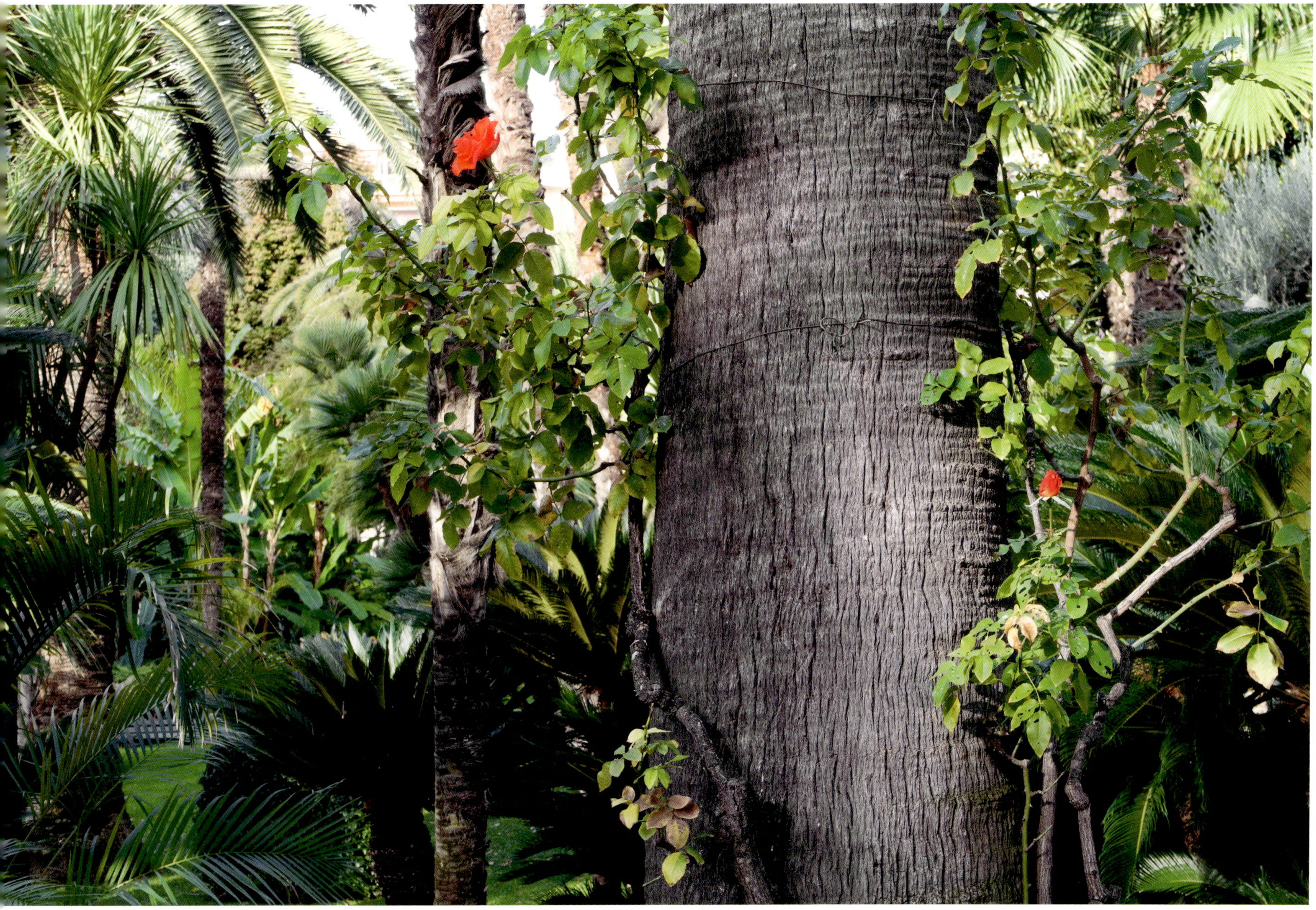

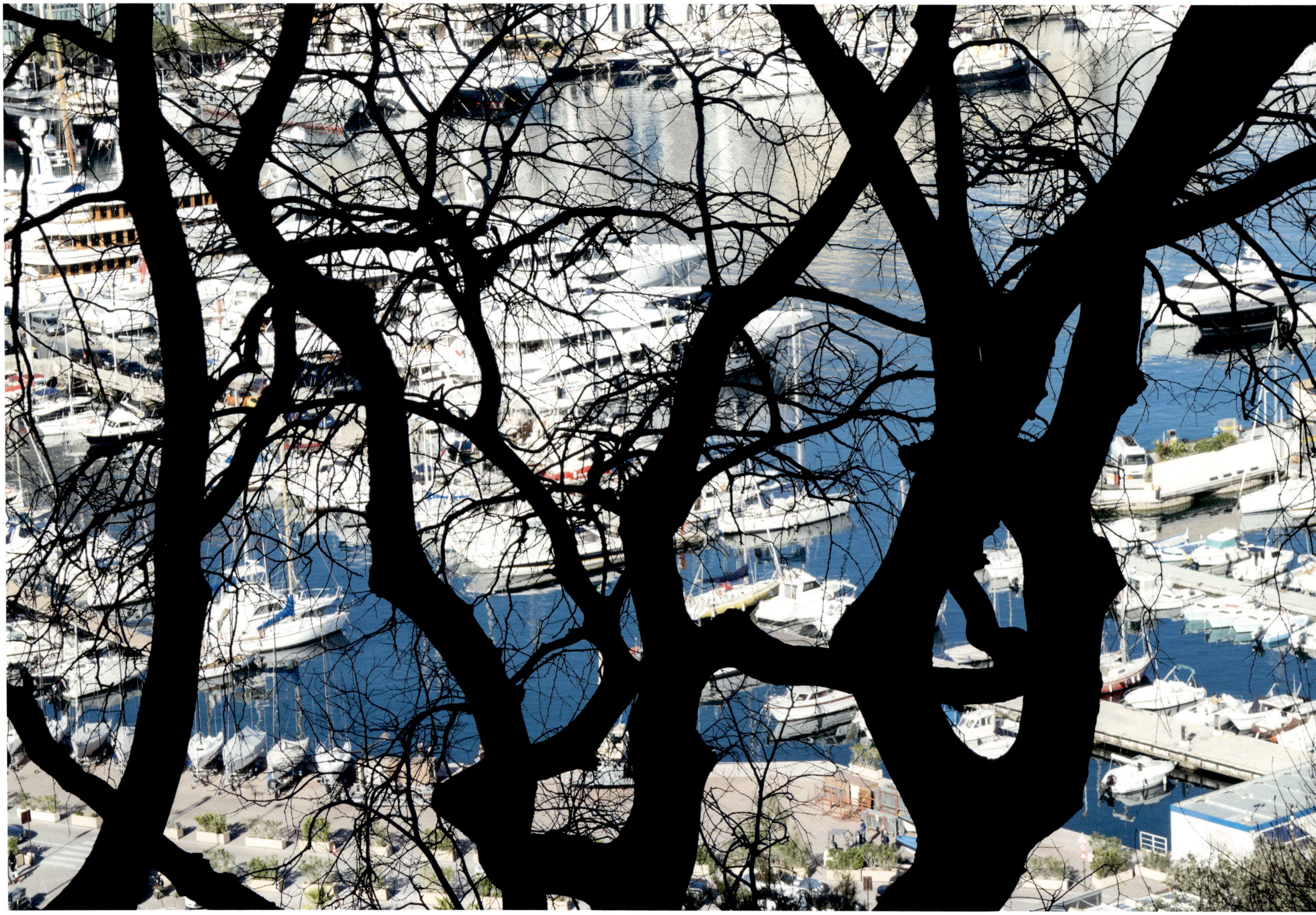

Rue des Remparts provides glimpses of Port Hercules through the silhouettes of denuded trees on a winter's morning, before the new leaves of spring start to conceal it once more.
Left page, February 21, 2016, 3:23 p.m. Right page, April 10, 2016, 10:45 a.m.

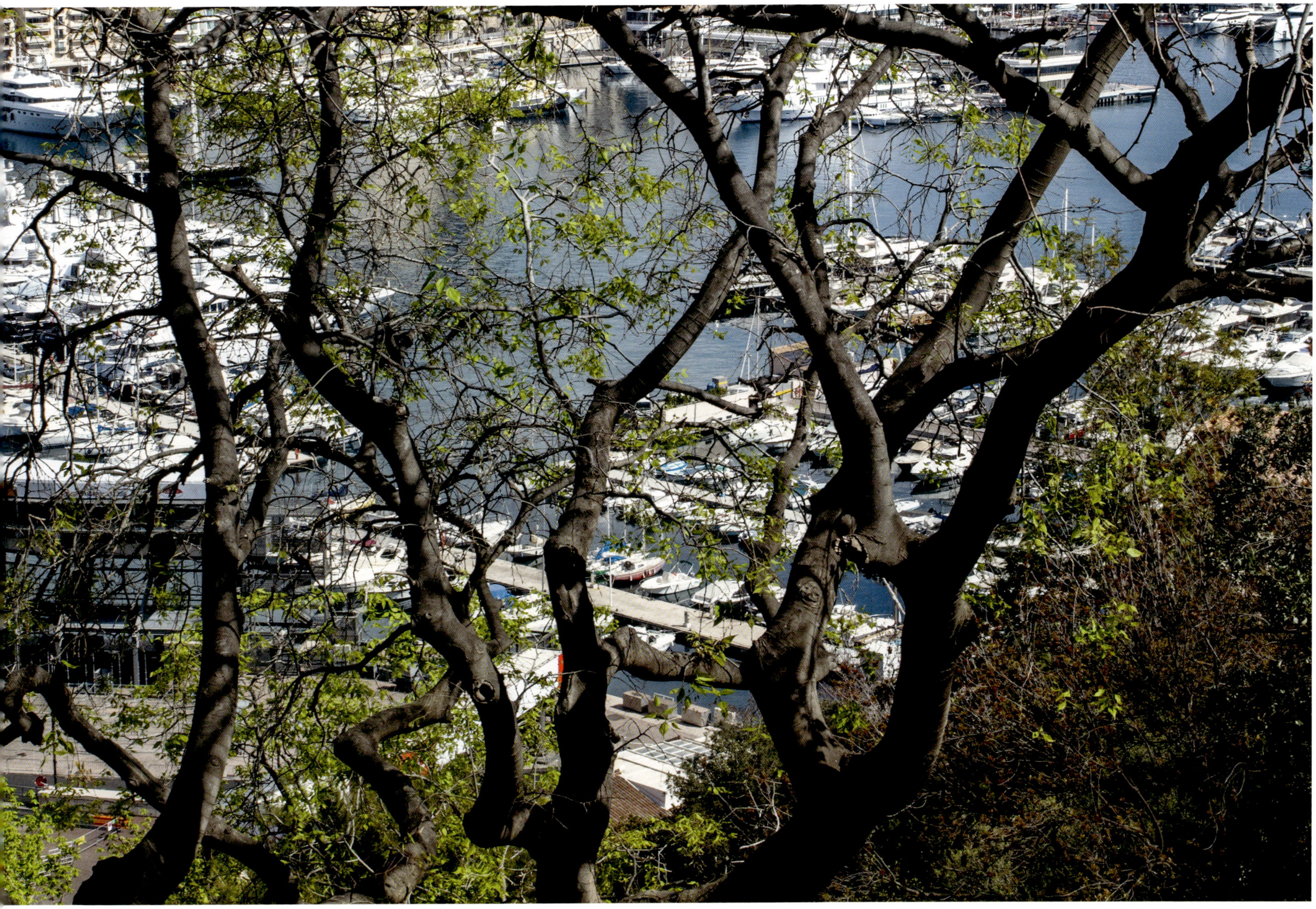

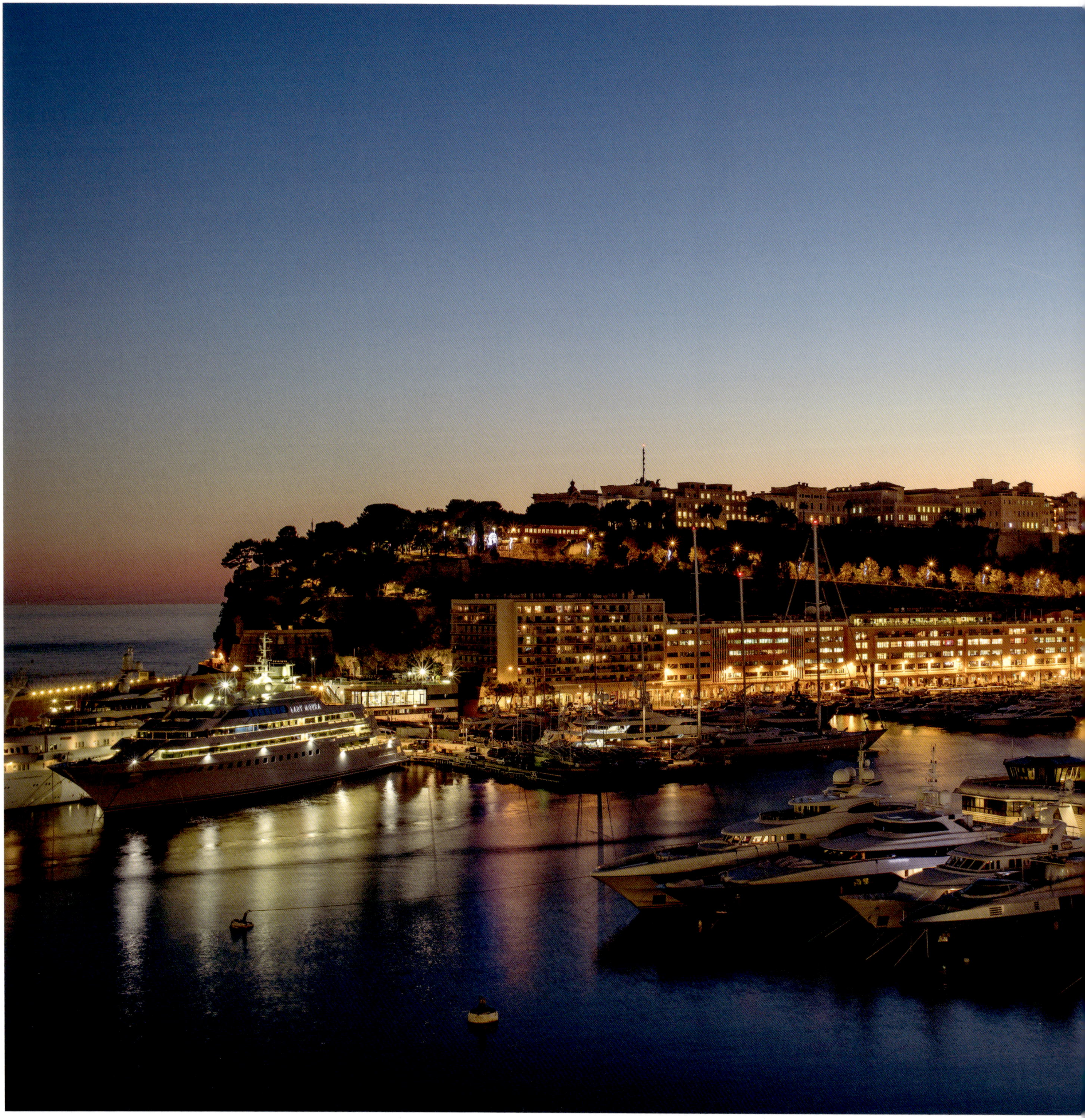

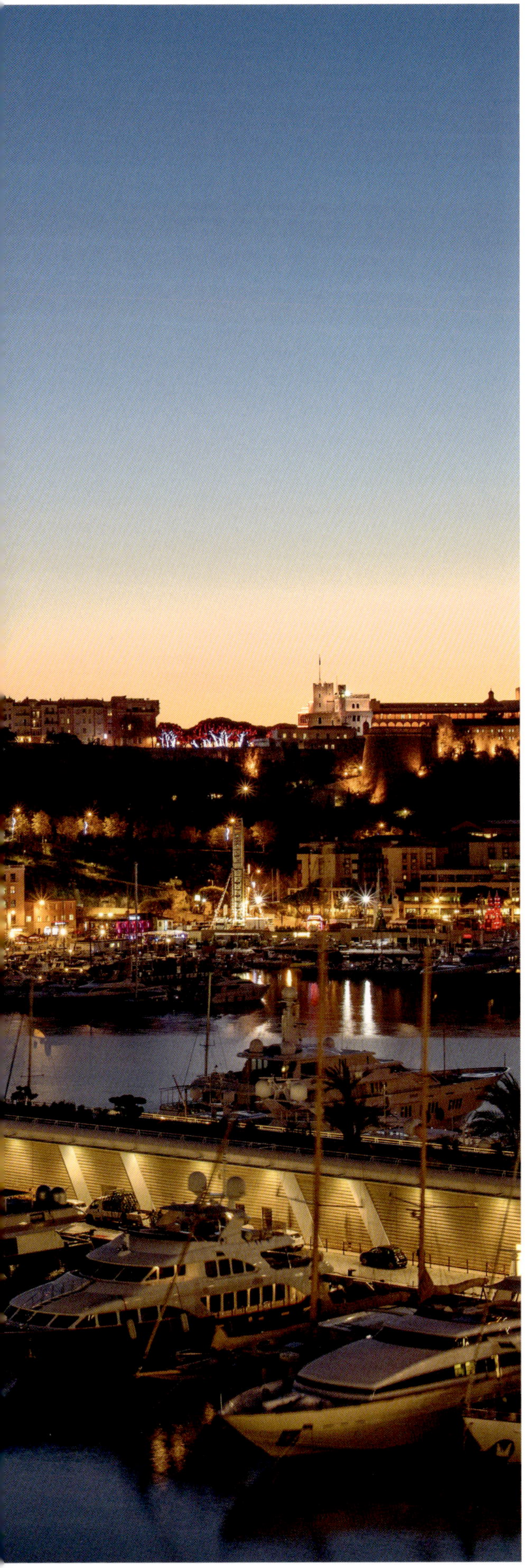

V

BEAUTY AFLOAT

In 1888 Guy de Maupassant published *Afloat (Sur l'eau)*, an account of a cruise he made off the Mediterranean coast aboard his yacht, the *Bel Ami*, and the first book published on yachting. He describes the beautiful skies, the colors, the landscapes, the dramatic role the winds play, his encounters while ashore, and the emotions he felt as a sailor on the sea. This is how he described the joy of hunkering down in his yacht: "I'm in my floating home which has wings, swaying to and fro like a pretty little nest, more comfortable than a hammock and which is drifting here and there on the water, following the whims of the wind, going wherever it chooses. To look after me and show me the way, I've got two sailors who do what I order them to do, a few books to read, and enough food for a fortnight. A whole fortnight without having to talk. What bliss!" Because of strong winds when he approached, Maupassant was unable to dock his yacht in Monaco. He had to stop at Antibes, then take a train to Monte Carlo to meet a friend. The Yacht Club de Monaco did not yet exist at that time, but the book's publication coincided with the founding of the Société des Régates by Prince Charles III and his son, Albert I, at the former Hôtel d'Orient on what is today boulevard Albert I. It was created to promote water sports for the international clients who vacationed in Monaco during the winter. The society moved to avenue d'Ostende in 1904, while Monaco was emerging as the premier destination for wealthy sailing and motorboat enthusiasts. The first Yacht Club de Monaco was founded in 1953 by Prince Rainier III. It took over the sailing component of the Société des Régates (which continued to represent rowing under the name of the Société Nautique) and is characterized by its philosophy: to achieve its yachting ideals while serving the interests of the Principality.

Unlike Maupassant who only shared his thoughts with his readers, the yacht club is intended to promote—in the words of the sovereign prince, its president since 1984—a certain *"art de vivre la mer"* in every sense of the phrase: courtesy, solidarity, elegance, respect for others, and also preservation of the environment, according to the prince's mission. A new club headquarters was opened in 2014, designed by the British high-tech architect Norman Foster, winner of the Pritzker Prize and recipient of the Gold Medal from the French Academy of Architecture. His other designs in France include the Carré d'Art in Nîmes, the Millau Viaduct, and Vieux Port in Marseille. Viewed from the outside, the building stretches along Quai Louis II like a "miniature city" and resembles an elegant ocean liner with terraces designed "like decks on a boat." The project was carried out in collaboration with the Monegasque architect Alexandre Giraldi and the interior design was the work of Jacques Grange with Fendi Casa. It is a rare treat to be able to sit on a Blixen chair at a Serengeti table and to dream of Africa, which is itself within reach aboard one of the yachts moored just a few feet away! Inside the building, everything is bright, from the muted tones of the furniture to the white cushions embroidered with the club's emblem. With twelve hundred members, sixty nationalities, the world's most prestigious yachts, and twenty-six marina berths for superyachts from ninety to two hundred feet, this unique and world-renowned club encourages classic yachting as well as modern yachting. It also offers sports sections for young people and adults, a fleet of sailors, a flagship, and many activities throughout the day and year, ensuring that Port Hercules never sleeps. In 1995, the sovereign prince acquired *Tuiga,* which means "giraffe" in Swahili. This long sailboat, described as "one of the most beautiful yachts in the world" by Eric Tabarly, became the yacht club's flagship and icon of Monaco Classic Week, the prestigious race for classic yachts. The ninety-four-foot gaff cutter with four-cornered sails was built in 1909 in Fairlie, Scotland, the birthplace of yachting. With its crew composed of members of the yacht club, *Tuiga* takes part in all classic yachting events and is instantly recognizable whenever it takes to the seas.

Prince Albert II redeveloped Port Hercules for yachting and its seven hundred berths along the jetties of the marina now welcome boats of all kinds and from all countries. Strolling along the waterfront, various unique vessels can still be found bobbing between the huge yachts, including traditional *pointu* fishing boats, the water taxi that crosses the harbor between the Quai des États-Unis and Quai Rainier I, and *Lulou,* a fishing boat that proudly rubs elbows with true ocean celebrities like *Lady Moura, Atlantis II,* and *Madame GU.* "The yachts just keep growing," says ***Lulou's*** owner, a retired fisherman, philosophically. Other recreational boats display poetic and evocative names—*Strangers in the Night, Odette, Sister Act,* and *Garfield*—while *Dédé,* the small boat of the port's last fisherman, prepares to leave from the end of Quai Antoine I. The ingenious semifloating breakwater, commissioned by Prince Rainier III in the early 2000s to protect the port from east winds, can accommodate colossal cruise ships such as the *Riviera* on its way to Venice, the *Silver Cloud,* which stops in Portofino, and the *Star Legend,* as it heads for Cannes.

The marina at Fontvieille is more intimate. In this reclaimed land between the walls of the Rock, Anse de la Grue, Pointe Sainte-Barbe, and a pier lined with modern buildings, the 275-berth harbor shimmers with charm. Sailboats and motor yachts float side by side, such as the Hollywood schooner *Zaca* and the more "rock 'n' roll" *Black Legend.* Behind the Rock's ramparts, Prince's Palace towers above, along with several of the upper town's old houses with their colorful pink façades and green shutters.

Previous spread. Evening light from the sky, sea, and land creates a scene of perfect harmony over Port Hercules. November 30, 2015, 6:35 p.m.

From avenue d'Ostende, flower and sun petals frame the huge yachts moored at Quai Rainier III. Left, December 10, 2015, 11:49 a.m. Right, April 10, 2016, 11:34 a.m.

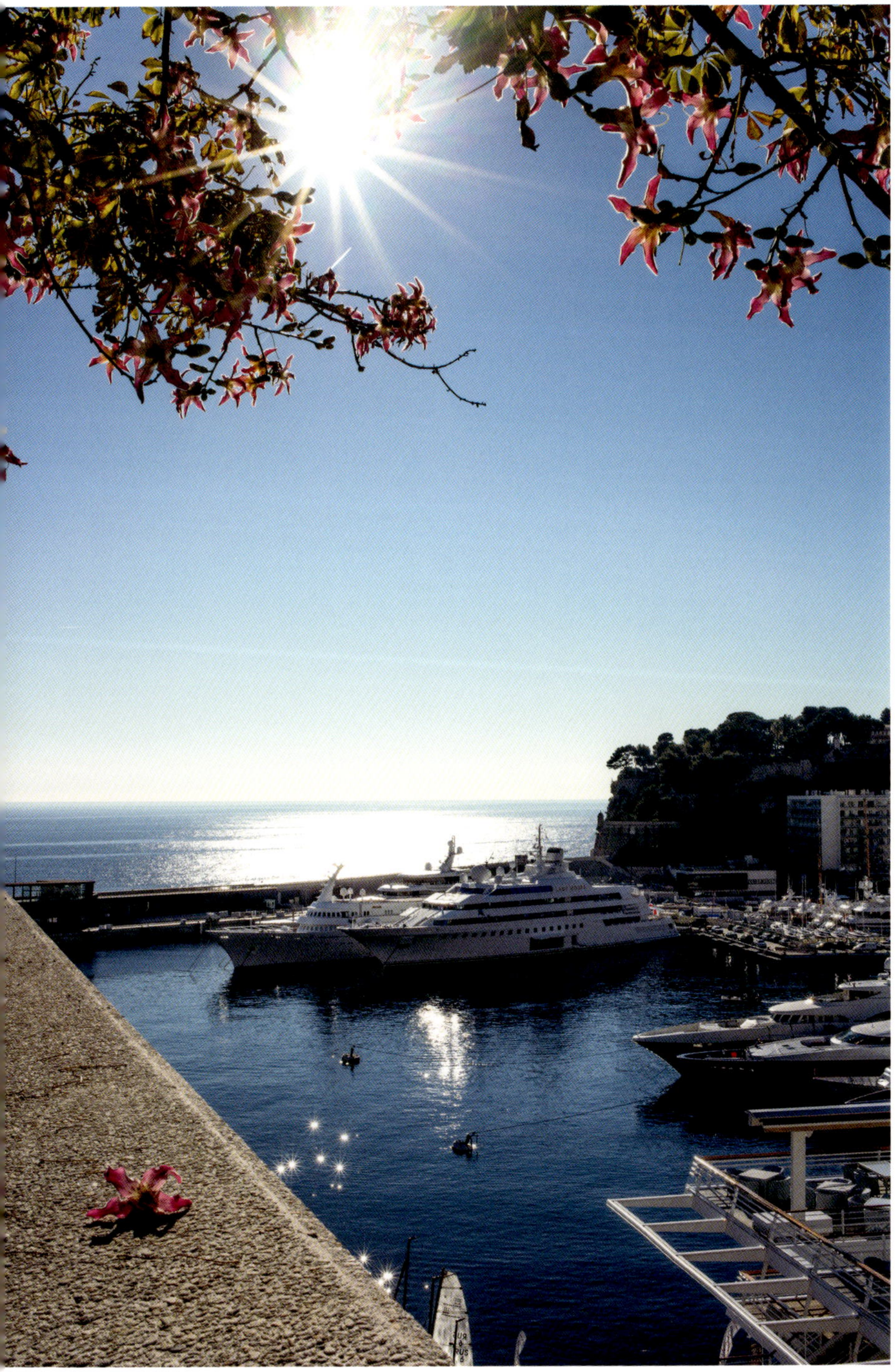

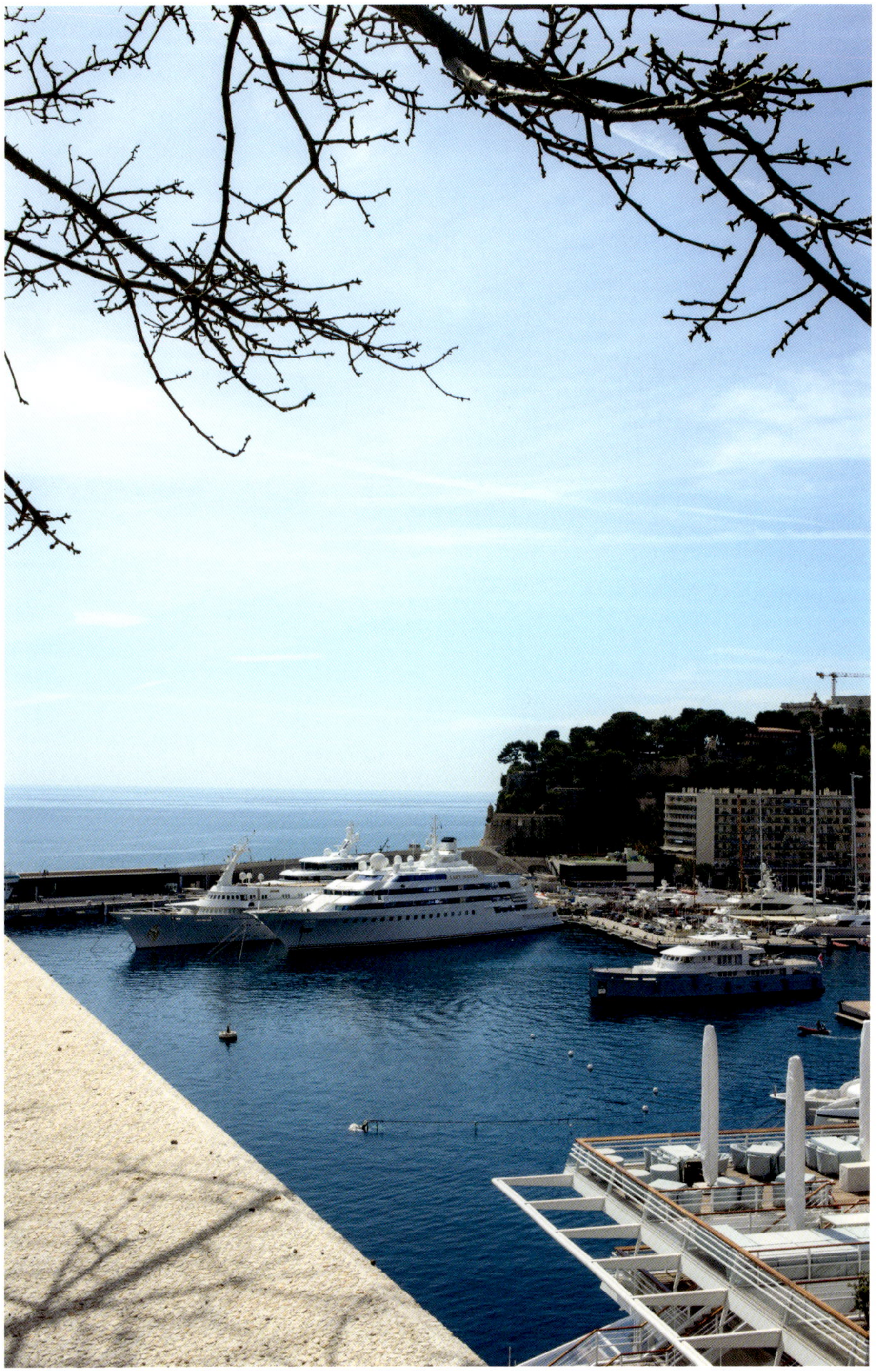

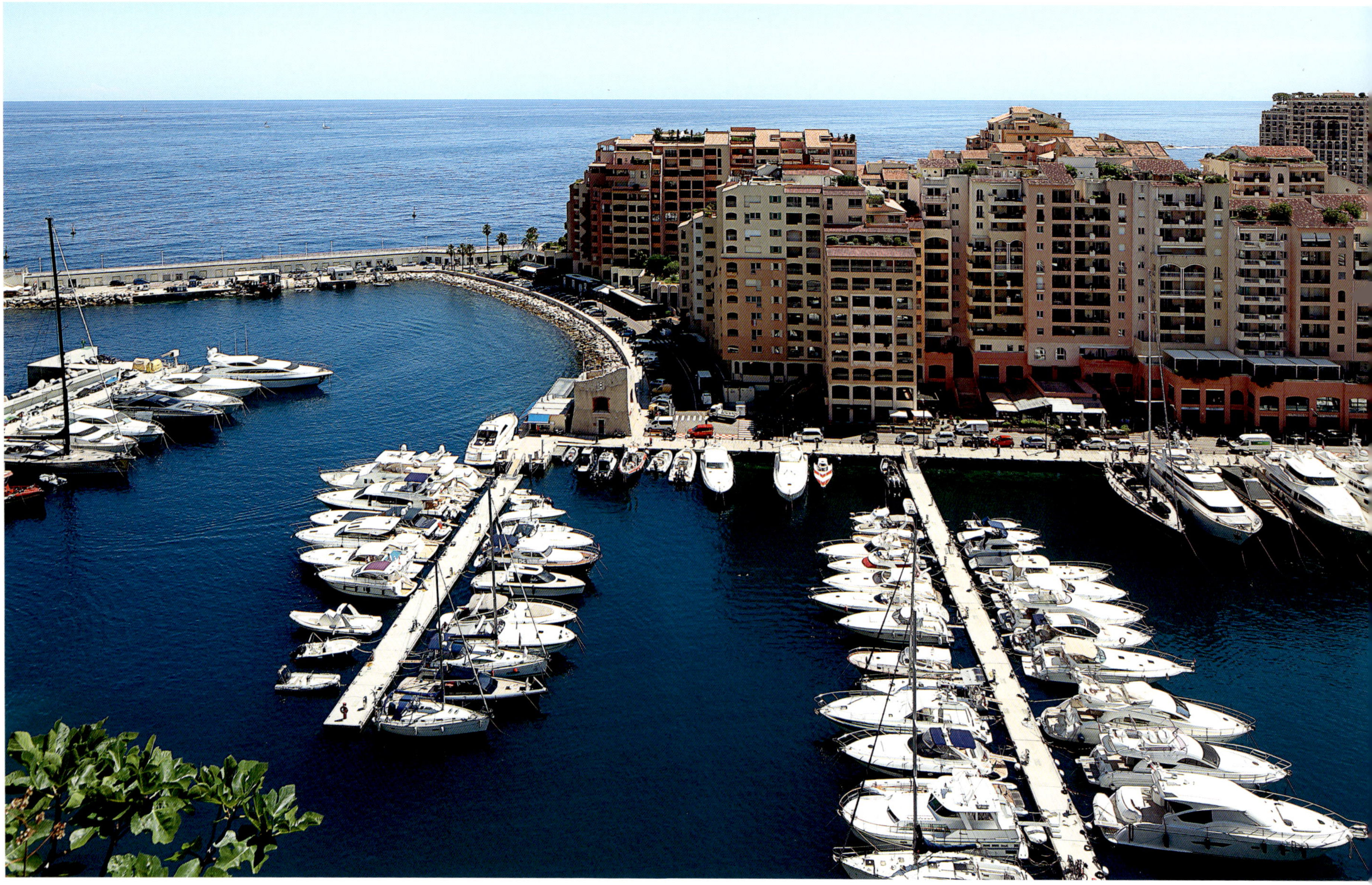

The calm of Fontvieille's harbor is interrupted by a small boat tracing
a white line with its ephemeral wake.
June 25, 2015. Left page, 2:11 p.m.; right page, 20 seconds after 2:11 p.m.

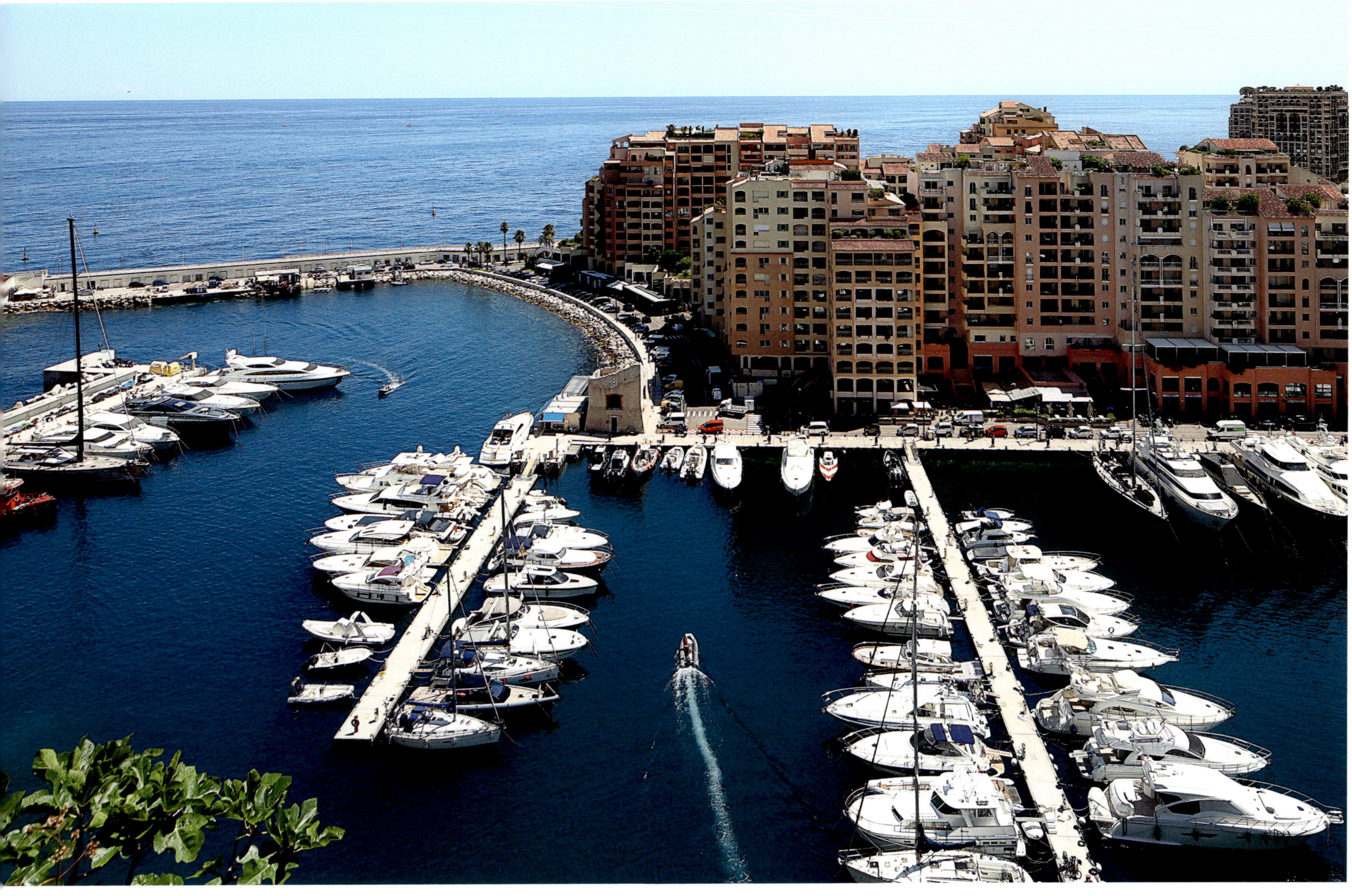

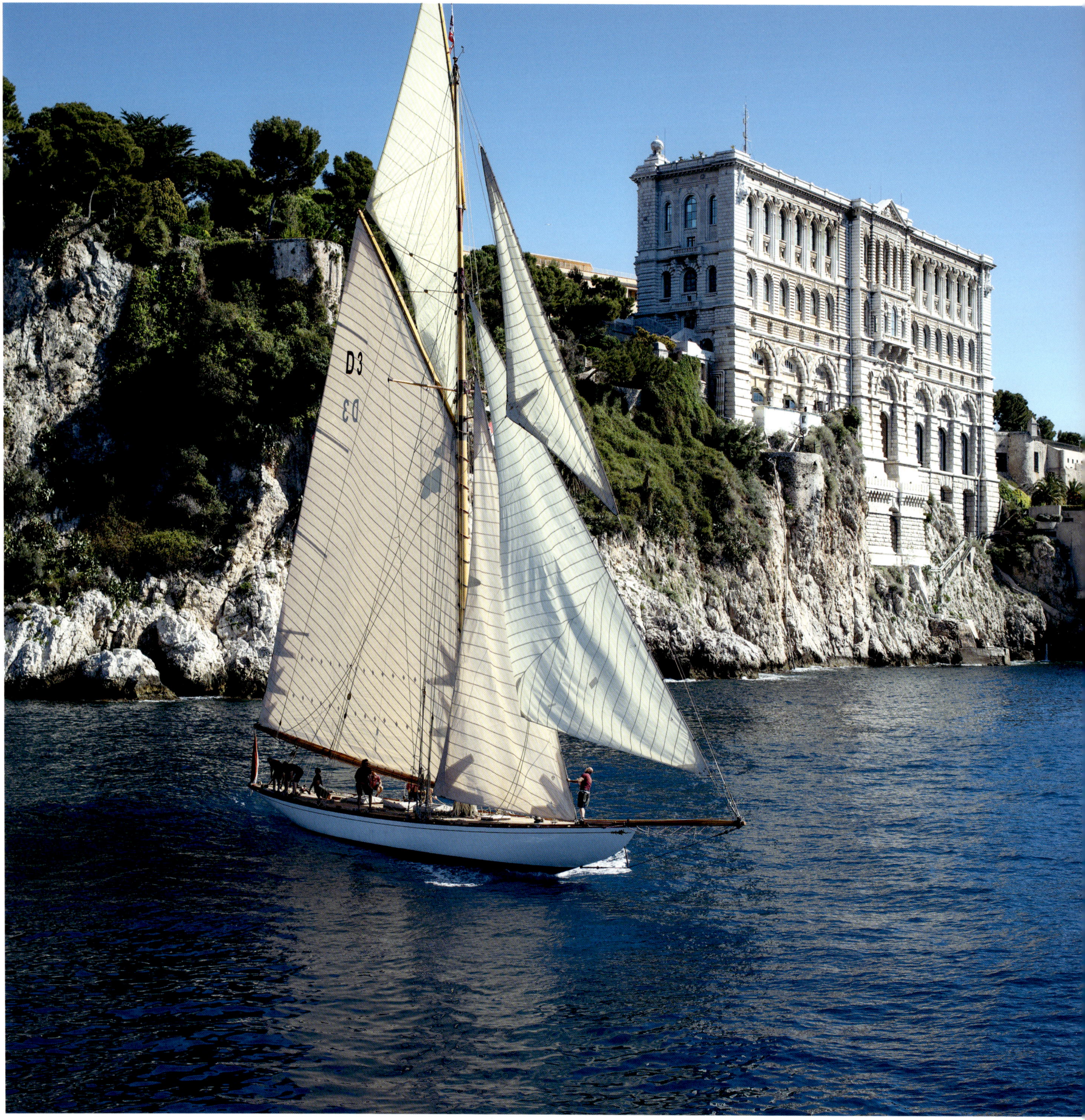
D3

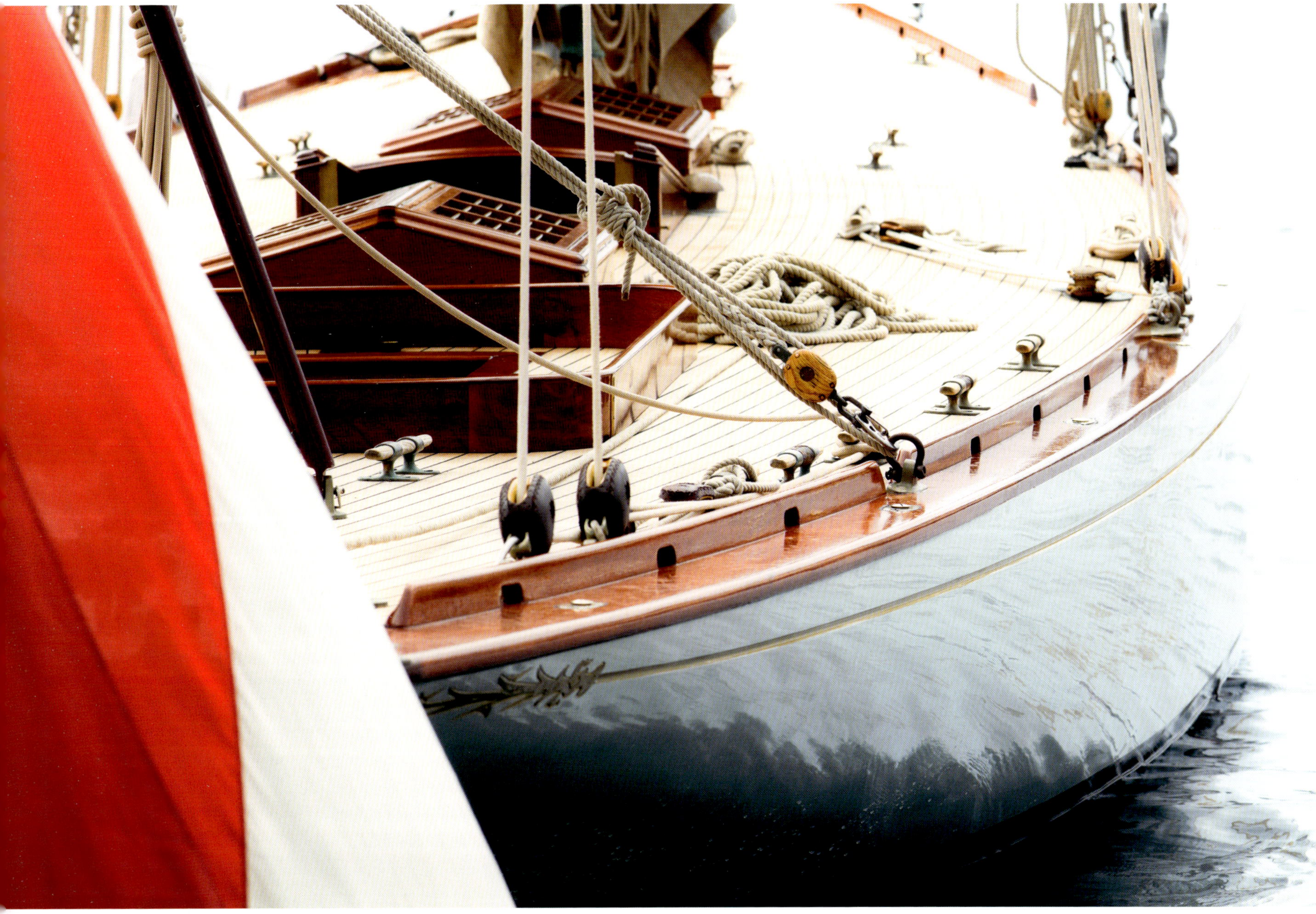

Tuiga, the Yacht Club de Monaco's flagship with its crew dances in the seas
below the south façade of the Oceanographic Museum and Saint Nicholas Cathedral on the Rock.
May 20, 2016. Left page, 9:07 a.m.
Following spread, left page, 9:08 a.m.; right page, 2:01 p.m.

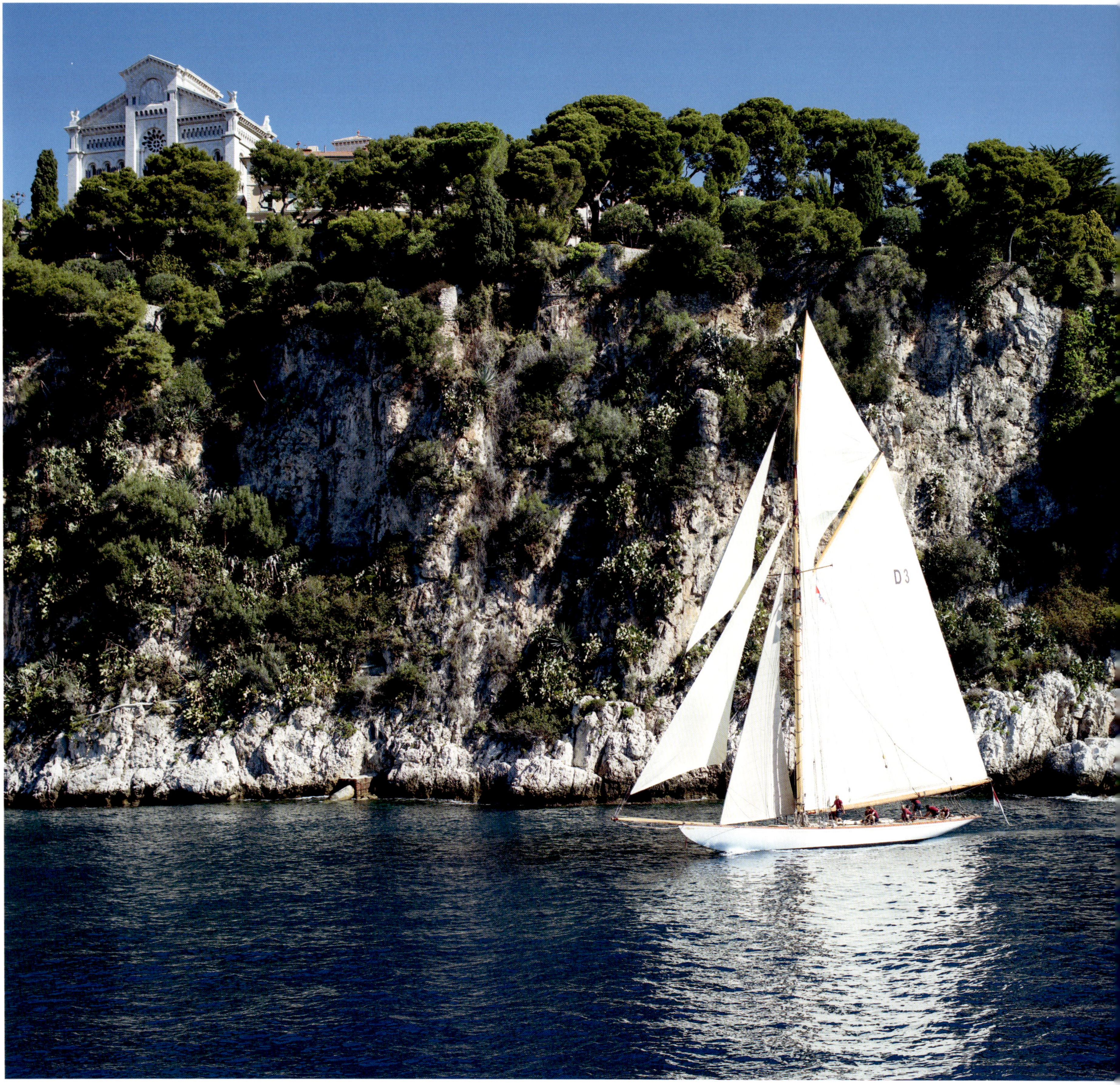
D3

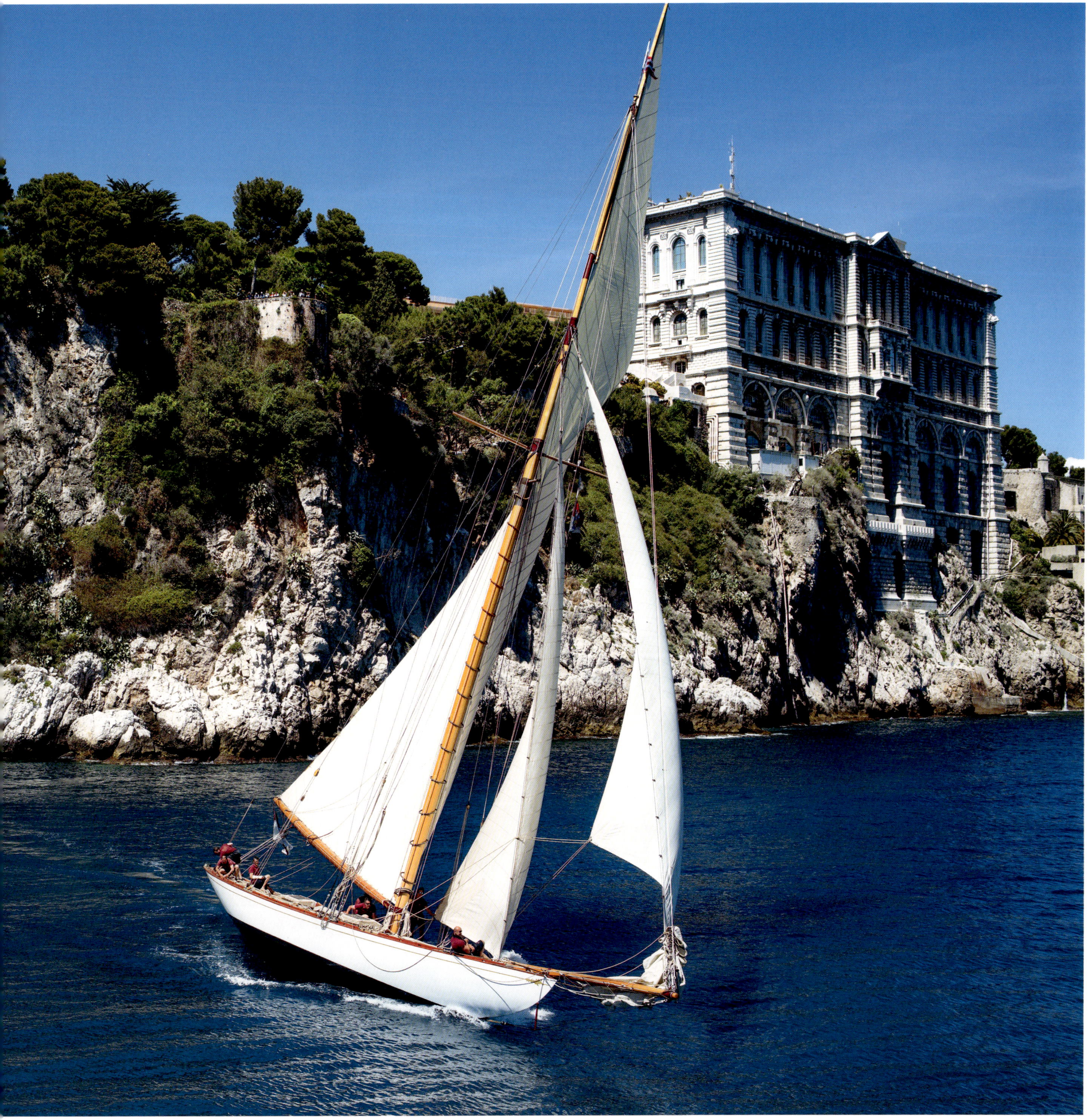

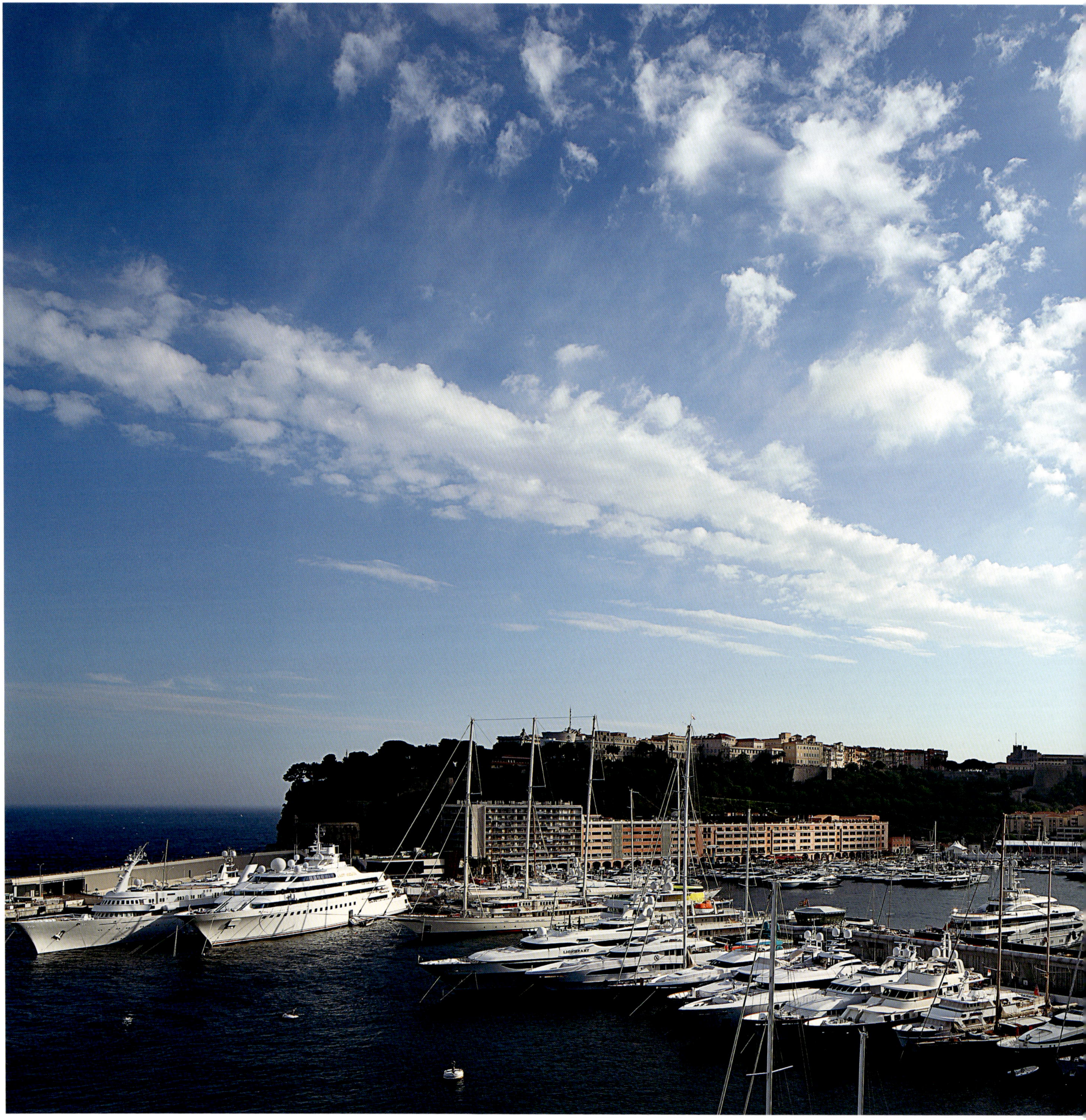

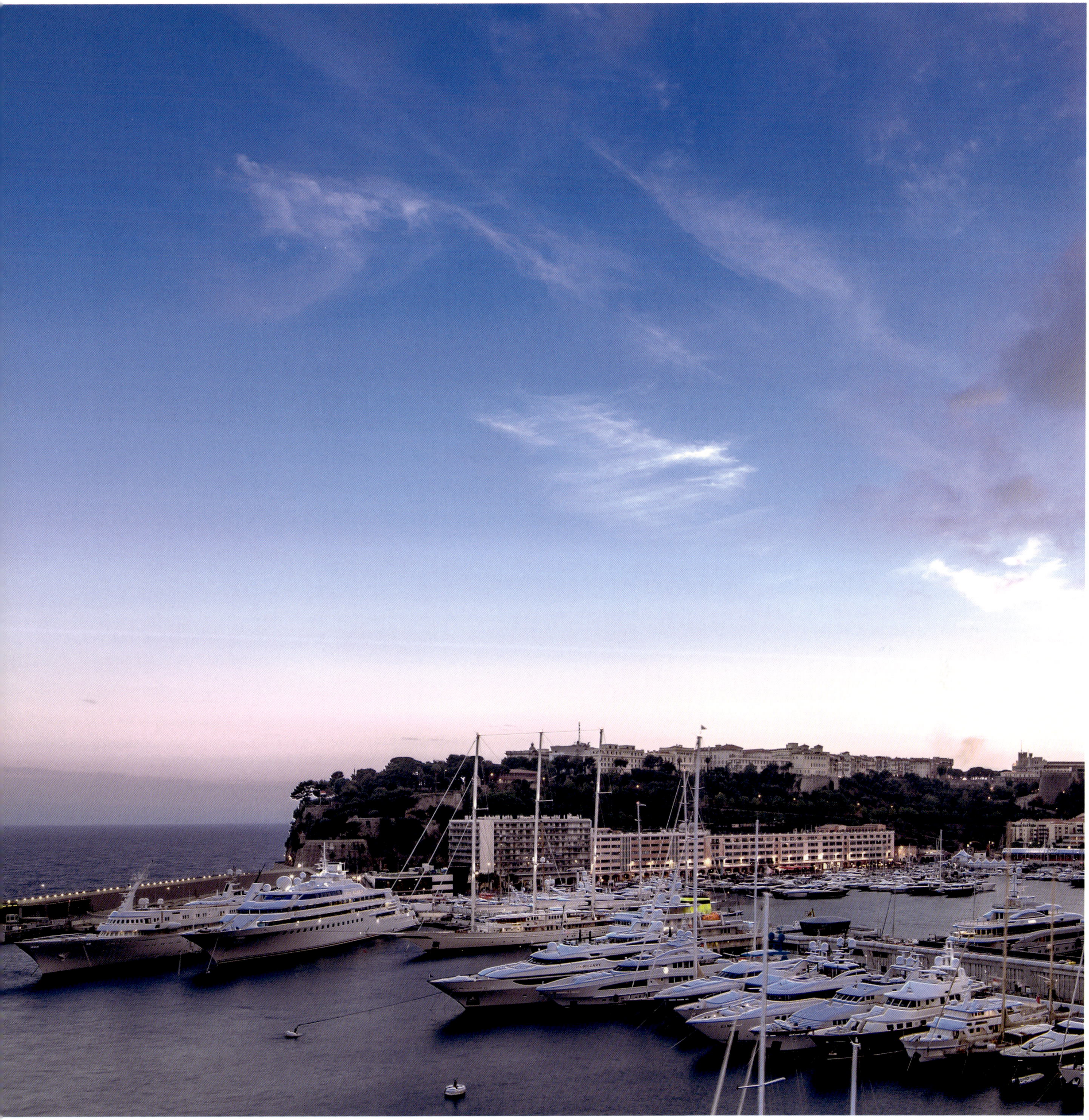

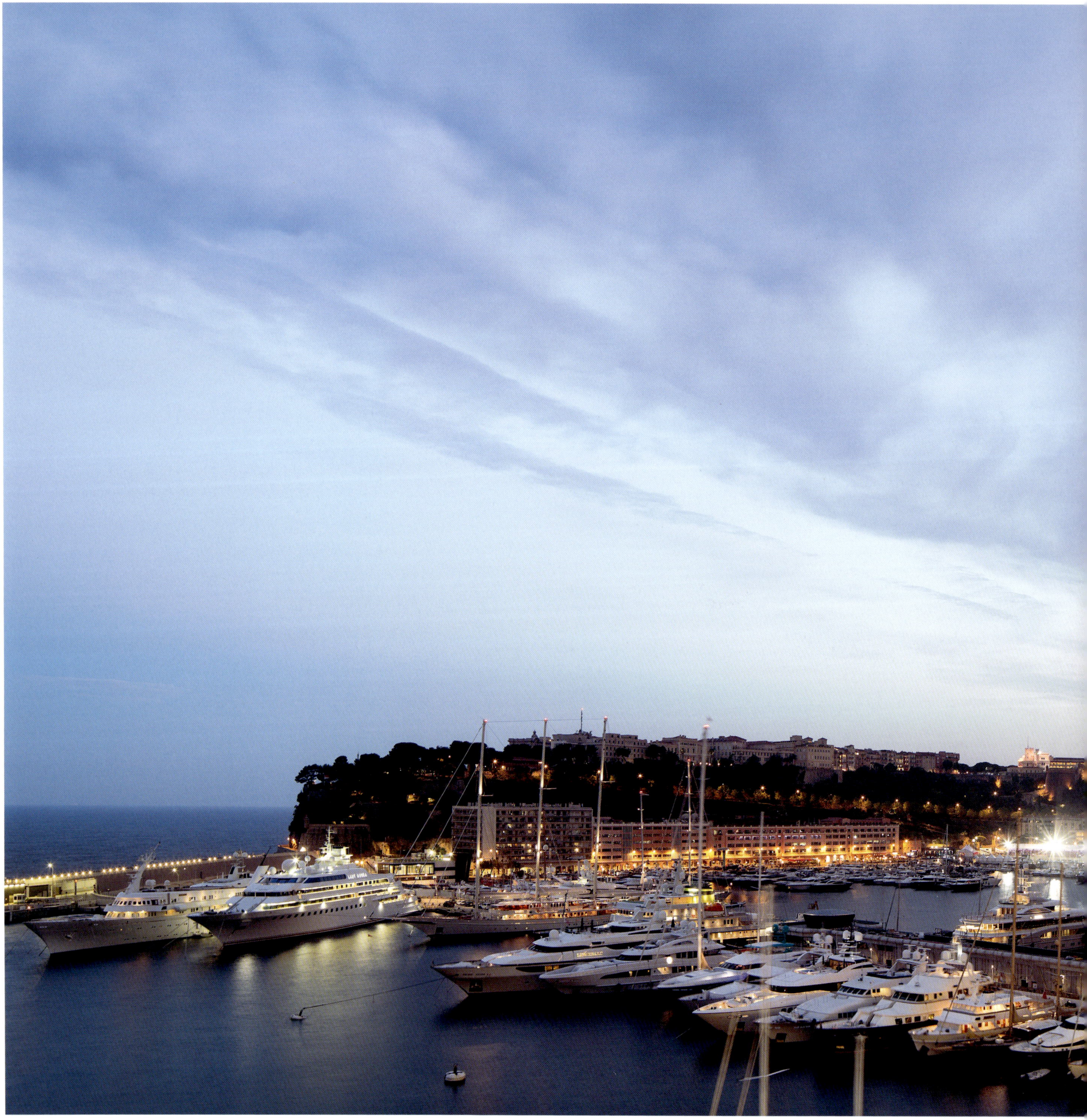

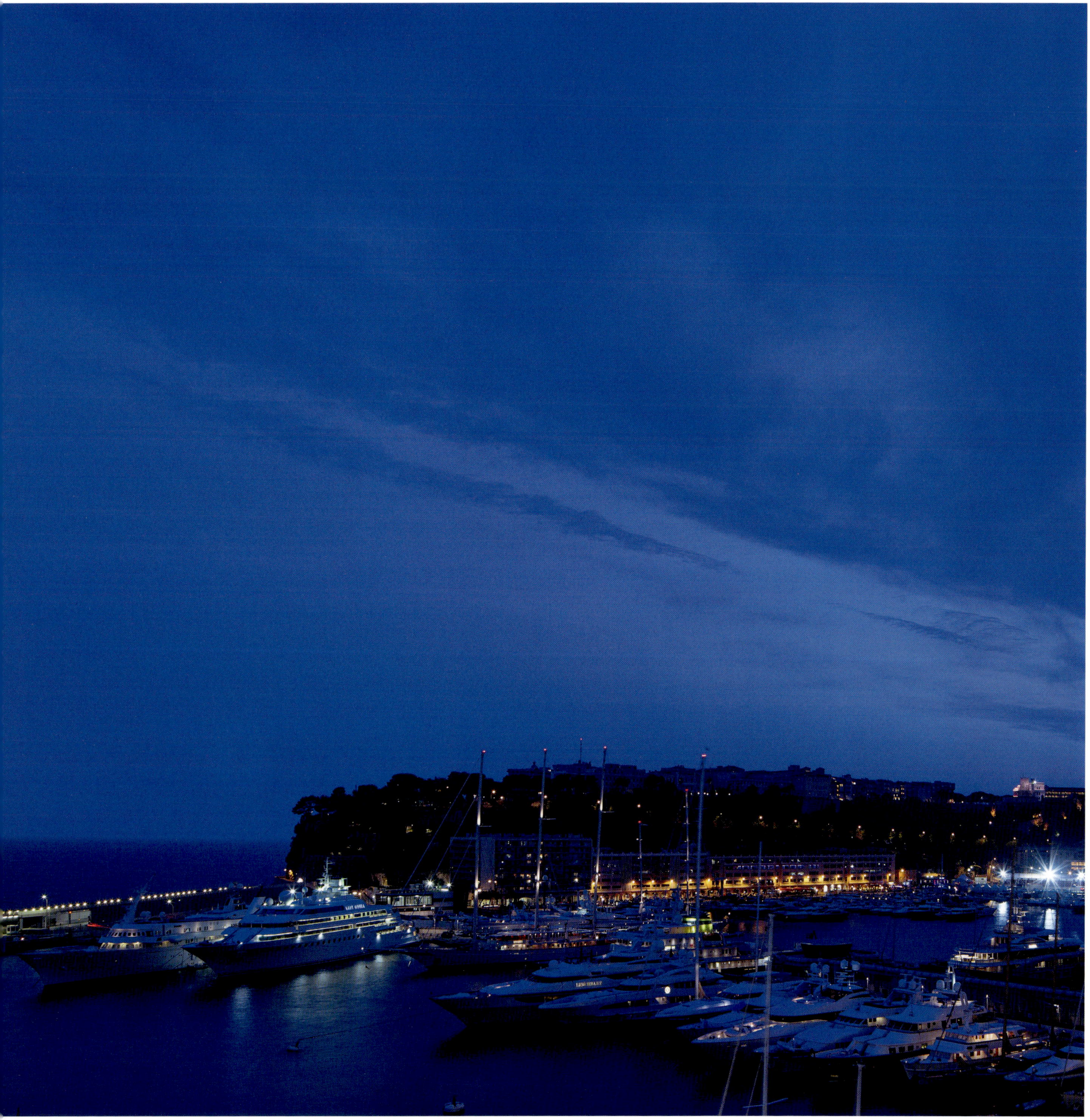

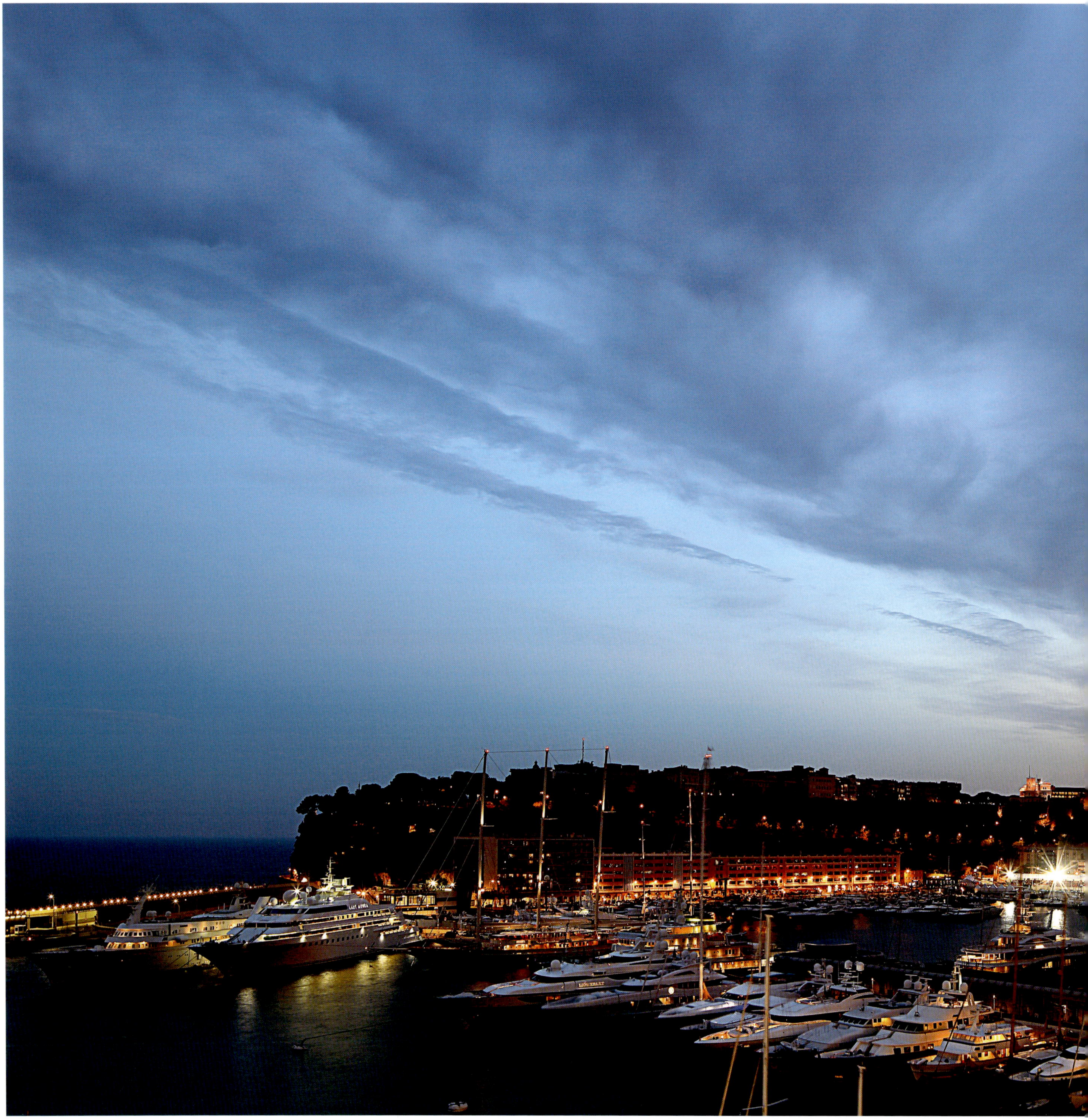

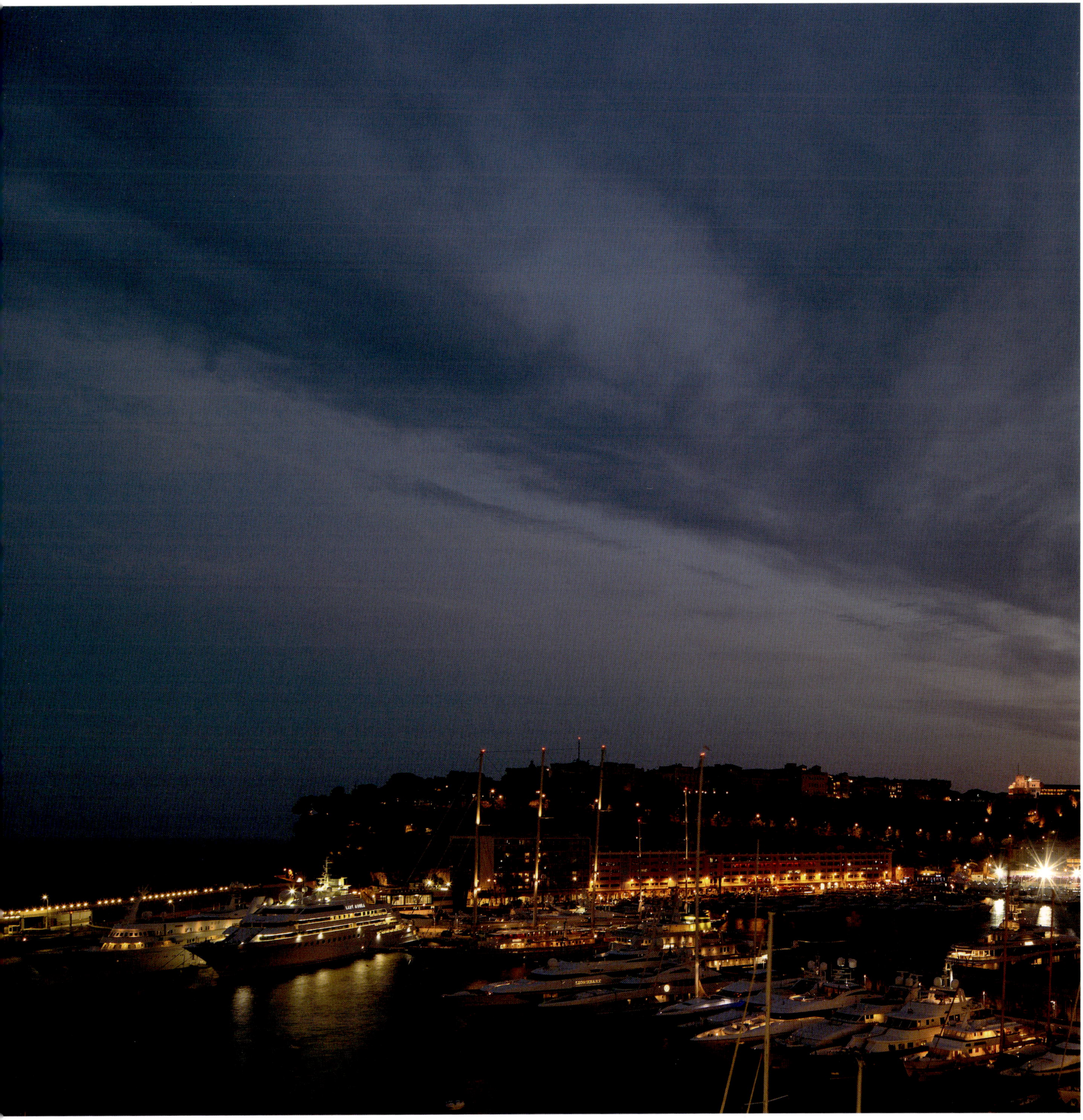

Previous spreads. Colors through the lens of time over Port Hercules. June 23, 2016. First spread, left page, 5:53 p.m.; right page, 8:10 p.m. Second spread, left page, 8:36 p.m.; right page, 8:38 p.m. Third spread, left page, 8:41 p.m.; right, 9:00 p.m.

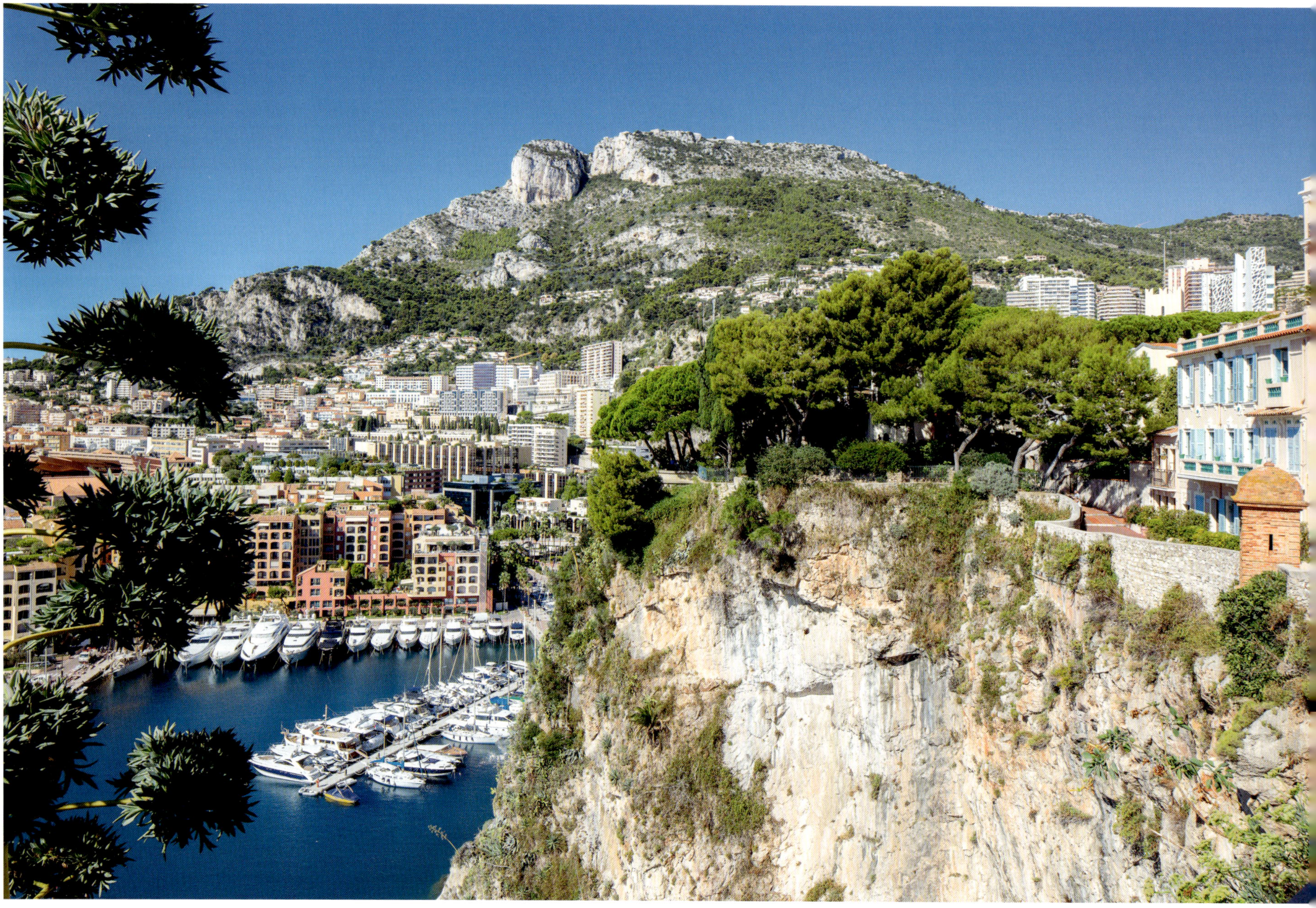

The sun's passage over Fontvieille's harbor as seen from the Rock.
Left page, September 23, 2015, 11:23 a.m. Right page, December 28, 2015, 2:53 p.m.

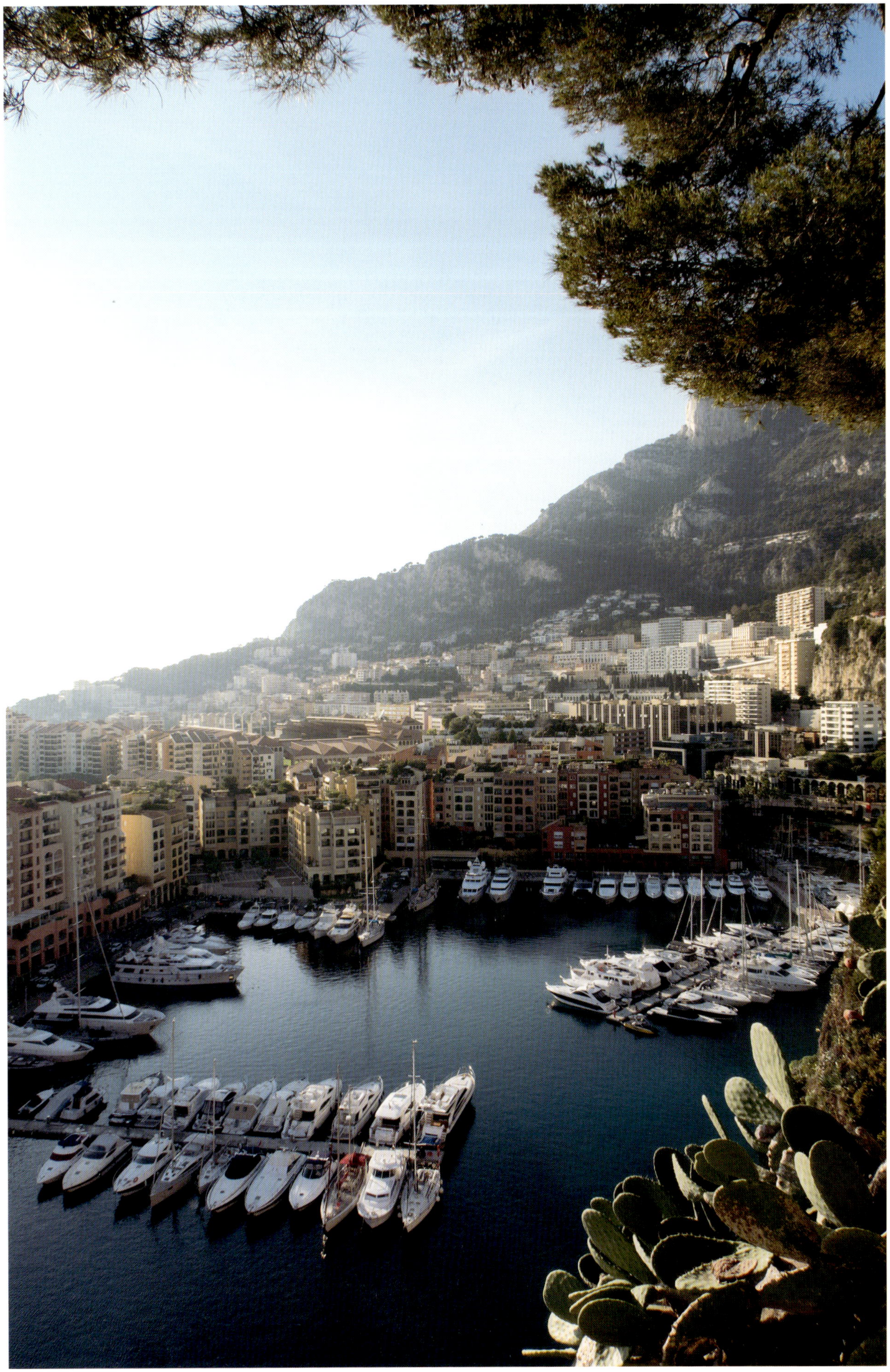

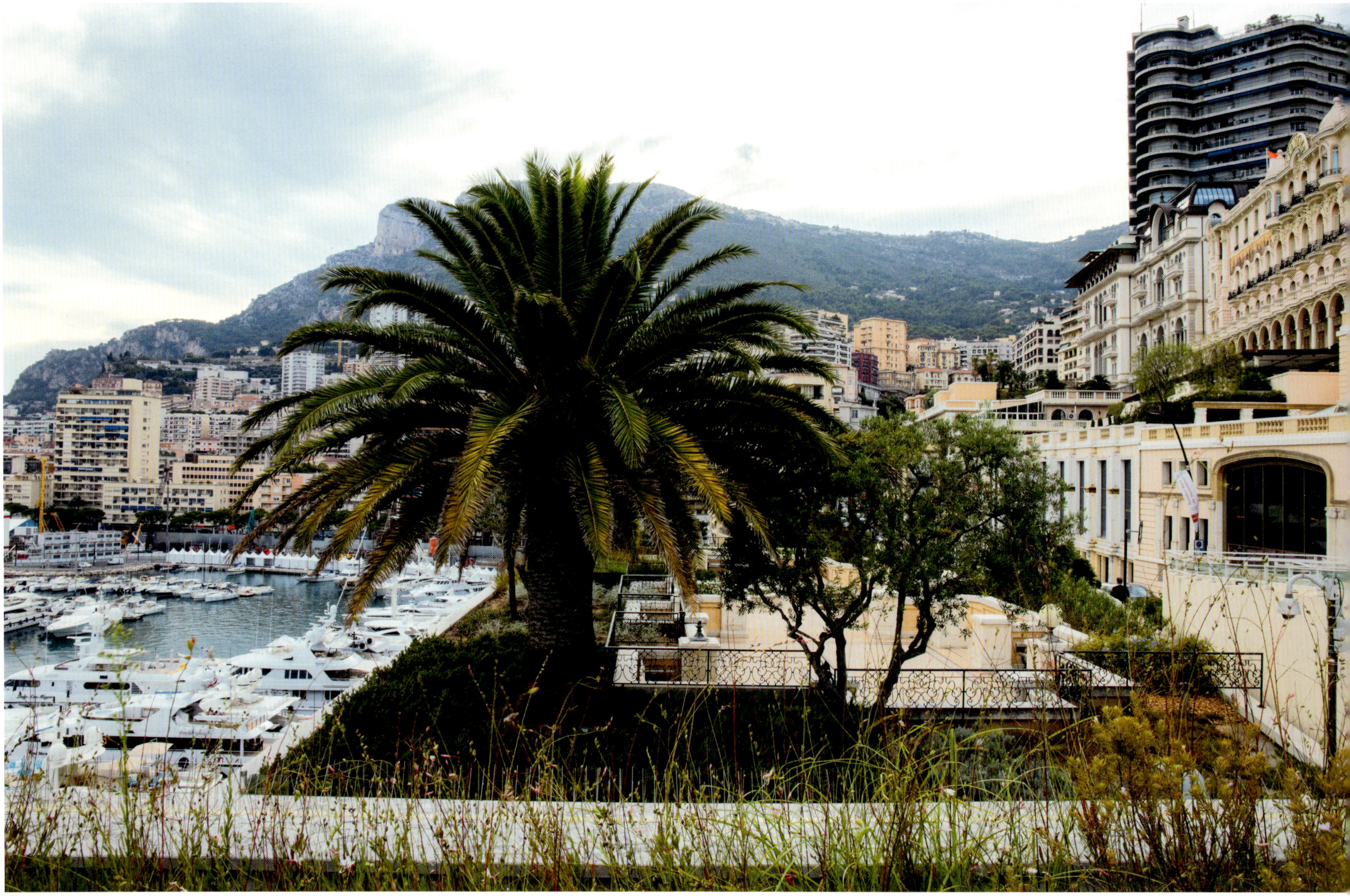

Night falls on a green roof garden between avenue d'Ostende and Port Hercules.
September 14, 2015. Left page, 6:28 p.m.; right page, 7:55 p.m.

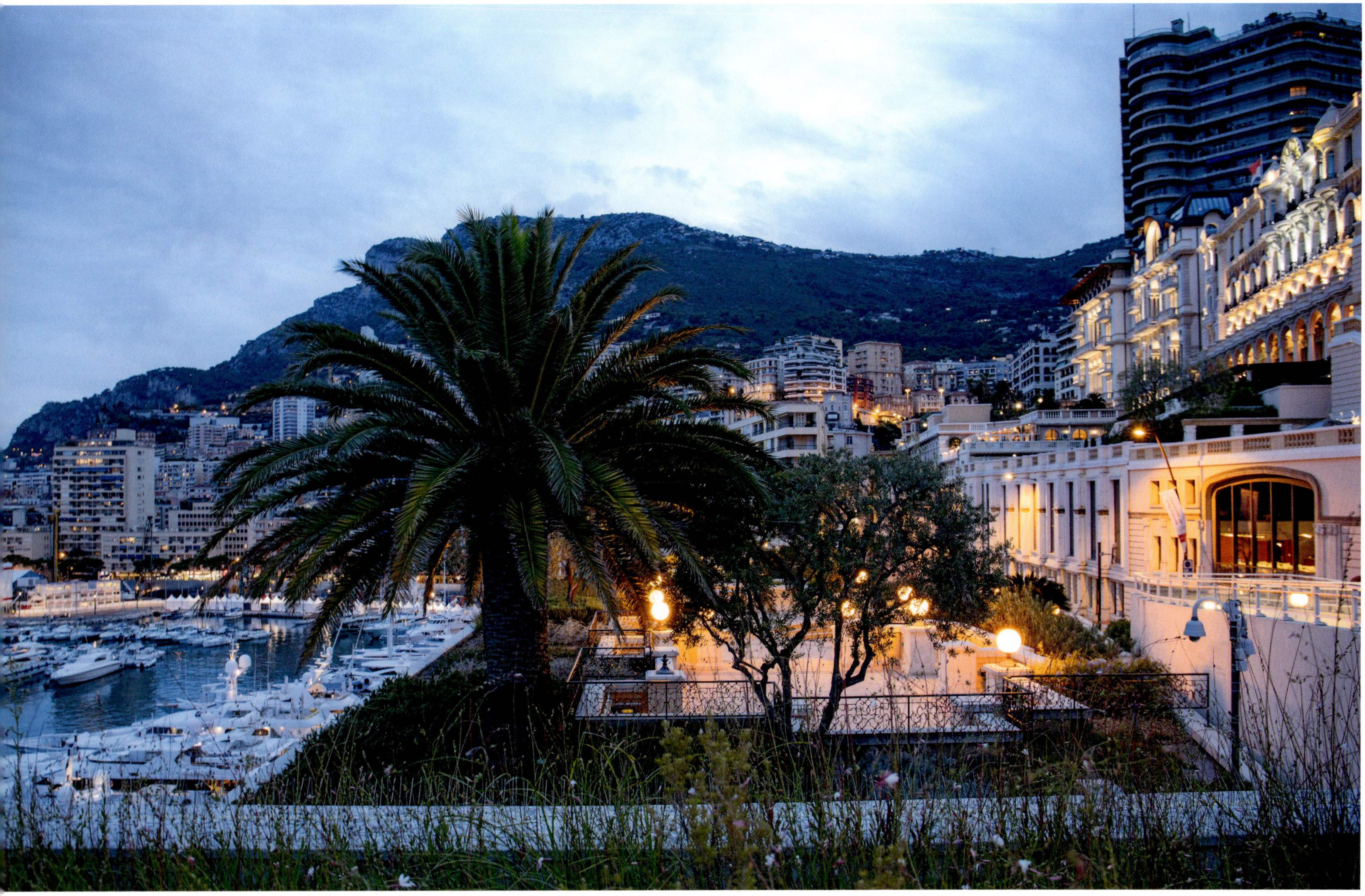

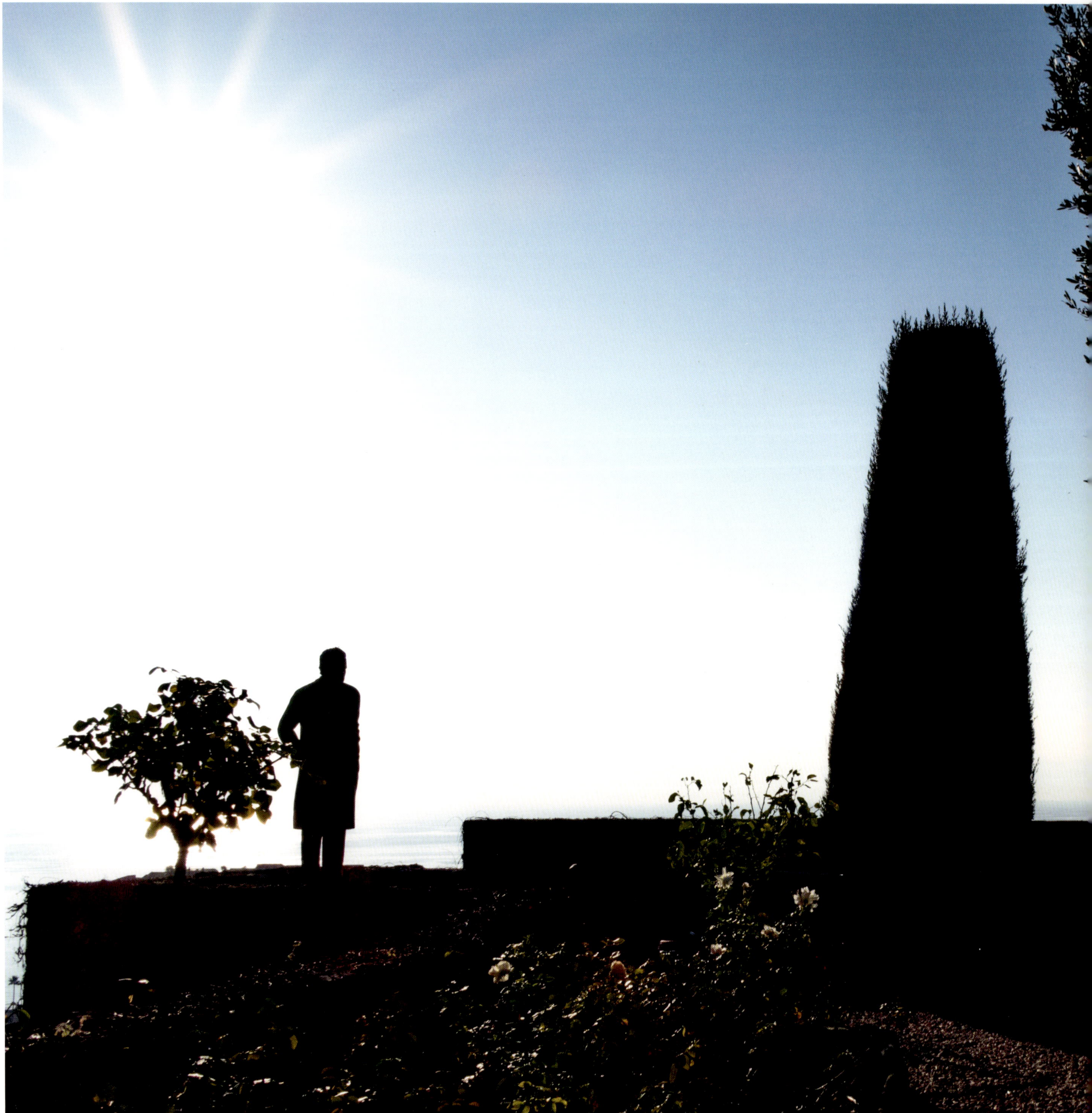

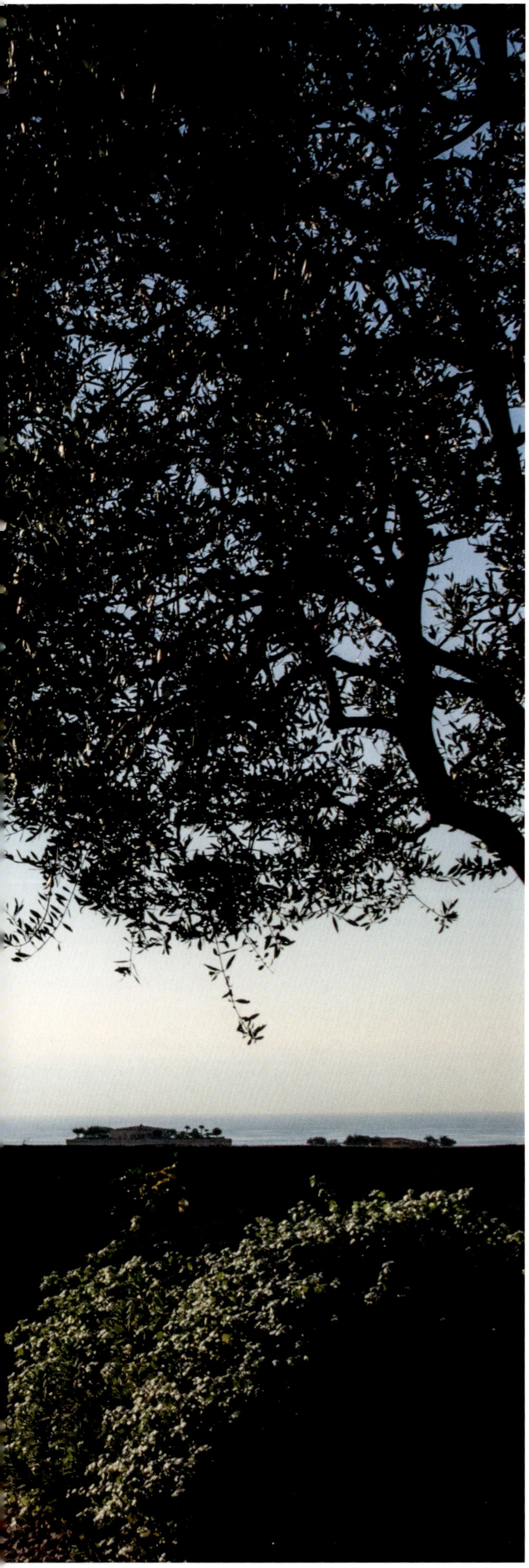

VI

ENDURING MEMORIES

On Lucciana Jetty, just a few steps from Quai Louis II, two monumental sculptures sparkle in the sun: *Ulysses,* a bronze by Anna Chromy, which was previously displayed on the south jetty near to the old yacht club building, and *Sfera Enigma,* by the Venetian Gianfranco Meggiato, which was installed in summer 2014. It is an exceptional location to view these works of art: under the sky, by the sea, looking inward to Port Hercules or out over a superb panorama toward Italy. Backdrops include the yacht club, the buildings of avenue de Monte-Carlo, the domes of the casino, and perhaps a boat leaving the harbor. Desperately clinging to the steering wheel, *Ulysses* struggles to decide his destiny as it hangs in the balance. A little farther, *Sfera Enigma* is a beautiful golden sphere trapped in a nest of silver triangles, through which the artist invites us to guess its story.

Having practiced it himself in his workshop at his retreat Roc Agel, Prince Rainier III was passionate about sculpture and wanted to share his love of contemporary art in the city and its gardens, thus turning the Principality into an outdoor sculpture museum. A sculpture trail can be found in the Fontvieille district providing visitors with the opportunity to view some forty works, while also taking in Fontvieille Park, the Princess Grace Rose Garden, the port, the Zoological Gardens, the Museum of Stamps and Coins, the Naval Museum, and The Prince of Monaco's Vintage Car Collection. The trail then heads into the city for another seventy new masterpieces, which involves taking the slopes up to the Rock, descending into La Condamine, strolling to Monte Carlo, then onward to the Grimaldi Forum. Construction work and limited space have meant that certain monuments have been moved. This includes the statue *Sitting Cino Del Duca* by Lajos Barta, which was in the gardens of Villa Sauber. He now sits smiling and mulling over his production projects near the Théâtre des Variétés. The curious who tread their own path are treated to some lovely surprises, like discovering the *Cairn* by land artist Andy Goldsworthy, hidden under the foliage in La Petite Afrique, as well as another twenty installations that have been added to the collection since the official trail was created in 2001. Fans of Colombian painter and sculptor Fernando Botero and his proportionally exaggerated figures will love *Woman Smoking a Cigarette* in the gardens of Fontvieille and *Adam and Eve* on the terraces of the casino. Sport and dance enthusiasts can find *Pas de deux* by Sauro Cavallini upon leaving the Princess Grace Rose Garden, *Le sport* by Kees Verkade at the entrance to Louis II Stadium, and *Plongeur* by Emma de Sigaldi on the access road of Stade Nautique Rainier III. Those who wish to contemplate the works that pay homage to the Grimaldi family should head to the Rock and to Place du Palais. Here, *Malizia* depicts Francesco Grimaldi, disguised as a monk in an effort to seize the fortress at the time of the Guelph and Ghibelline conflicts. The elegant femininity of the statue of Princess Grace sits in the heart of the rose garden that bears her name, and Prince Rainier III stands regally underneath the fortifications along Rampe Major. All of these are the work of the same artist, Kees Verkade. Another statue of the Builder Prince by Daphne Du Barry is located in a private area of the palace. It depicts Prince Rainier III standing on top of the ramparts contemplating his life's work, Fontvieille. In Fontvieille, in Monte Carlo, and on the Rock, César, Arman, Folon, and Calder have all contributed to this extraordinary trail with their world famous creations. In April 2016 Monaco celebrated its first ever Nuit Blanche, an invitation for all lovers of contemporary art to head out into the streets of Monaco for a night of surprises, exhibitions, performances, concerts, and innovative shows.

Another route proposed in 2007 as part of the exhibition The Grace Kelly Years, Princess of Monaco aimed to continue this tradition while paying tribute to the woman who helped raise the Principality's international reputation. The three-and-a-half-mile Princess Grace trail comprises twenty stops at some of the Principality's most famous sites, featuring photos and captions that explain Grace Kelly's contribution through charitable actions, inaugurations, and commemorations. Stretching from the Grace Kelly Rose Garden in Fontvieille in the west, to the Sporting Club in the east, then returning via the boulevard des Moulins to the Jardin Exotique, the trail includes a stop at the Opéra de Monte-Carlo to remember the fiftieth anniversary of the Ballets Russes, which was celebrated by a performance of *Prelude to the Afternoon of a Faun* by Serge Lifar in 1969.

In an effort to revisit the concept of heritage and use it to drive a new outlook on the future, the Principality opened the Nouveau Musée National de Monaco (NMNM) in 2010, which presents temporary exhibitions of modern and original art at two historic sites: Villa Sauber and Villa Paloma. Villa Sauber is a superb Belle Époque villa and former home of London painter Robert Sauber. It was built around 1900, possibly by Charles Garnier, near Larvotto Beach, which was then just a small dirt road along the sea. Visitors can now climb a few steps into a citrus garden before entering the villa and a world of imaginative visual design and performance. Villa Paloma is near the Jardin Exotique. Across an "antique-style" garden designed by Octave Godard, protégé of the landscape architect Édouard André, visitors find themselves on a terrace with a stunning view. Dating from about 1913, the villa still retains its original stained glass, columns, and mosaics. Inside, the exhibition spans three floors and reveals a little-known collection and heritage. On the terrace and in the garden, visitors can sit and contemplate what they have just seen in front of a majestic panorama that takes in the Rock, the harbors, and the crowns of olive trees in Princess Antoinette Park, ensuring they remain part of Monaco's heritage too.

Previous spread. Under the sun, the silhouette of the statue of Prince Rainier III by Daphné du Barry looks out over Fontvieille's harbor from the palace gardens. December 28, 2015, 10:18 a.m.

Like an apparition, Princess Grace of Monaco, sculpted by Kees Verkade, serenely contemplates her favorite flowers in the rose garden in Fontvieille that bears her name. April 25, 2016, 4:06 p.m.

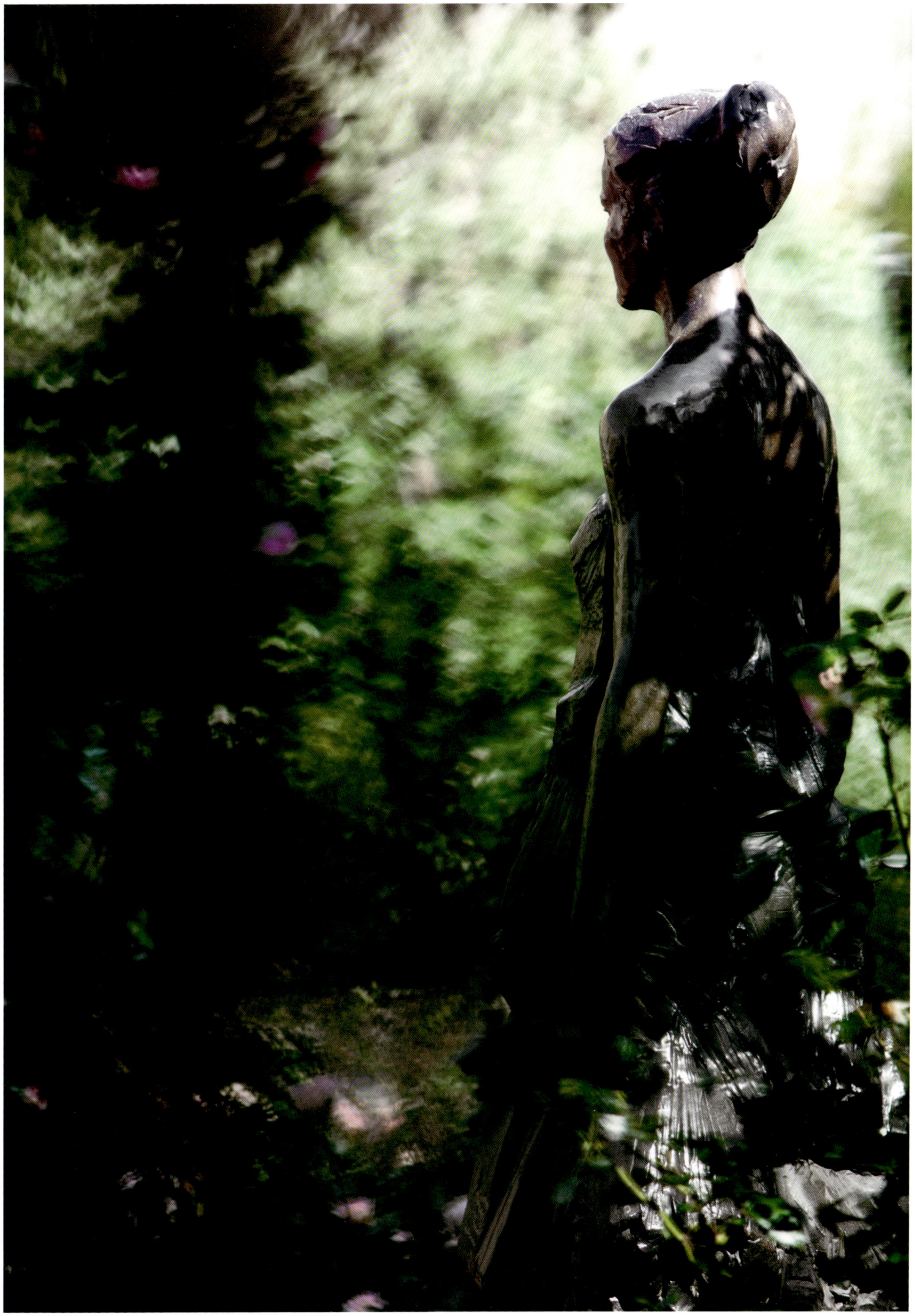

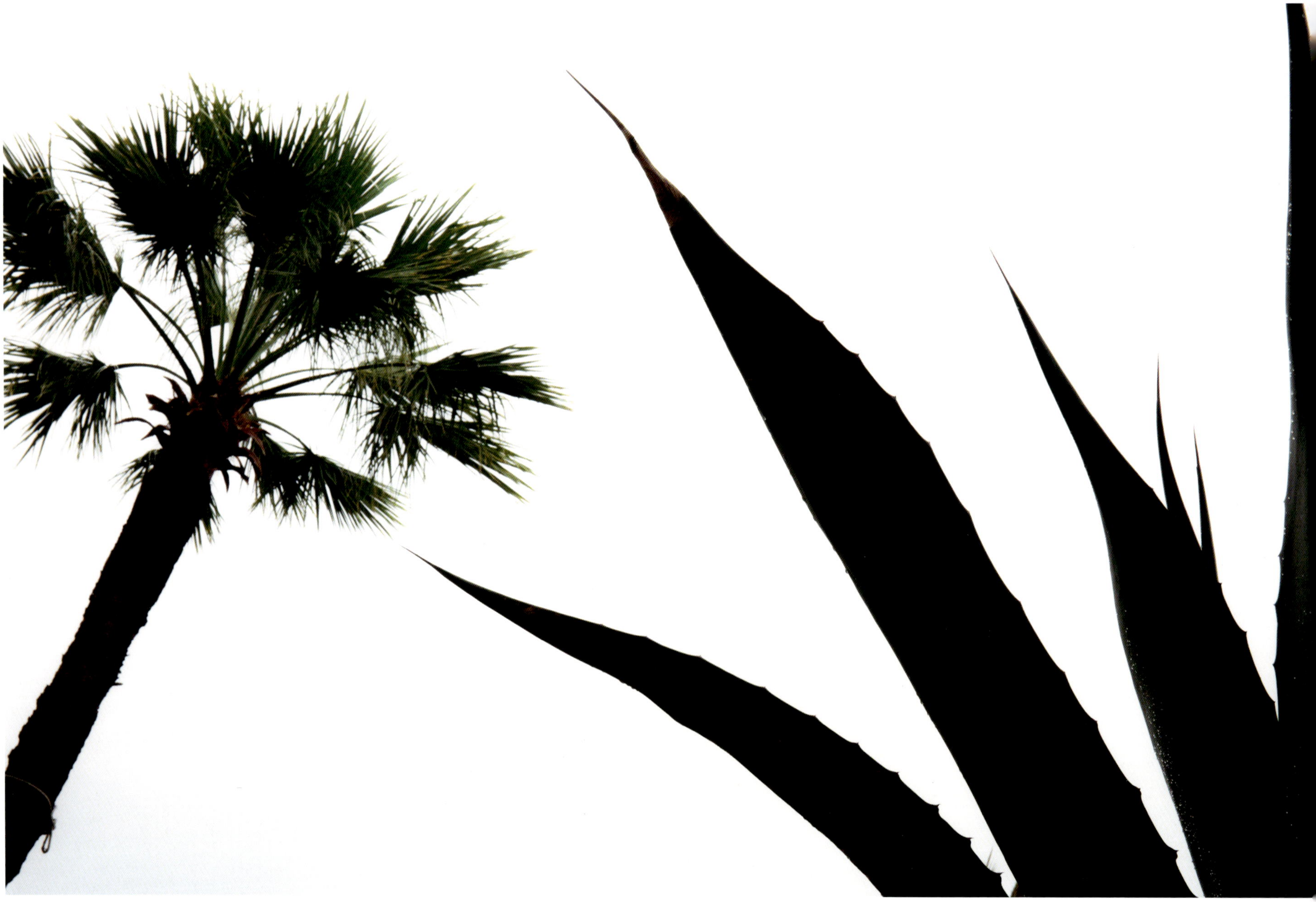

At the water's edge, two of nature's stars put on their daily show against an ever-changing backdrop of color. Left page, September 13, 2015, 12:00 p.m. Right page, September 14, 2015, 5:53 p.m.

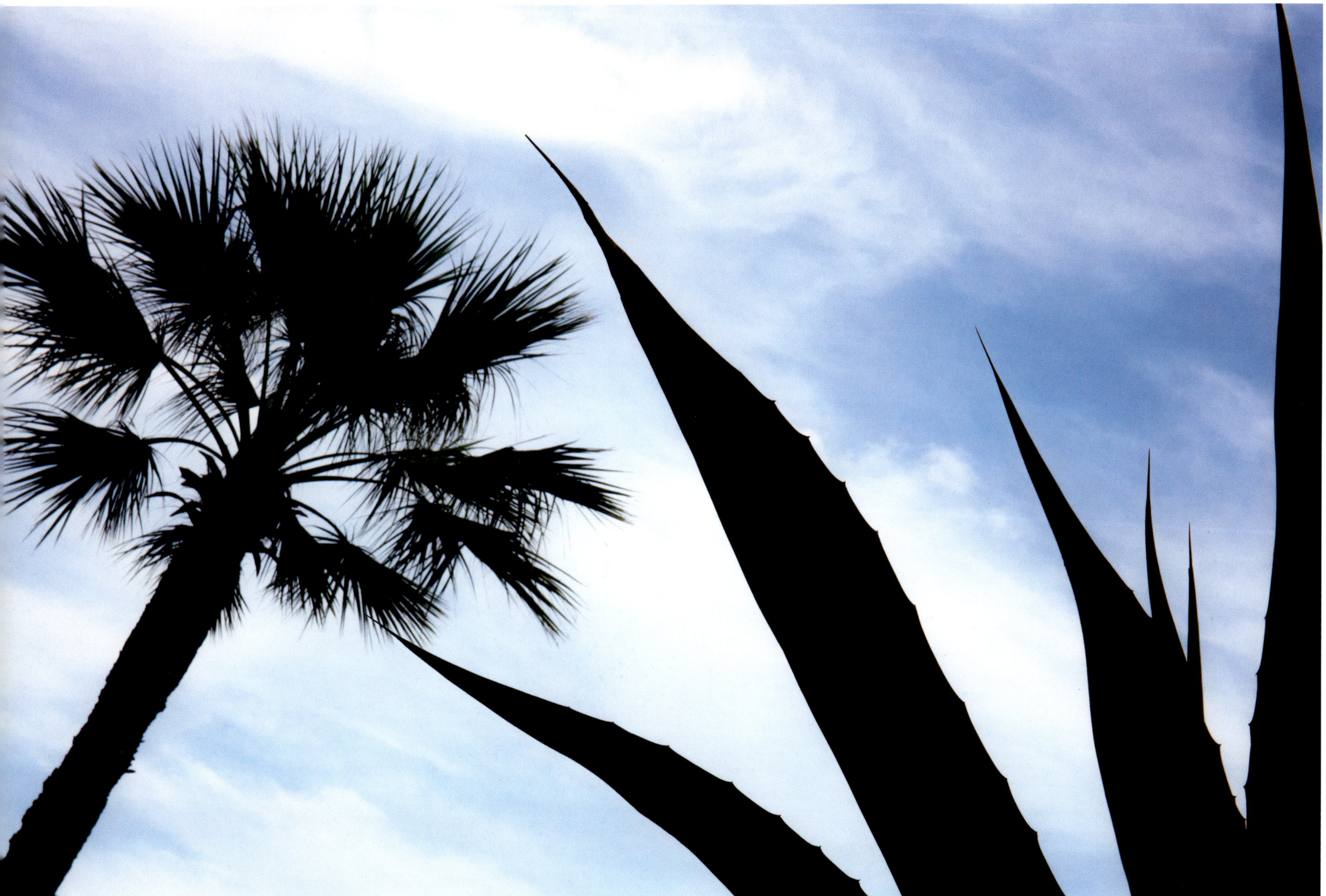

Following spread. Sculpted by François Cogné, Prince Albert I stands at the wheel of *Hirondelle* as it sets sail from the Oceanographic Museum.
Left page, June 22, 2015, 5:02 p.m. Right page, September 23, 2015, 10:36 a.m.

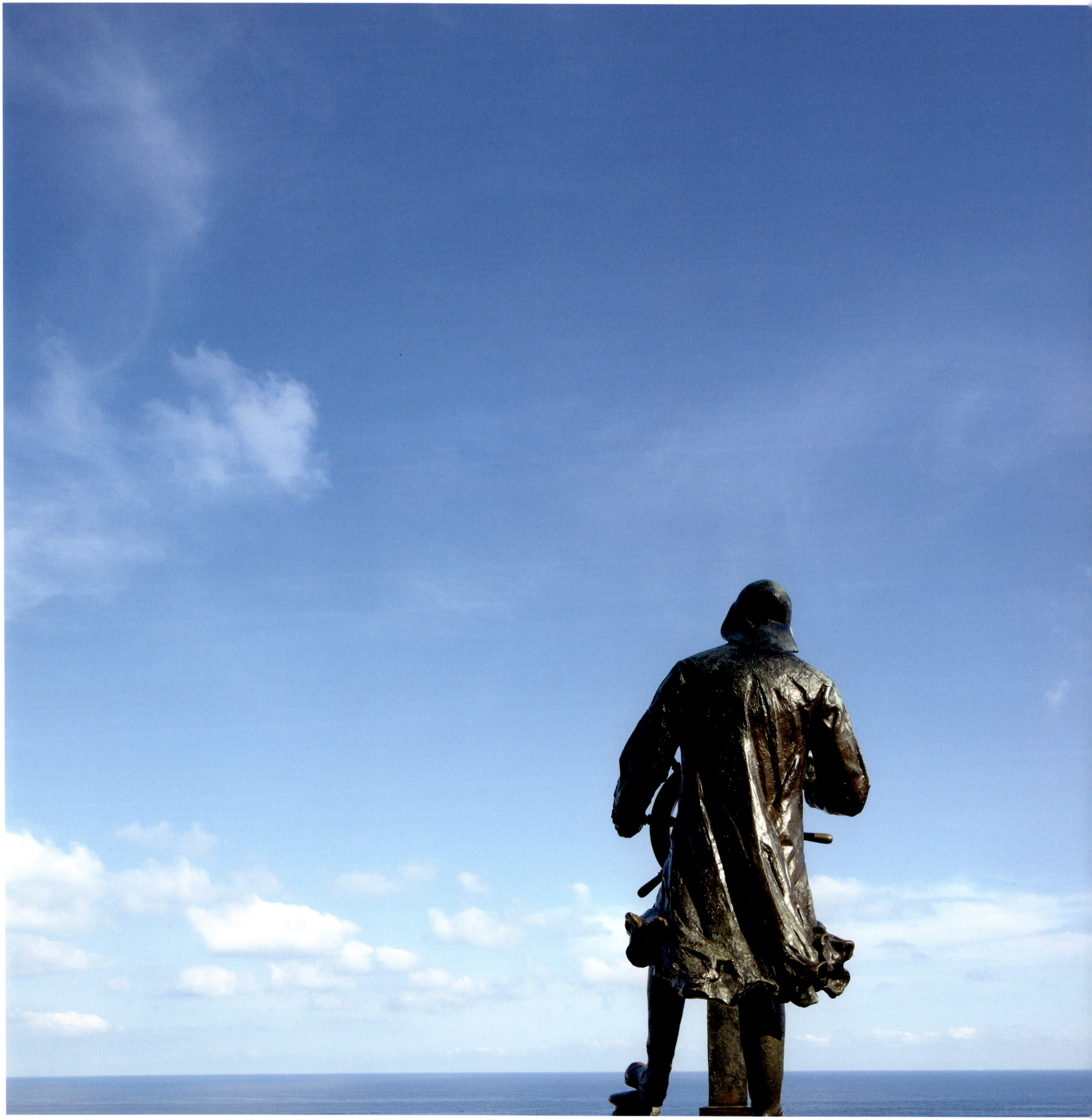

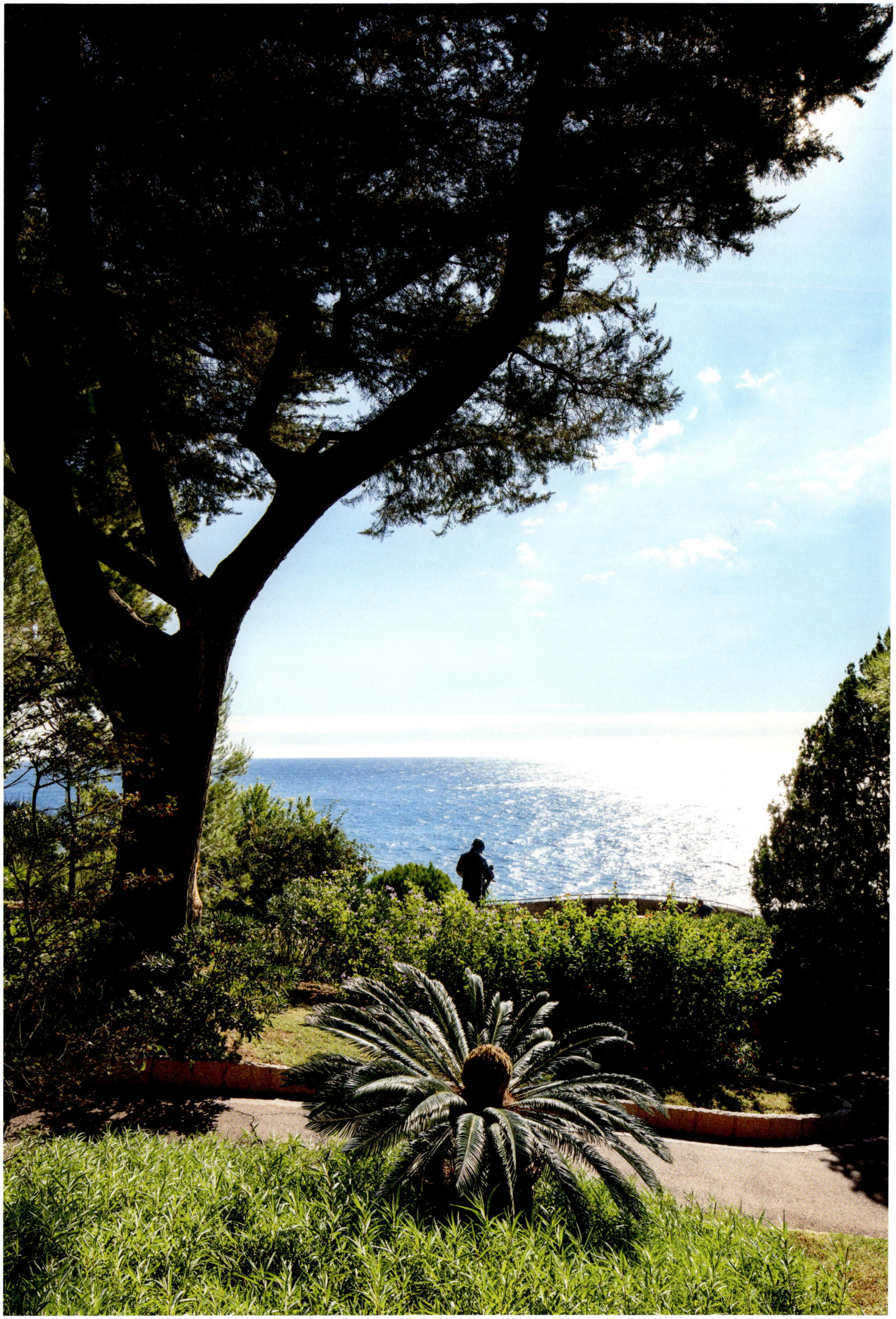

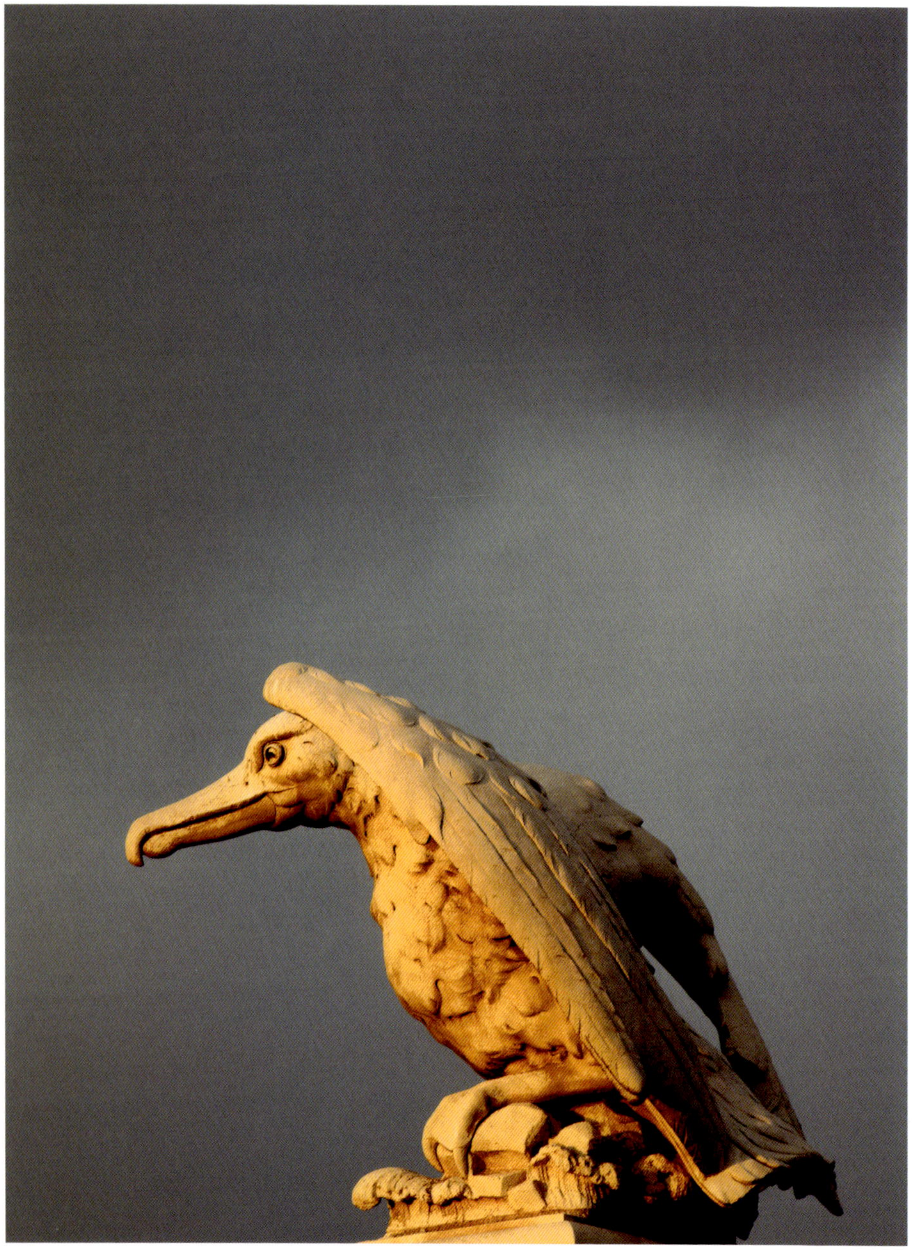

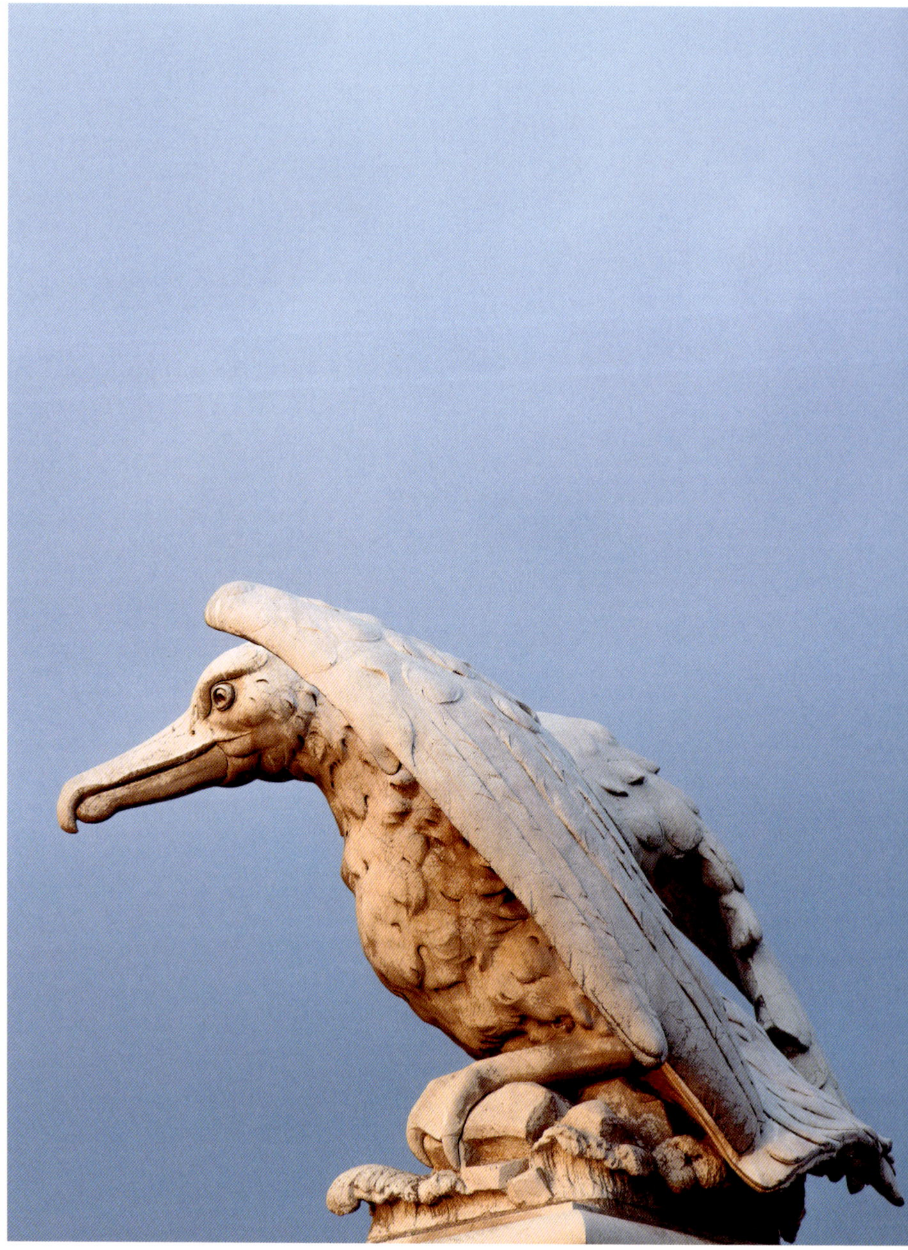

An albatross on the roof of the Oceanographic Museum wears the colors of the passing hours.
From left to right: January 31, 2016, 5:22 p.m., 5:31 p.m., and 5:41 p.m.;
February 4, 2016, 2:14 p.m.

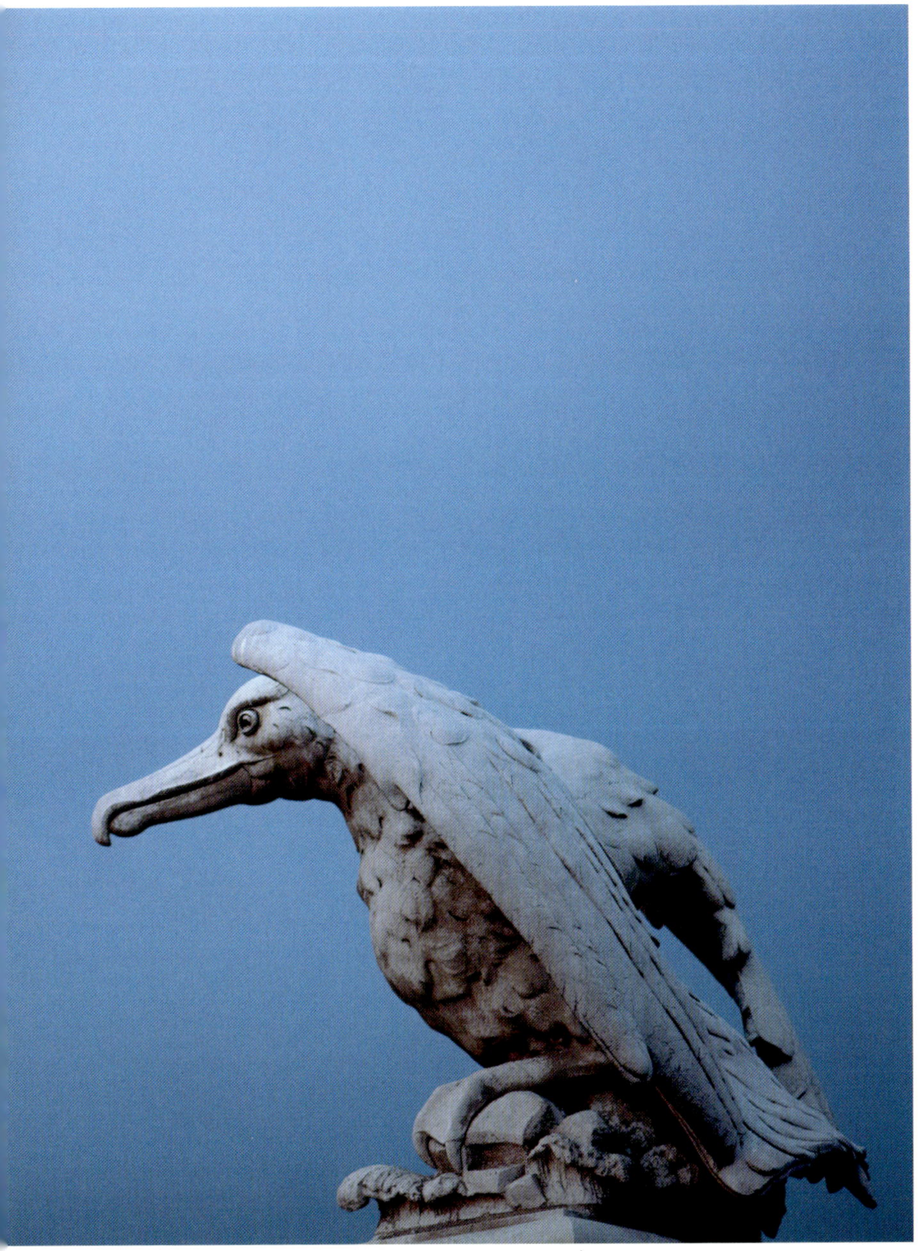
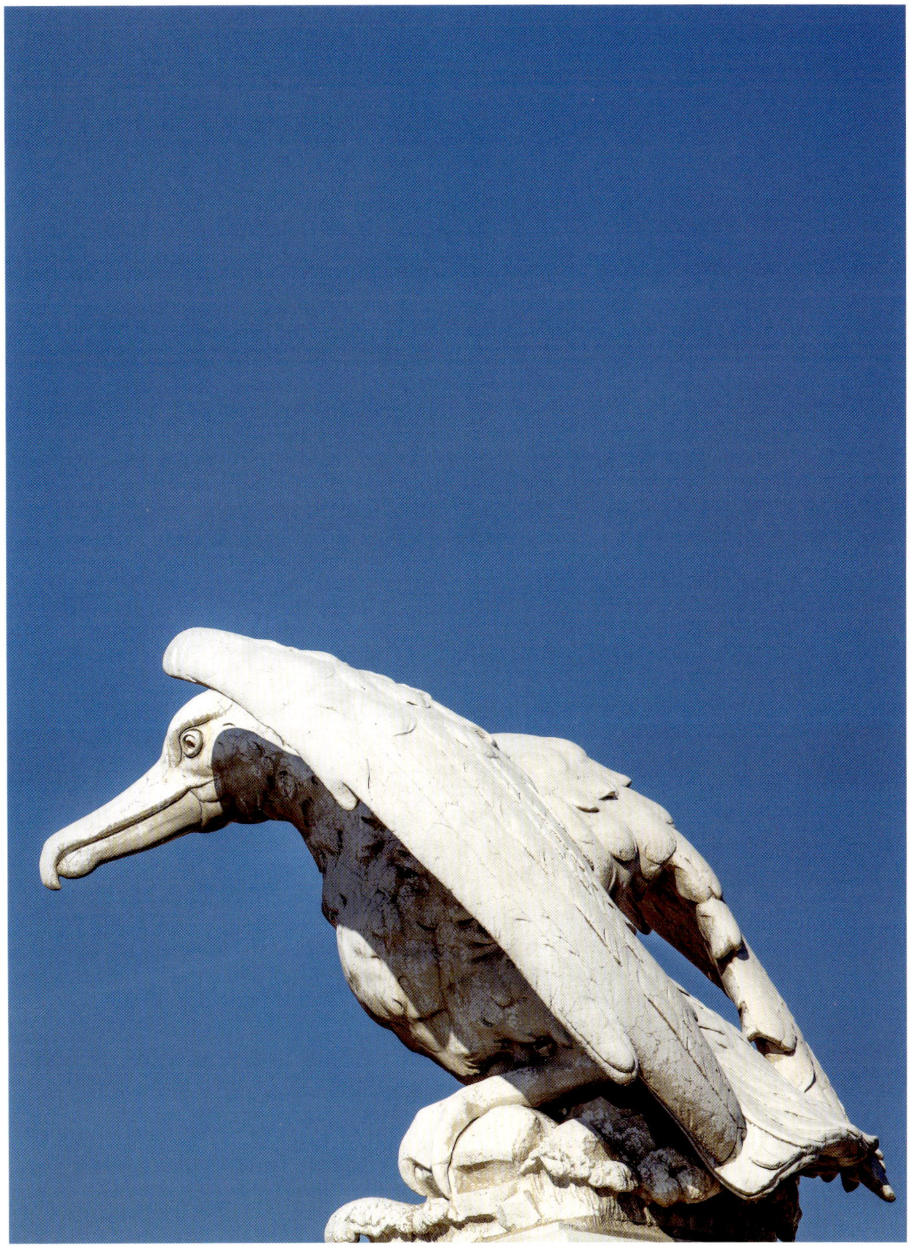

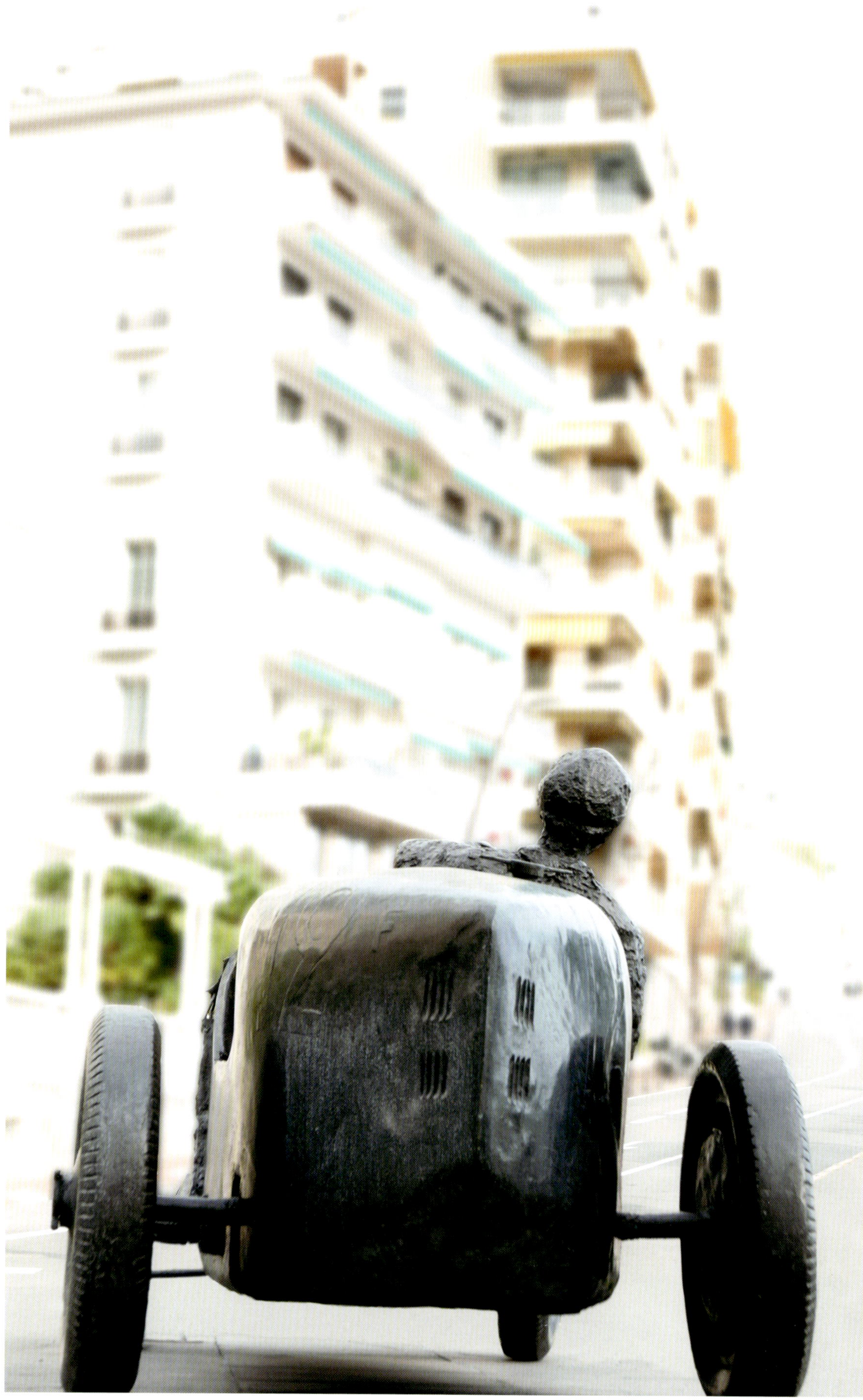

Color effects between sculptures and modern façades. François Chevallier's Bugatti 35B gets ready to race down avenue d'Ostende; while Thalia, the Muse of comedy, brandishes her flame in front of the Théâtre des Muses on boulevard du Jardin Exotique. Left page, November 29, 2015, 1:56 p.m. Right page, January 26, 2016, 12:51 p.m.

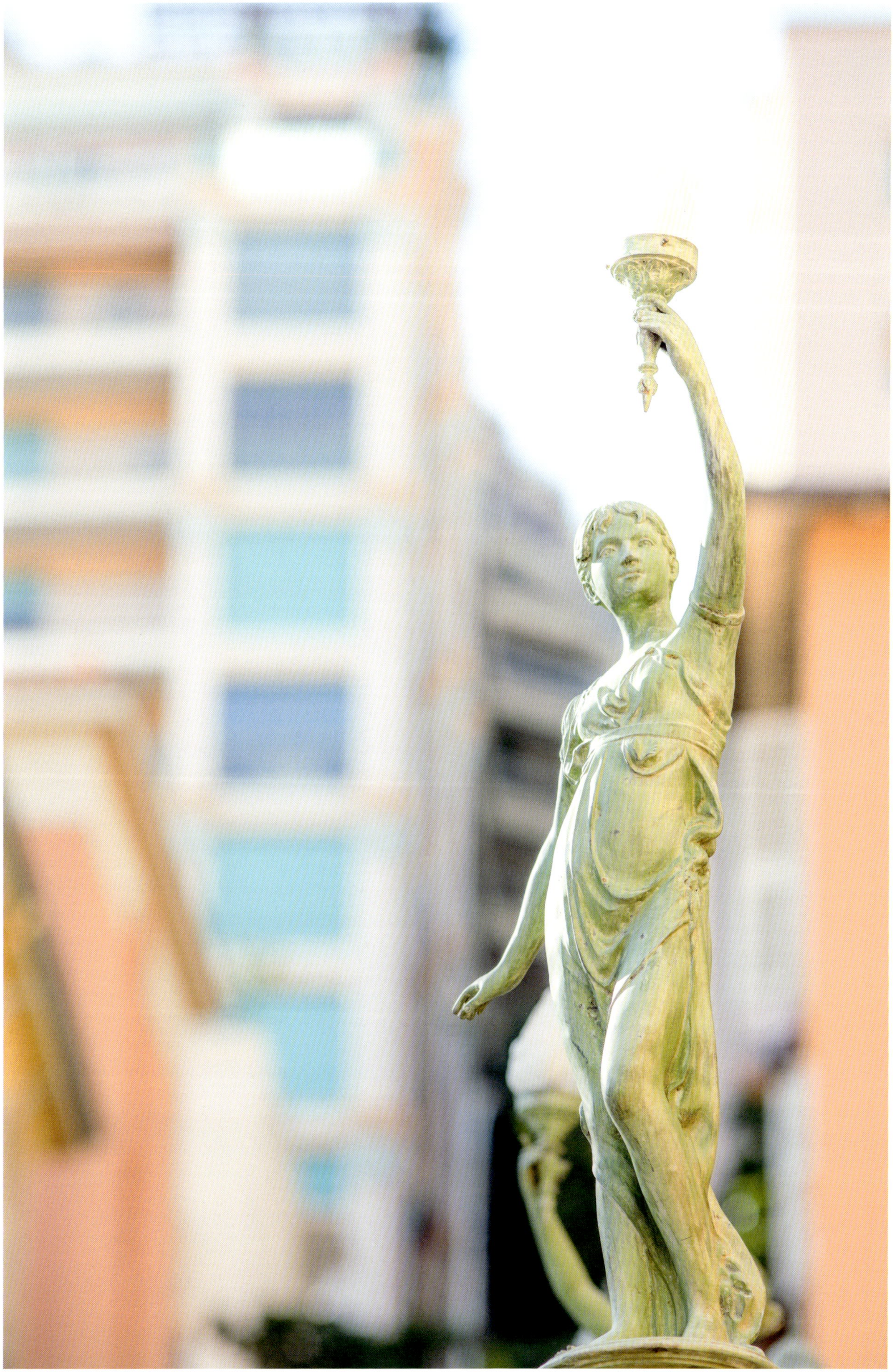

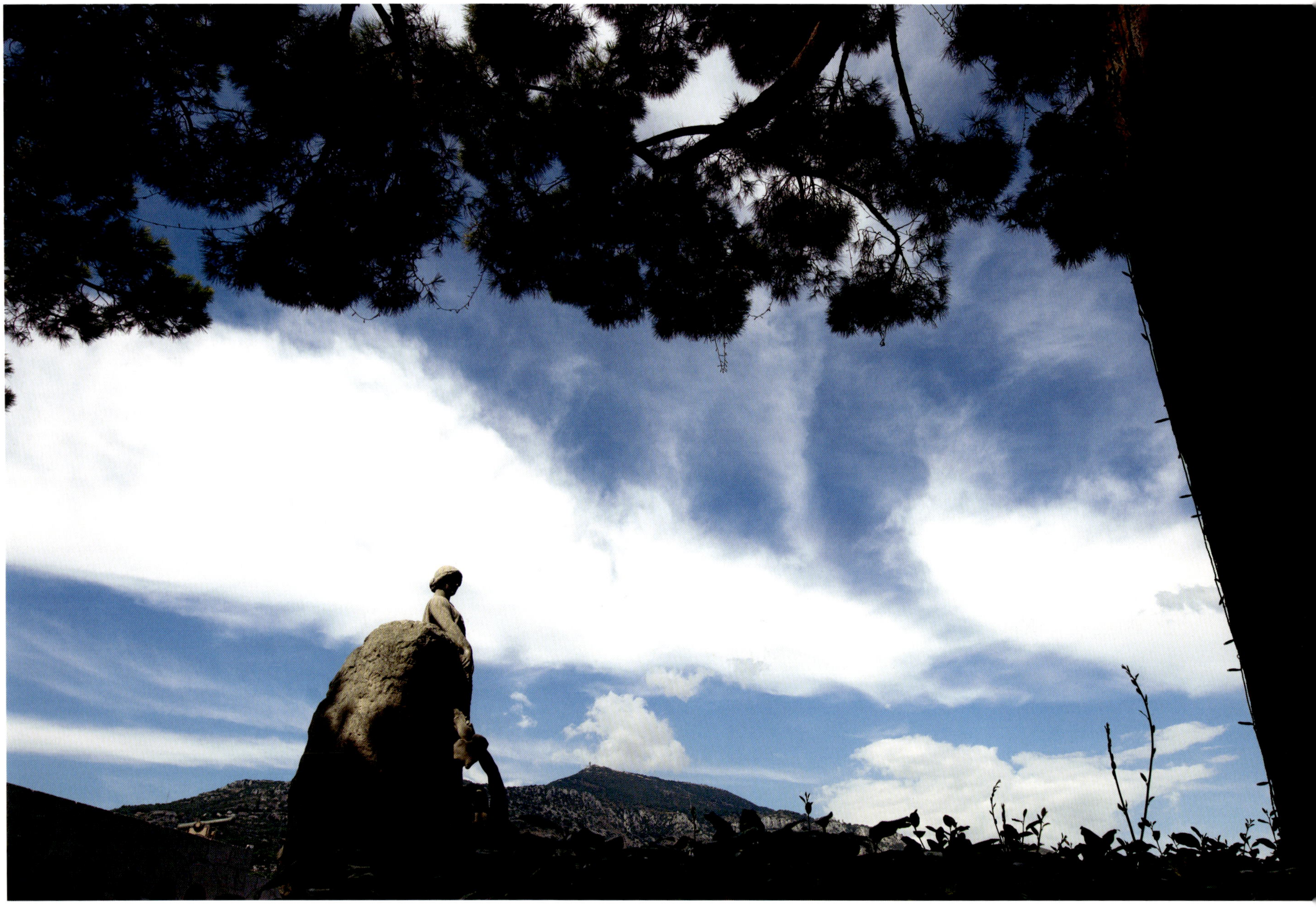

Oleanders and pine trees frame *Science Discovering the Riches of the Ocean* by Constant Roux in Place du Palais. Left page, August 20, 2015, 3:11 p.m. Right page, April 25, 2016, 5:25 p.m.

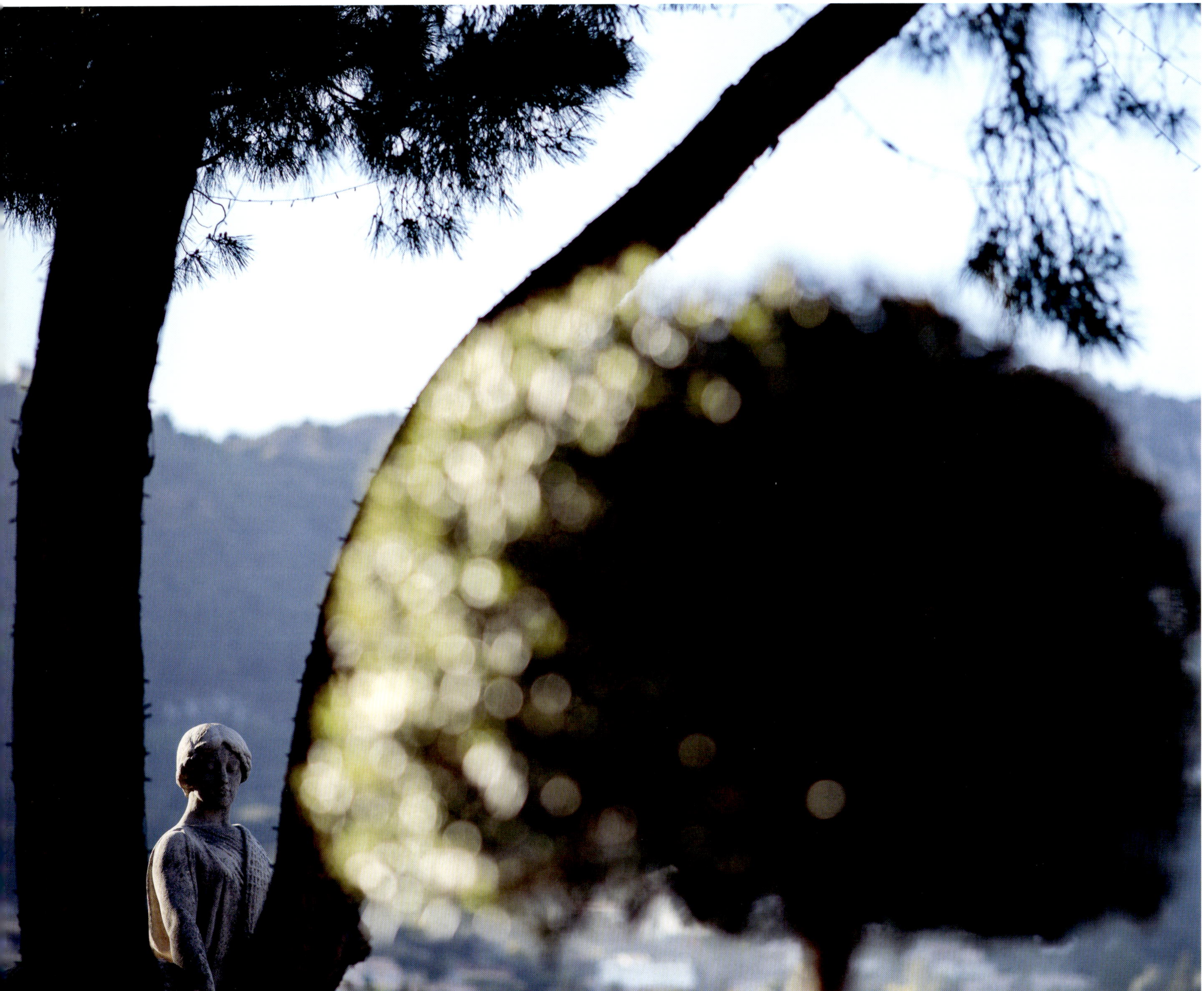

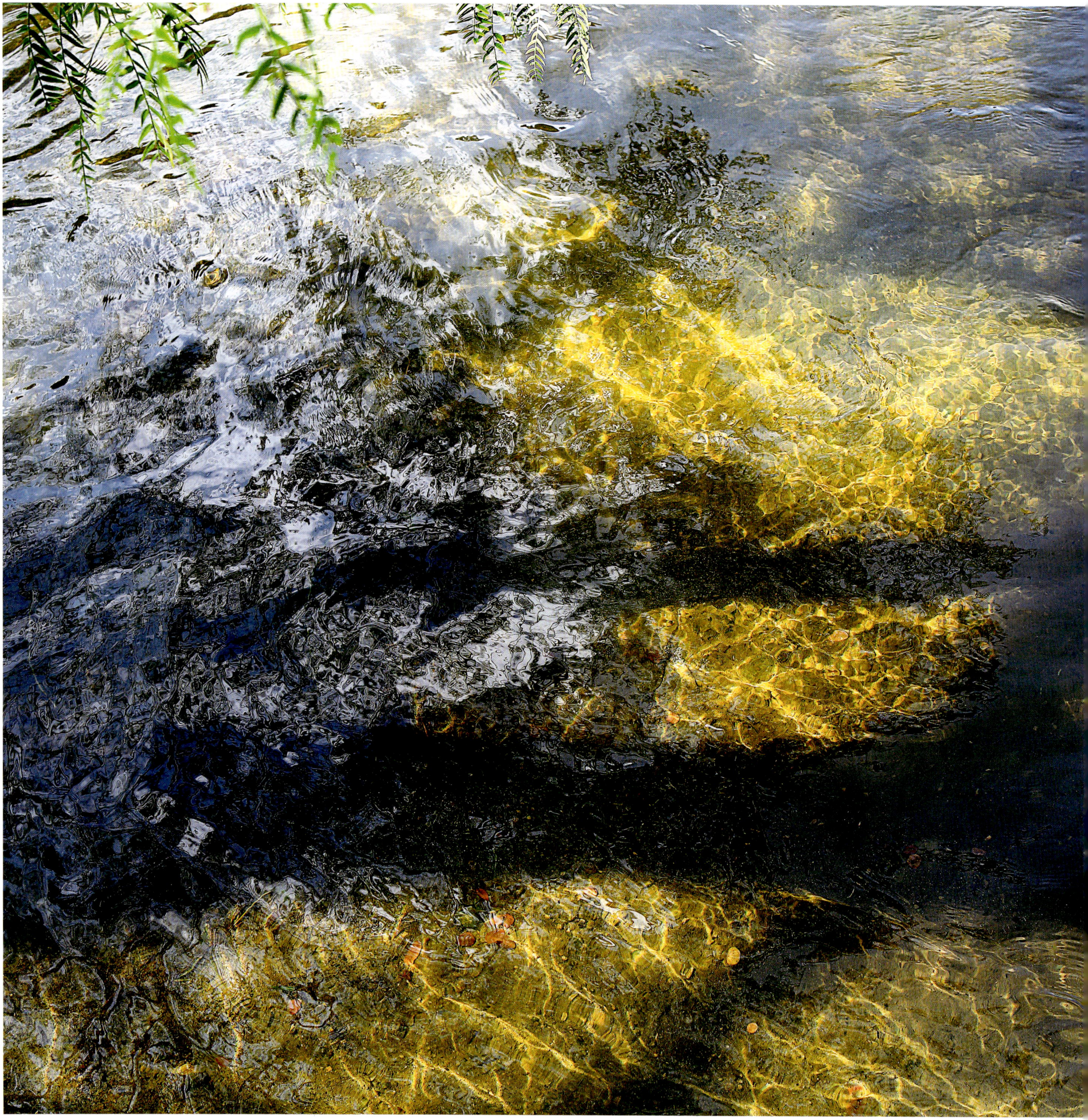

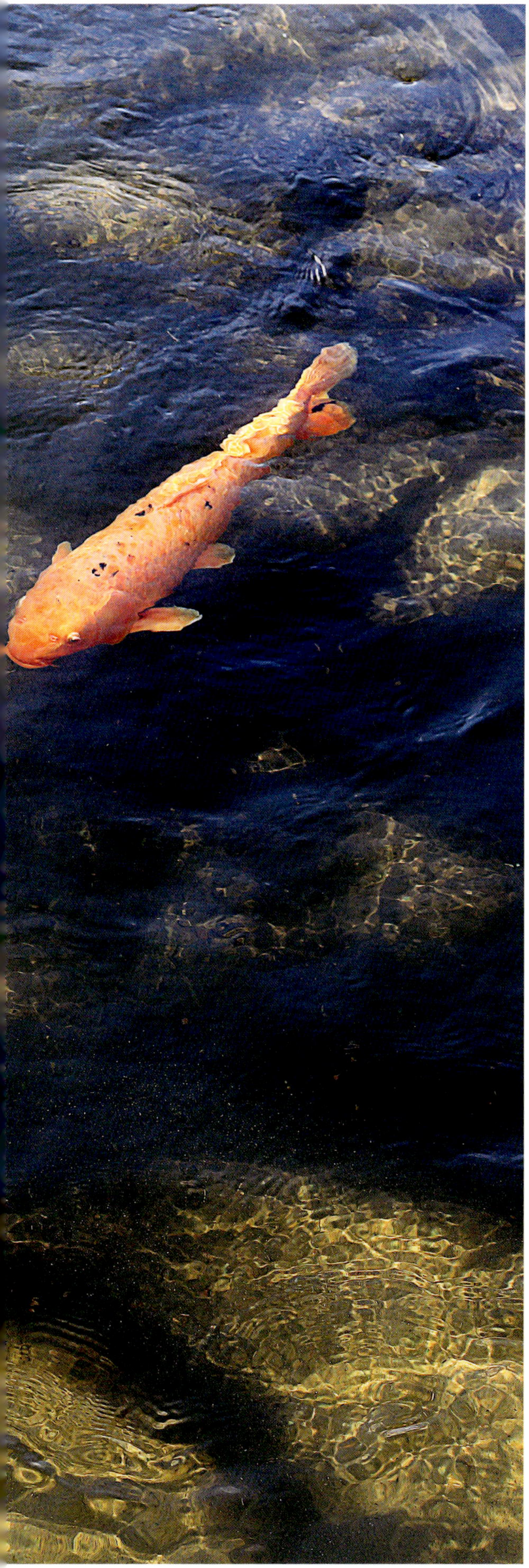

VII

CAPTIVATING MOMENTS

Those who walk around Monaco will encounter exquisite little moments that seem to mute the bustle and slow the pace of the surrounding city. Sitting on a bench in the Japanese garden is an unforgettable escape, where the singing of birds, wind in the foliage, and lapping of water combine to replace noise from the street. Plunging into the depths of the Oceanographic Museum to witness the dance of marine creatures in the silent shadows is a fascinating and enlightening voyage into the world's seas.

Similar emotions are evoked at one of the grand shows of the country, where art is an inseparable part of its heritage. Witnessing an enchanting performance at the Opéra de Monte-Carlo, founded in 1879 by the Société des Bains de Mer, is a magical experience in an unrivaled setting overlooking the sea. Sitting in front of the red curtain of this elegant theater, it feels like an honor to respect the traditions of the court of Antoine I, the Musician Prince. Words from *Deianira*, *Don Quixote*, or *The Child and the Spells*—major operatic works that were performed here for the first time—spring to mind, as do the famous artists who have graced the venue with their presence: Alphonse Visconti, Léon Barsacq, Picasso, and the star of Diaghilev's Ballets Russes in particular, Vaslav Nijinsky.

Ballet has been an integral part of Monegasque tradition ever since. The current company, directed by Jean-Christophe Maillot, includes an academy, holds a festival every year, and regularly tours the globe to perform its original choreography. A short walk from the opera house, the former Théâtre des Beaux Arts, founded by the SBM in 1930 and unused since 1958, was renamed the Théâtre Princess Grace in 1981 in honor of her involvement in its restoration. The theater features a varied artistic program with a special emphasis on plays. For classical music, amateur and professional theater, movies, and conferences, there is the Théâtre des Variétés in La Condamine. And for something more eclectic, the Théâtre des Muses on boulevard du Jardin Exotique provides a stage for a fascinating program of performing arts. Just three years old, this one-hundred-seat theater built in a former bakery has big ideas for such a small place.

Previous spread. Morning colors in the reflections and translucent water of a koi pond in the Japanese garden. June 21, 2015, 9:05 a.m.

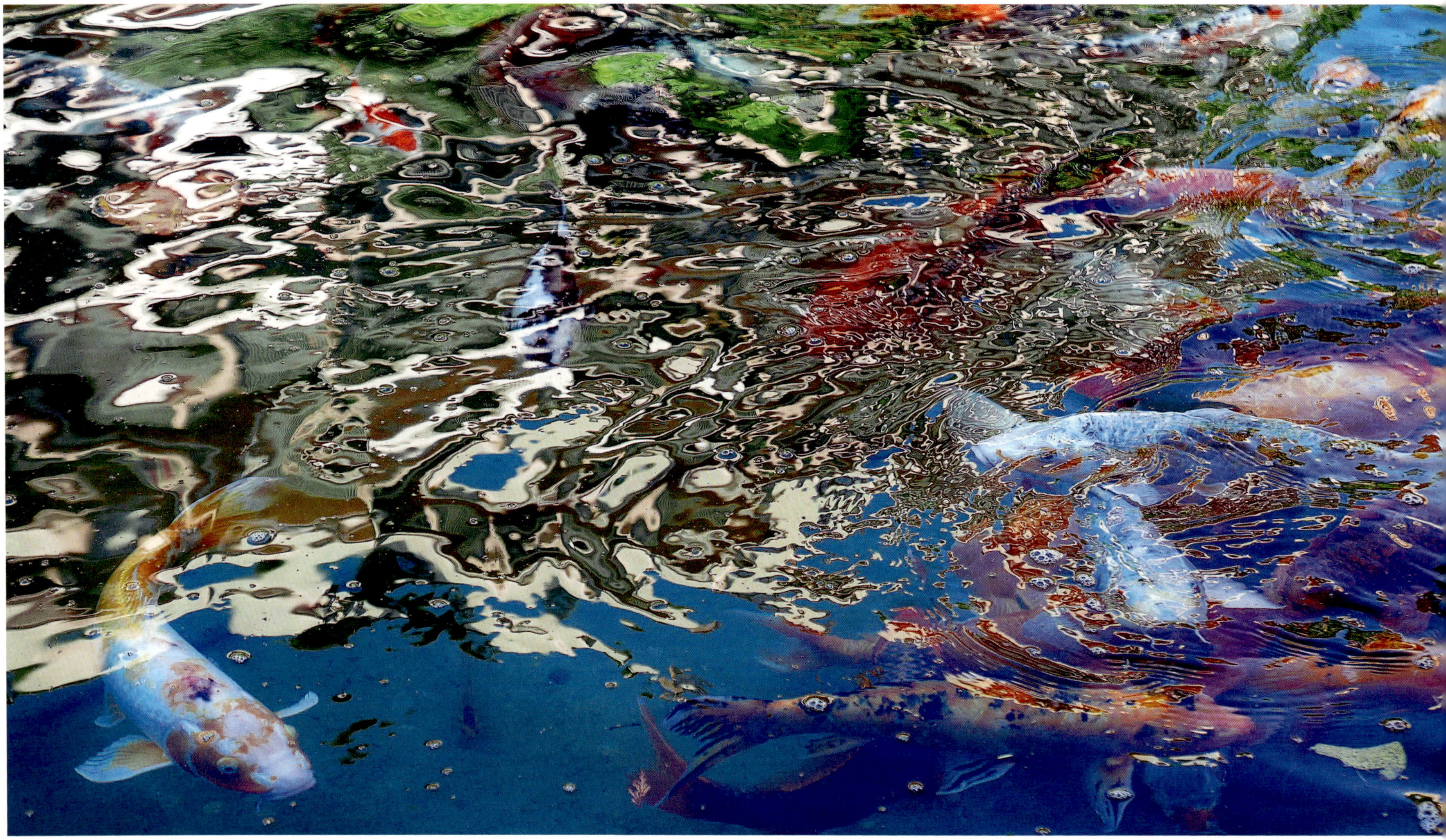

Koi glide and whirl around a Japanese garden pond, while roses bloom through the mist of a water jet in the Princess Grace Rose Garden.
Left page, December 2015, 1, 12:22 p.m. Right page, May 10, 2016, 4:33 p.m.

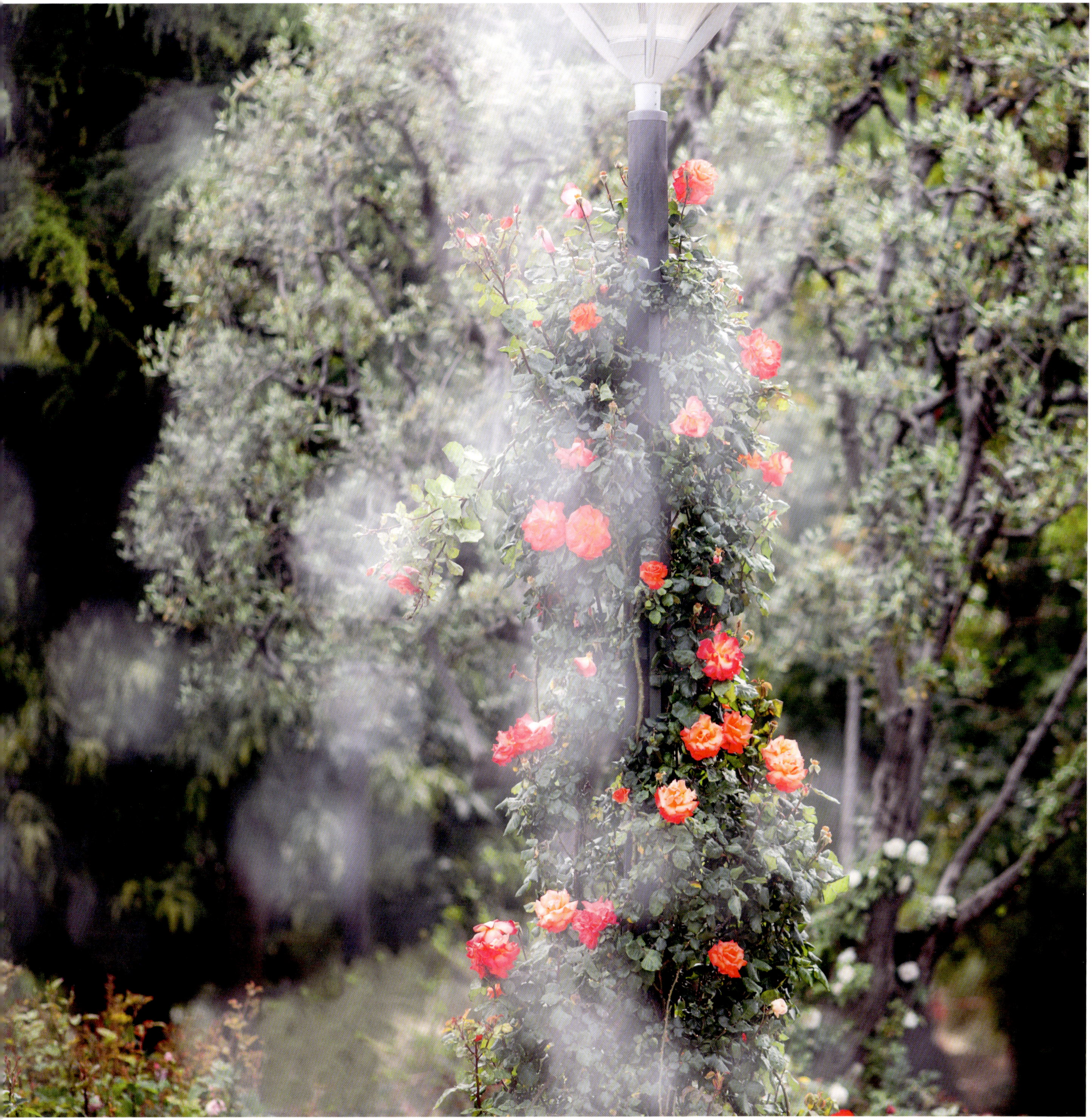

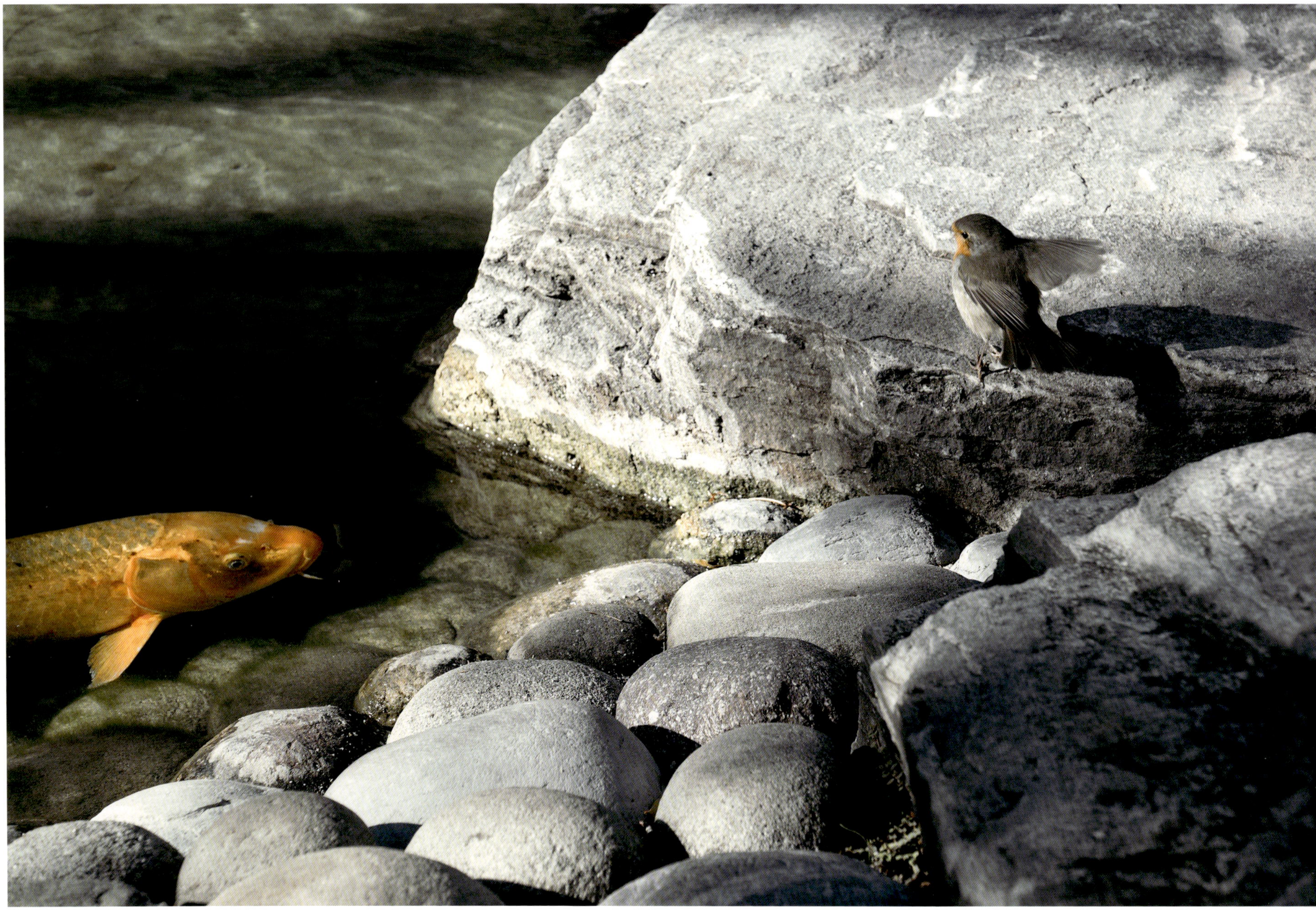

After waiting 15 minutes, the first moment of an encounter which results in a delightful face-to-face meeting! November 22, 2015. Left page, 12 seconds after 12:50 p.m.; right page, 13 seconds after 12:50 p.m.

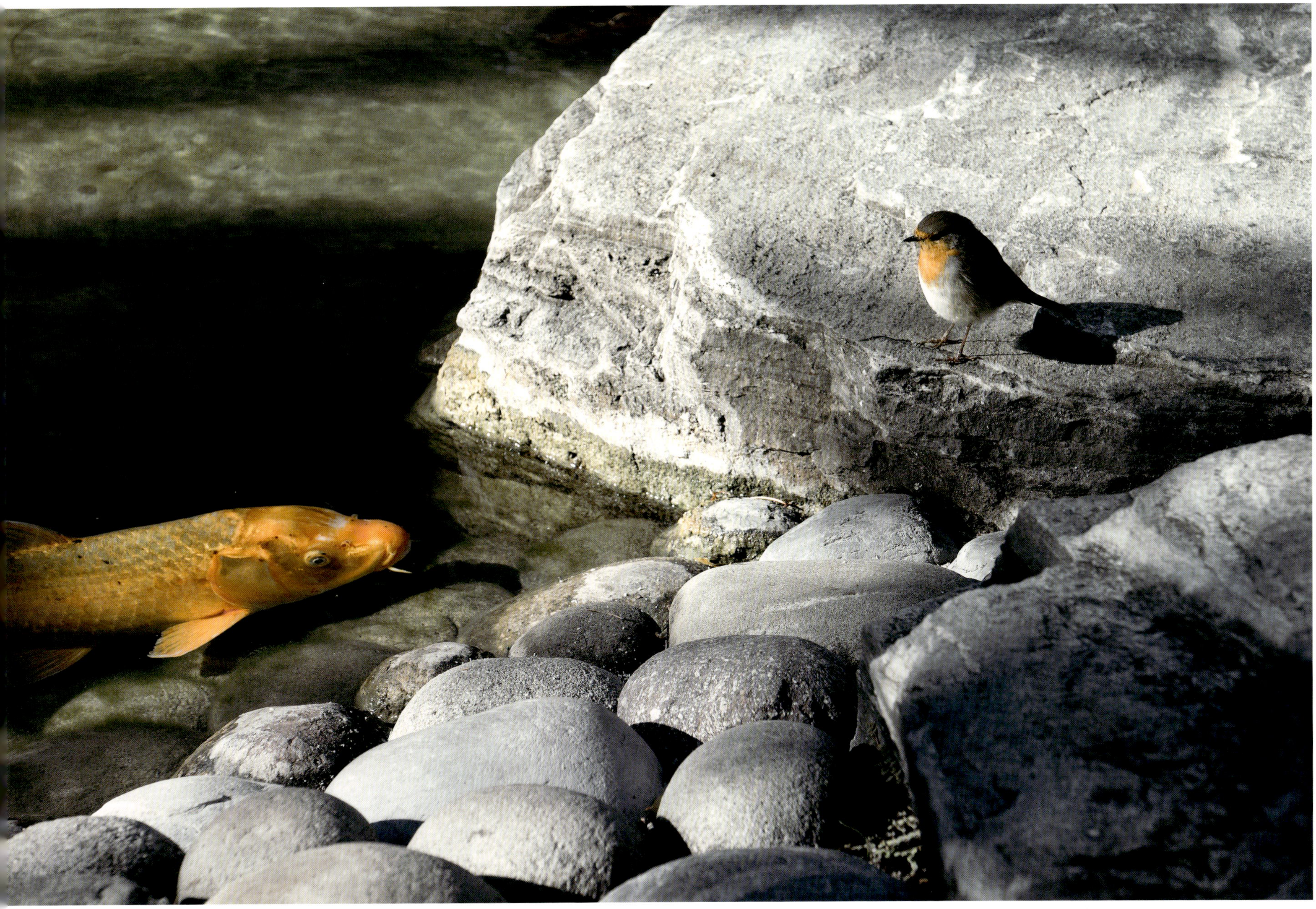

Following spread. The shark lagoon at the Oceanographic Museum provides an exhilarating sense of immersion in an underwater world. February 4, 2016. Left page, 4:27 p.m.; right page, 4:56 p.m.

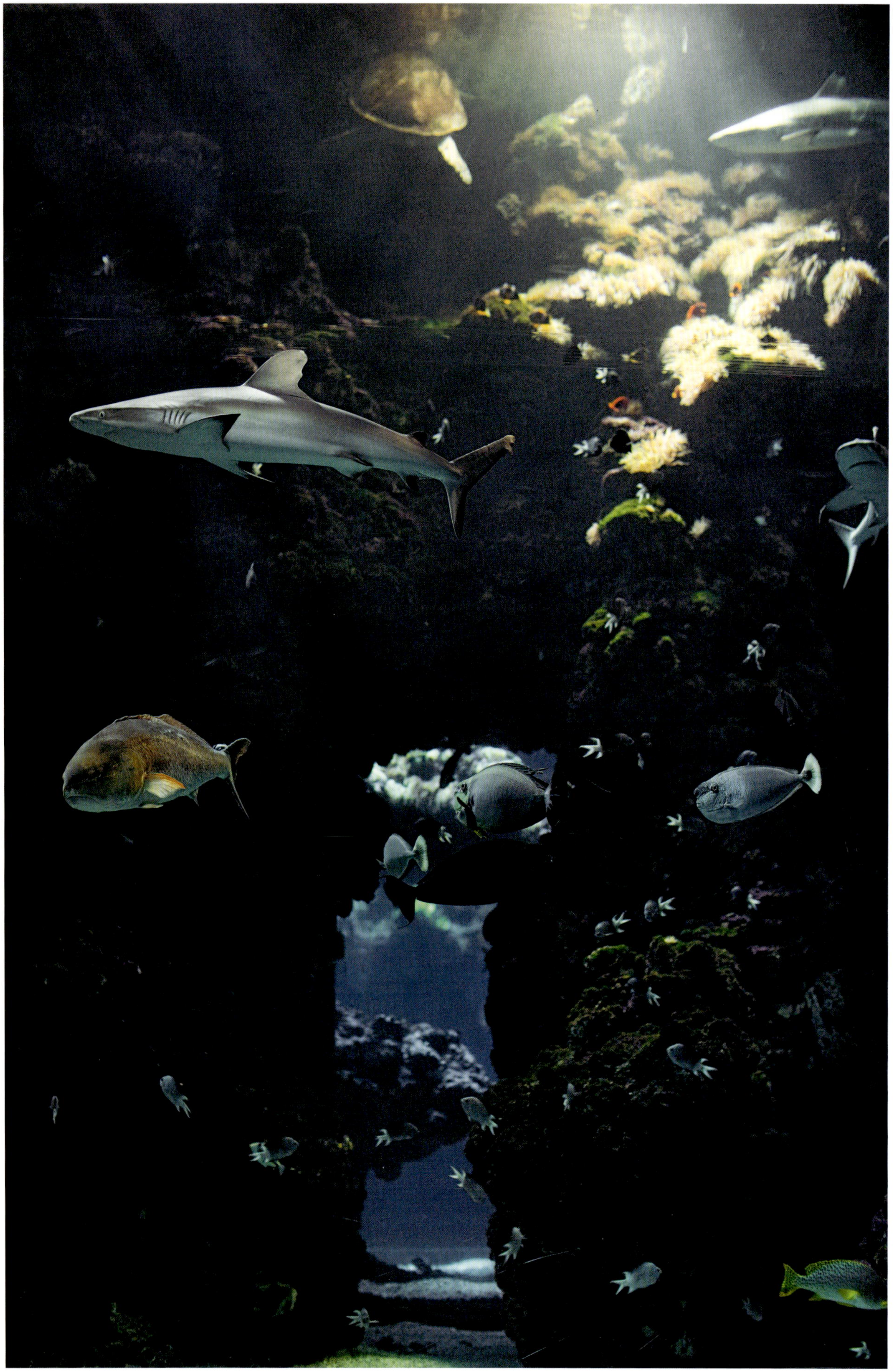
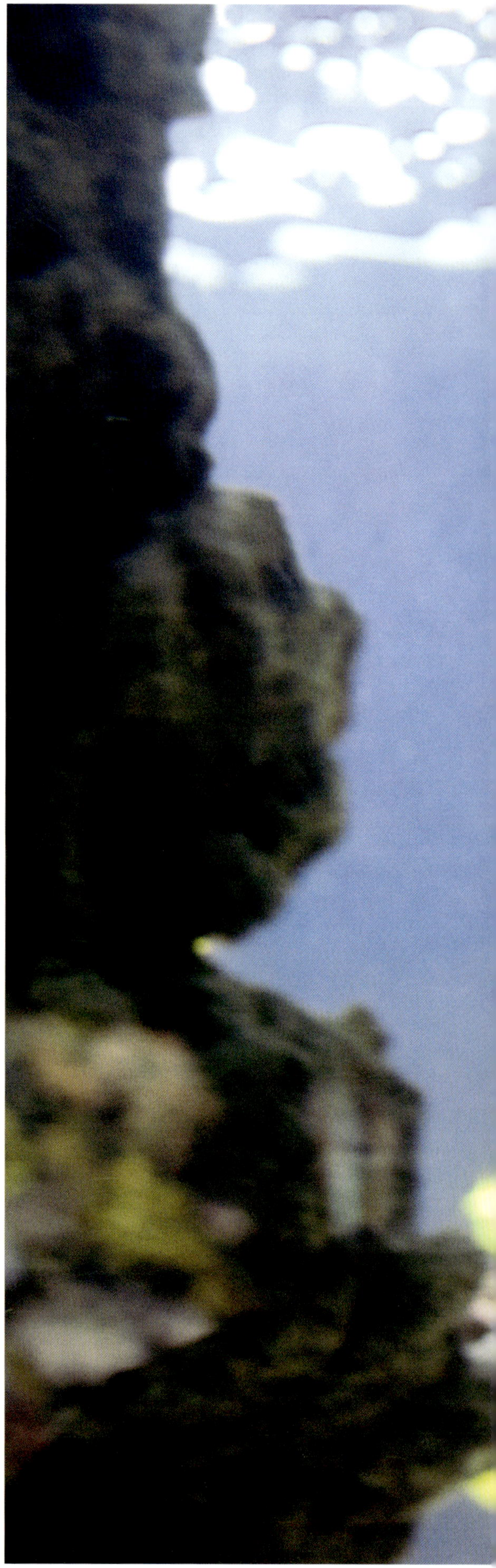

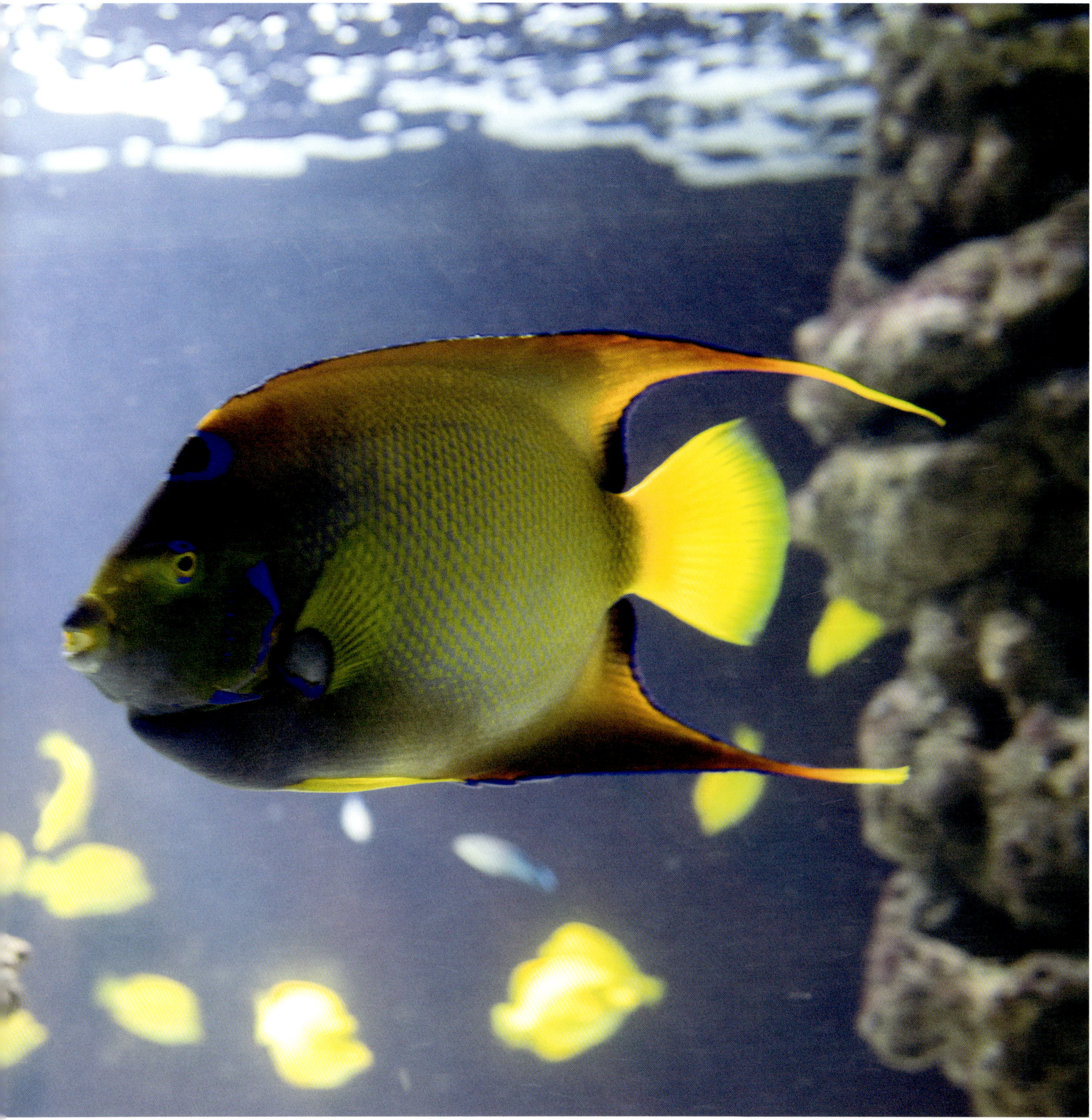

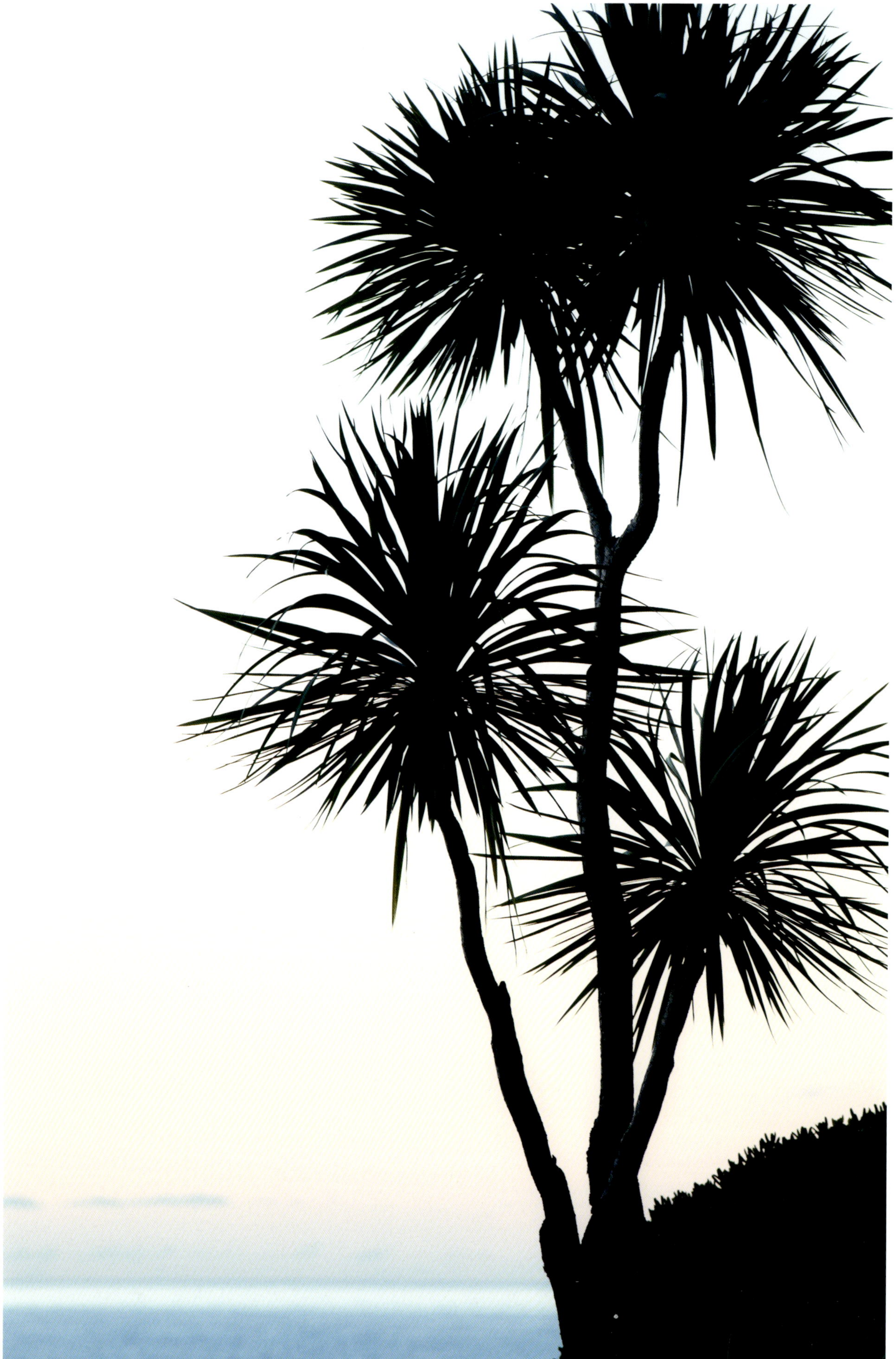

Trees show off their ornate silhouettes against a morning's pastel tones, as the sun's rays break through the clouds and shatter into millions of silver fragments on the sea.
Left page, December 1, 2015, 8:37 a.m. Right page, January 22, 2016, 11:20 a.m.

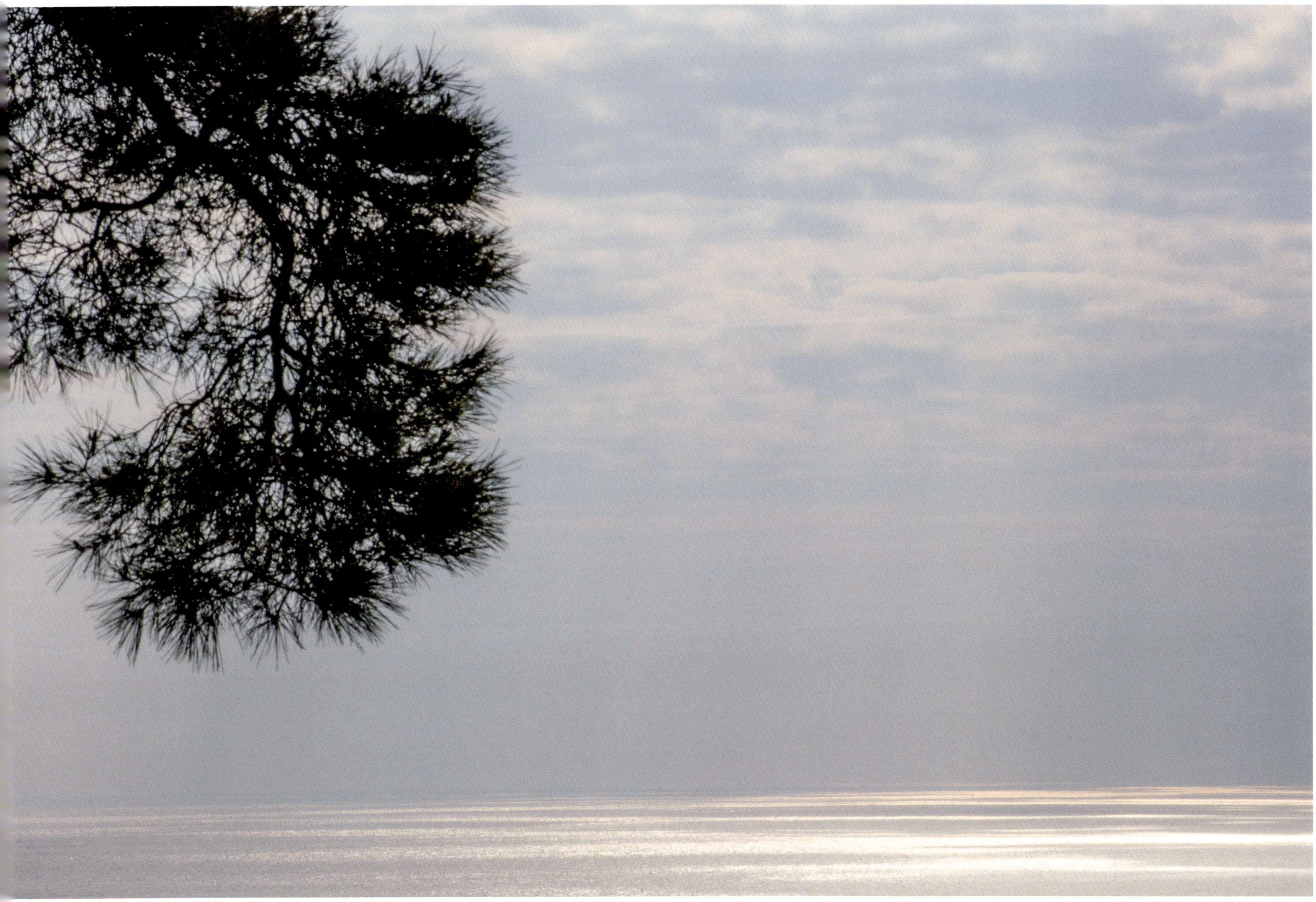

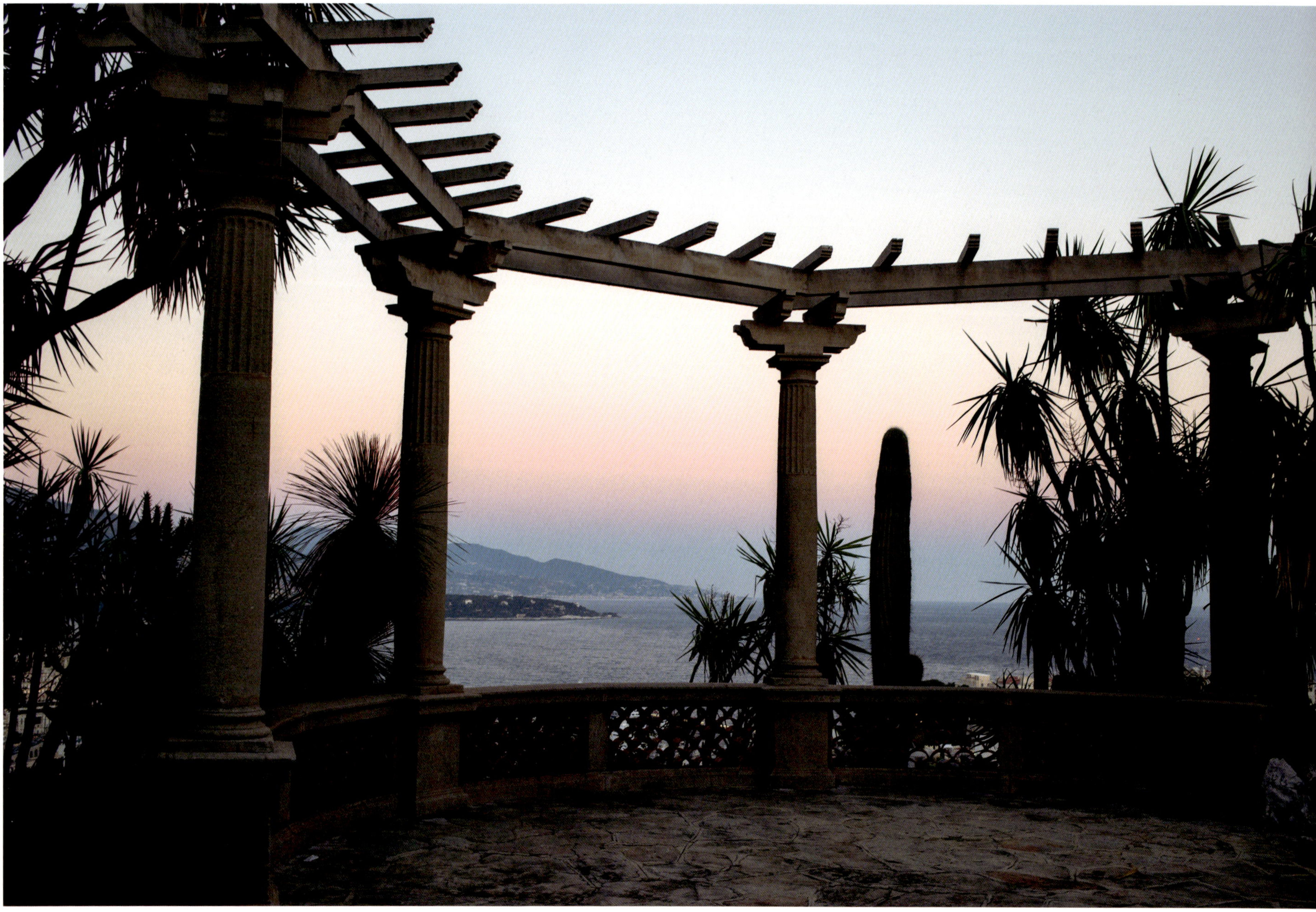

Leaving the Jardin Exotique, a pergola provides the setting for the arrival of dusk over Monaco and the French and Italian coasts.
October 31, 2015. Left page, 6:29 p.m.; right page, 6:50 p.m.

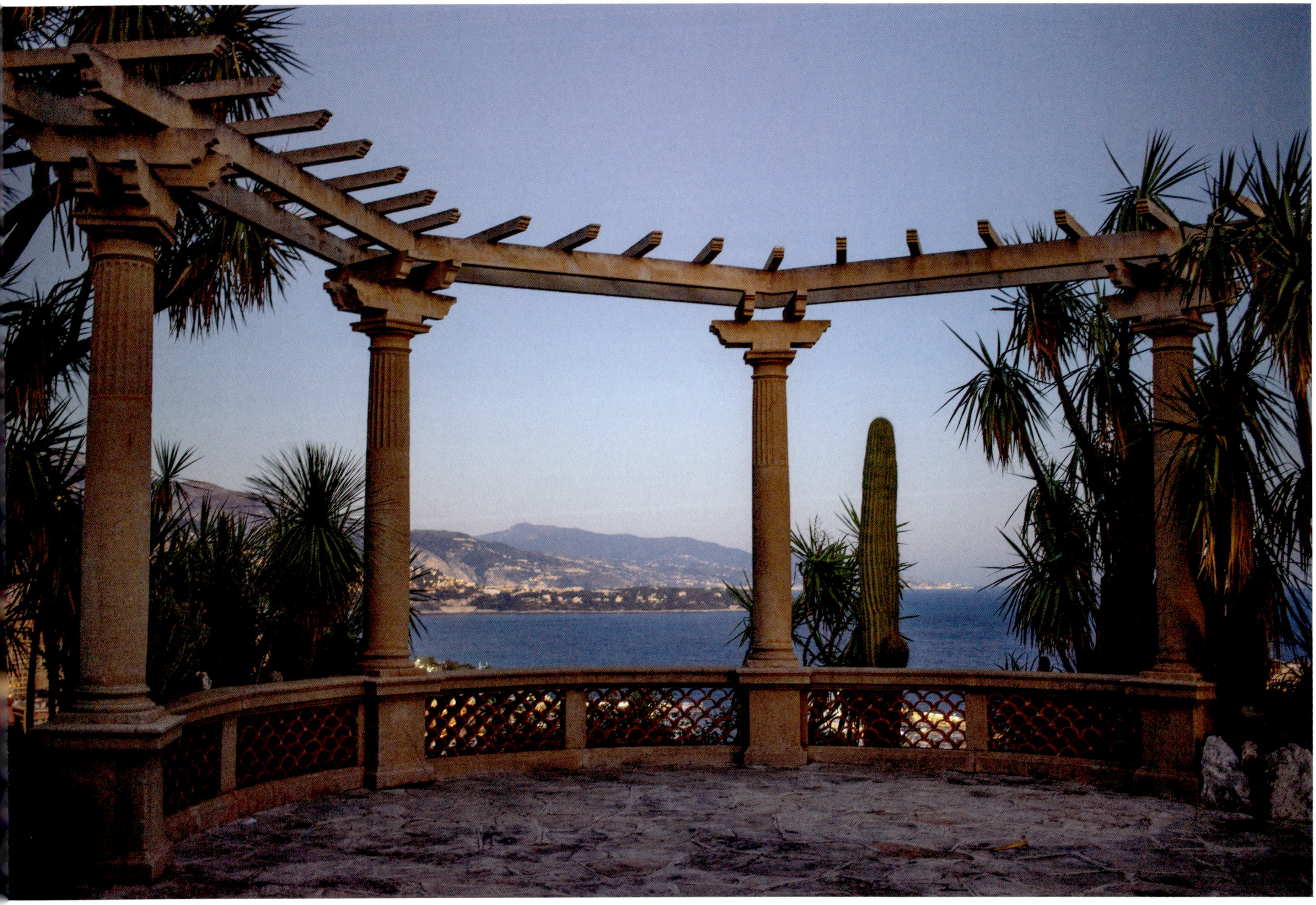

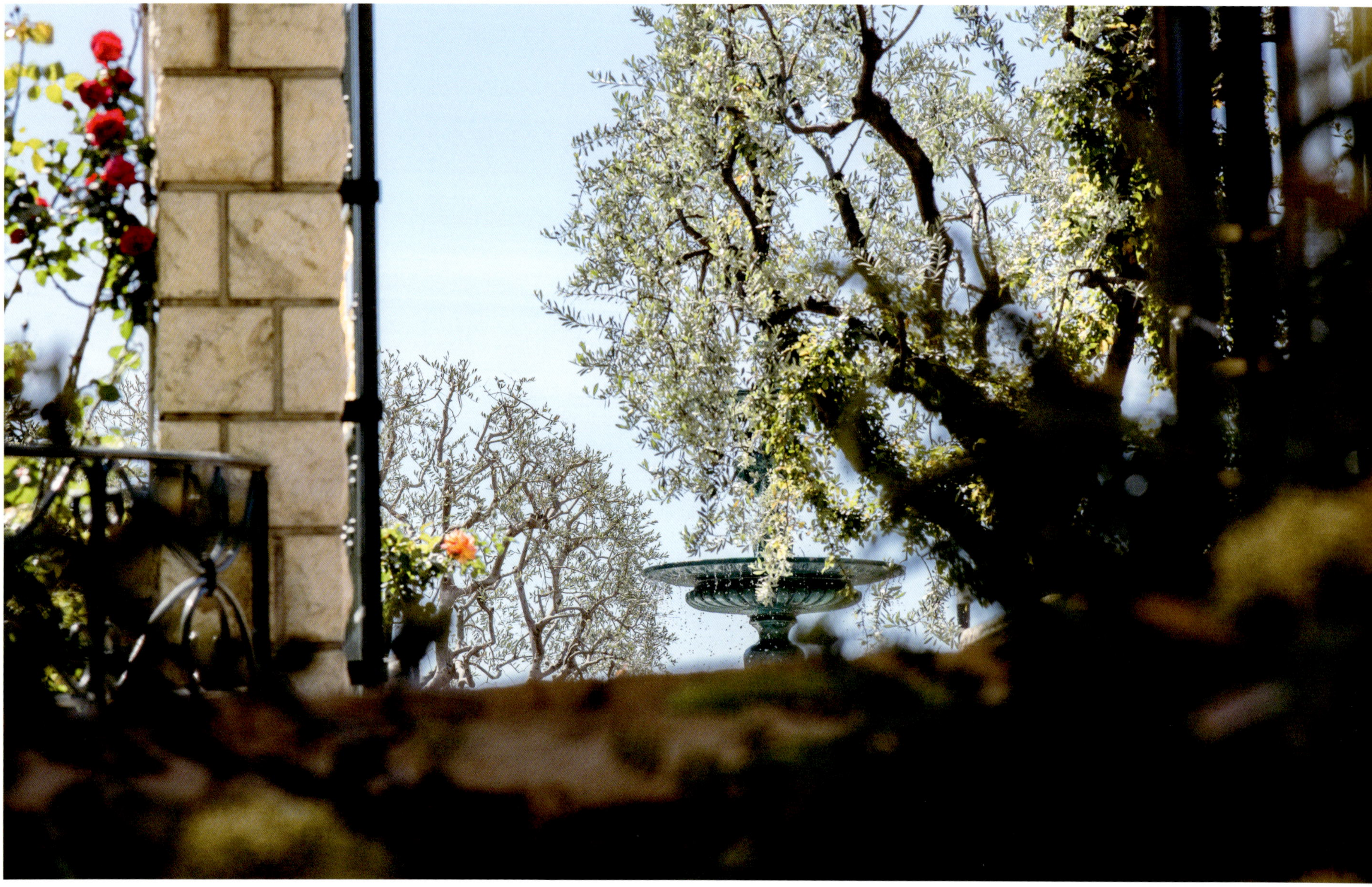

Spring shows the Princess Grace Rose Garden in all its glory.
April 16, 2016, 10:43 a.m.

ACKNOWLEDGMENTS

We extend our sincere gratitude to HSH Prince Albert II of Monaco for allowing us to create this book and for contributing his words to the preface.

Our warmest thanks also goes to Rolex S.A., Mr. Arnaud Boetsch, and Ms. Sandra Weiss.

We would also like to thank:
The Private Secretariat of HSH the Sovereign Prince
Mr. Hervé Irien, Curator of the Princely Collections

And:

- Angélique Alonso, Head of the Urban Planning Division, Department of Forward Studies, Urban Planning and Mobility, and Deputy Frédéric Kappler
- François Bonne, Head Gardener at the Prince's Palace
- Robert Calcagno, Director of the Oceanographic Museum
- Olivier Campana, Operations Manager, Buildings and Marina, Monaco Yacht Club
- Astrid Claudel-Rusin, Head of Section, Department of the Environment
- Annick Daniel, Head of Films and Exhibitions, Société des Bains de Mer
- Georges Restellini, Head of Gardens Section, Department of Urban Amenities
- Jean-Marie Solichon, Director of the Jardin Exotique
- The Department of Cultural Affairs
- The Nouveau Musée National de Monaco team, Villa Sauber and Villa Paloma for their hospitality
- Anthea Sogno, Director of Théâtre des Muses
- The Tourist and Convention Authority
- Meteoconsult and Groupe Figaro

My thanks would not be complete without expressing my gratitude to Pierre Finot for his constant support and patience in the design of my work; Mic Chamblas-Ploton for his inspiring words, which always push me to grow as a photographer; Canon France and Arta Photo for their technical support; Corinne Schmidt, Gaëlle Demouth, and Florent Roger from Éditions de La Martinière; and the Imprimerie Escourbiac team.

Bibliography

Arthaud, Christian et Paul, Éric L., *La Côte d'Azur des écrivains*, Édisud, 1999.
Bowlt, John E., Tregulova Zelfira, Rosticher Giordano Nathalie (dir.),
"Étonne-moi", *Serge Diaghilev et les Ballets Russes*, Skira, 2009.
Cars, Jean (des), *Colette et Monaco*, Éditions du Rocher, 1997.
Cars, Jean (des), *La Saga des Grimaldi*, Éditions Perrin, coll. Tempus, 2012.
Castans, Raymond, *Pagnol et Monaco*, Éditions du Rocher, 2000.
Chamblas-Ploton, Mic, *Dans les jardins des Grimaldi*, photographies
de Jean-Baptiste Leroux, préface de S.A.S. le Prince Albert II de Monaco,
Éditions du Chêne, 2008.
Colette, *L'Ingénue Libertine*, Le Livre de poche, 2015.
Erlanger, Philippe, *Fascinant Monte-Carlo, Principauté de Monaco*,
photographies d'Italo Bazzoli, Épi Éditions, 2015.
Laplace, Pierre, *Les Anciennes Villas et leurs Hôtes à Monaco*, Éditions V. Gadoury, 2015.
Maupassant, Guy (de), *Sur l'eau*, édition de Jacques Dupont, Gallimard,
coll. Folio Classique, 1992.
Mille, Raoul, *Sarah Bernhardt et Monaco*, Éditions du Rocher, 2005.
Novella, René, *Monaco, huit siècles d'art et d'architecture*,
photographies de Luca Sassi, Épi Éditions, 2003.
Pauvert, Jean-Jacques, *Apollinaire et Monaco*, Éditions du Rocher, 1999.
Renaudot, Patrick, *Cocteau et Monaco*, Éditions du Rocher, 1999..

Credits for the works of art represented on the photographs

Pages 8-9: *Vagues*, Brigita Lekše for Zepter International
S.A.S. le Prince Albert II de Monaco, Daphné du Barry ©ADAGP, Paris 2016
Pages 82-83: *Malizia*, Kees Verkade ©ADAGP, Paris 2016
Pages 134-135: *Rainier III*, Daphné du Barry ©ADAGP, Paris 2016
Page 137: *La Princesse Grace de Monaco*, Kees Verkade ©ADAGP, Paris 2016
Pages 140-141: *L'Hirondelle*, François Cogné
Page 144: *Bugatti 35 B*, François Chevalier, frachevalier@gmail.fr
Pages 146-147: *La Science découvrant les richesses de l'océan*, Constant Roux

Despite our research, we have not been able to find some of the authors of the works reproduced into this book. They are welcome

Photographs: Jean-Baptiste Leroux
Graphic design: Pierre Finot
Translation from French: Primoscrib (Rob Latchford)

Library of Congress Number: 2016943681
ISBN: 978-1-4197-2516-6

Published in 2016 by Abrams, an imprint of ABRAMS

Printed and bound in France
10 9 8 7 6 5 4 3 2 1

ABRAMS The Art of Books
115 West 18th Street, New York, NY 10011
abramsbooks.com